Col. Frank Huger,
C.S.A.

Col. Frank Huger, C.S.A.

The Civil War Letters of a Confederate Artillery Officer

FRANK HUGER
Edited by THOMAS K. TATE

McFarland & Company, Inc., Publishers
Jefferson, North Carolina, and London

LIBRARY OF CONGRESS CATALOGUING-IN-PUBLICATION DATA

Huger, Frank (Francis Kinloch), 1837–1897.
    Col. Frank Huger, C.S.A.: the Civil War letters of a Confederate artillery officer / Frank Huger ; edited by Thomas K. Tate.
        p.   cm.
    Includes bibliographical references and index.

    ISBN 978-0-7864-6330-5
    softcover : 50# alkaline paper ∞

    1. Huger, Frank (Francis Kinloch), 1837–1897 — Correspondence.   2. United States — History — Civil War, 1861–1865 — Personal narratives, Confederate.   3. Confederate States of America. Army — Officers — Correspondence.   4. Soldiers — Confederate States of America — Correspondence.   5. United States — History — Civil War, 1861–1865 — Artillery operations, Confederate.   I. Tate, Thomas K., 1936–   II. Title.   III. Title: Colonel Frank Huger, Confederate States of America.
    E605.H888   2011
    973.7'82 — dc22   2011011941

BRITISH LIBRARY CATALOGUING DATA ARE AVAILABLE

© 2011 Thomas K. Tate. All rights reserved

No part of this book may be reproduced or transmitted in any form or by any means, electronic or mechanical, including photocopying or recording, or by any information storage and retrieval system, without permission in writing from the publisher.

Front cover image © Shutterstock 2011

Manufactured in the United States of America

McFarland & Company, Inc., Publishers
    Box 611, Jefferson, North Carolina 28640
        www.mcfarlandpub.com

Table of Contents

Preface and Acknowledgments 1
Introduction 3

Chapter One — Frank and His Family 7
Chapter Two — West Point 22
Chapter Three — The War Letters 38
Chapter Four — Letters from the Trans-Mississippi 114
Chapter Five — Postwar Letters 127
Chapter Six — Benjamin Huger 149

Appendix I: Technical Developments at Harpers Ferry 165
Appendix II: Supplemental Letters 173
Appendix III: Ordnance Chief Colonel Henry Knox Craig on Civilian Superintendents of the National Armories 184
Appendix IV: Men at West Point When Frank Huger Attended 188
Appendix V: Report of the 1840 Board of Ordnance 192
Chapter Notes 195
Bibliography 199
Index 203

Preface and Acknowledgments

Without encouragement and help from Robert K. Krick I would not have attempted to bring Frank Huger's Civil War letters to the reading public. In fact I would not have known Frank Huger wrote any letters that survived the war. Until his retirement several years ago, Krick held for thirty years the position of chief historian of Fredericksburg and Spotsylvania National Military Park. A noted authority on General Robert E. Lee's Army of Northern Virginia, he is the author of numerous books and articles.

The project began in mid–2009 when Krick sent me copies of typewritten transcriptions of Frank Huger's letters, letters he received from one of Frank Huger's descendents, Lloyd Smith. Through Krick's efforts Smith was agreeable to having his ancestor's letters published. Then I checked the transcriptions against the originals contained in the Huger Family Papers held by the Virginia Historical Society in Richmond, Virginia. To the original typist credit is due; the transcriptions were very accurately copied. Most of the mistakes in spelling and punctuation were made by Frank Huger himself, writing as he did under trying conditions in the field. Krick helped additionally with suggestions on research material and provided help in making identifications of people named in these letters. He provided Frank's standings at West Point and also supplied the letter written on April 15, 1861.

I am further indebted to Robert K. Krick for his reading of portions of the work. "Make the subject act," were his words of advice for avoiding not only passive voice but also weak sentences. In some of mine the subject, rather than act, limped lamely along. Whatever vitality one may find in the forthcoming prose is the result of his advice.

Following close upon Robert K. Krick's heels in offering help to me is his son Robert ("Bobby") E.L. Krick, historian at the Richmond National Battlefield Park. Those of us fortunate enough to call Bobby our friend will have no trouble appreciating the remark made by Edward Porter Alexander about his friend Frank Huger. Alexander called Huger "the most loveable comrade that the Lord could make in the pattern of man." Bobby offered advice, helped to identify persons and places named in Frank Huger's letters and provided good information concerning Richmond newspapers during the Civil War years. He also helped to describe Richmond neighborhoods during those years. Both of the Kricks, father and son, were helpful in locating photographs of Frank Huger. In this regard I am indebted through Bobby Krick to Jimmy Blankenship of the Petersburg National Battlefield Park for the picture of Frank Huger in uniform.

Many thanks are due to Frances Pollard and her able staff at the sedate Virginia Historical Society and to Graham T. Dozier of that society who arranged to have the Huger Family Papers available. It was encouraging to work inside such a comfortable setting that is virtually within the shadow of the statues on Richmond's Monument Avenue.

I am indebted to Michael P. Gabriel, History Department chair, Kutztown University, for his comments and suggestions following his reading of the manuscript. He too has the editor's hawk eye to snatch passive voice rodents hiding in the verbal foliage. His help was especially appreciated because he had to interrupt his own work to be of help in this project.

The style of the editing I selected is to precede each letter with an introduction explaining and identifying persons, places and things named in the letter that follows. Footnotes provide the documentation for the identification. Unless noted otherwise all underlining as well as the use of parentheses are those of the original writer. Any insertions made by the editor for clarification are contained within brackets.

Introduction

Mail, especially from home, has always been a major morale booster to men and women in uniform, far away from family and friends. Today perhaps, with cell phones and the Internet, mail may not be as important as it once was, but it is still anticipated. Not receiving a letter or package at mail call remains a disappointment to persons of all ranks. The Civil War soldier, were he Billy Yank or Johnnie Reb, was no exception; mail was particularly important.

My most vivid example of the importance of mail to the service man or woman happened when I was at the U.S. Army Language School in Monterey, California, in 1959. One of the fellows there majored in journalism in his college years and subscribed to a number of newspapers. Although he received several papers every day he always complained after mail call that he failed to get a letter. His "letter drought" lasted for a number of days and he complained of his misfortune after every mail call.

Finally one day, in addition to receiving his regular supply of papers, there was a long envelope for him. We all gave him a cheer. Yet again after mail call he was still complaining. We asked what his problem was now; he had just received a letter. It was a bill for one of his newspapers.

The Civil War letters of Confederate artillery officer Frank Huger make it perfectly clear how the soldier of whatever period looks anxiously for mail. Nearly every one of Frank's letters, as well as those written by his father and two older brothers, begins with concerns for mail. Most of it arrived, eventually. Frequently it arrived in batches. The officers and men themselves were an important component of the postal service. Those who traveled from the front lines to a city or town of some size frequently carried letters from their comrades to be posted home. The following lines taken from several of Frank's letters are examples.

"I was surprised to find my mother's letter of the 20th received today that none of my letters home had been received" [April 24th, 1863].

Following the battle of Gettysburg Frank wrote the following to his mother on July 12, 1863: "Today we received our first mail since leaving Millwood, and I was most glad to get several from home, tho' of old dates."

When transferred to Tennessee with General James Longstreet's First Corps, minus Pickett's division that remained in Virginia, Frank wrote the following on October 18, 1863, to his younger brother, Thomas Pinckney Huger: "Lieut. J. Thompson Brown goes to Richmond in the morning to attend to some business and I will get him to deliver this to you."

If mail delivery was erratic within the main portion of the Confederacy, delivery was worse across the Mississippi River after the fall of Vicksburg in July 1863. Frank's father and his two older brothers were serving there in the Trans-Mississippi region. Writing to his father on New Year's Day 1864, Frank's letter began: "As one of our men is about to start on a furlough to Mississippi, and tells me he expects to communicate across the River."

For the most part Frank's letters are concerned with the conditions facing his family and friends. Writing to family loved ones required no explanation on Frank's part to explain just who someone was. As a result, some of the people he mentioned are impossible to identify precisely. The identity of Aunt Henderson who lived in Fredericksburg is such an example. The origin of the endearing term for his mother, "little Seve," is unclear. Frank's father, Benjamin Huger, used it in early letters prior to the Civil War and it must have been a familiar term to Frank and his brothers and sister.

Frank wrote only sketches of the battles in which he participated. There is a cheerful as well as an optimistic tone to his letters throughout the war. He commented to a degree on his superiors and the men around him. Frank's opinions are fair and honest. His harshest remarks are for generals Braxton Bragg and James Longstreet. It was Longstreet who blamed Frank's father, Major General Benjamin Huger, for Longstreet's own failure at the battle of Seven Pines. In letters to his father, a former ordnance and artillery officer, he wrote about technical problems with the artillery, problems he found frustrating. Expressing his young man's appetite for the charms of young women, Frank frequently asked family members, his younger sister, Celly, in particular, to remember him to a variety of young ladies.

Frank Huger's letters are part of the overall Huger Family Papers at the Virginia Historical Society in Richmond, Virginia. Companion with them are letters from his father and his two brothers, Benjamin Jr. and Eustis. They were written primarily from Trans-Mississippi. These letters show the relative comfort enjoyed by Frank's father and brothers in Trans-Mississippi compared to the hardships Frank faced in both Virginia and Tennessee. As staff officers the older Huger men had a roof over their heads and pretty good food in relative abundance. At the close of the war Frank's old comrade Edward Porter Alexander wrote him four letters included in this volume. They document the problems faced by former Confederate soldiers returning to a devastated

South and the efforts they made to support their families. Some of those proposed efforts were little more than schemes. Finally there are several letters written in 1896 that narrate Frank's duties at Gettysburg and his capture at Sailor's Creek in the spring of 1865.

The Hugers' prominence among South Carolina families stretched back to colonial times. To better understand Frank, I have included brief descriptions of some of his immediate relatives. I have provided a chapter on Frank's father, Benjamin Huger, concentrating on his long career as an important ordnance officer. The appendices contain much of the technical information so as not to fatigue the general reader. I have paid considerable attention to Frank's West Point years and his conduct there before the Civil War.

As a letter writer Frank displayed indifference to the use of the question mark and the apostrophe to show possession. Naturally enough he made some spelling mistakes because he spelled names the way they sounded. Writing often times while in a hurry to get the letter finished before a courier departed, Frank wrote as the thoughts came into his head and many of his letters are disorganized. Nevertheless the reader becomes acquainted with a generous and intelligent young man who loved his family, respected his superiors and formed lasting friendships with the men like Edward Porter Alexander, J. Thompson Brown and William Watts Parker with whom he served.

CHAPTER ONE

Frank and His Family

On June 12, 1897, the *New York Times* carried the following obituary: "Col. FRANK HUGER, Superintendent of Transportation of the Norfolk and Western Railway, died suddenly Friday in Roanoke, Va., from a stroke of apoplexy. Col. Huger was one of the oldest officers of the road. He served with distinction as Colonel in the Confederacy during the late war. He was sixty years of age."

An obituary supplies a very dehydrated summary of one's life. What filled his sixty years? What was distinctive about his service in the Confederacy? Who survived to mourn his passing?

Francis Kinloch Huger (September 29, 1837–June 11, 1897) or Frank, Confederate artillery officer, belonged to the sixth generation of the family since his great-great-great-grandfather Daniel Huger, a Huguenot merchant, left France in 1685 to settle on South Carolina's Santee River. His son, also named Daniel, was the father of five Huger brothers, all of whom served in the American Revolution. Raised on the plantation called Limerick and receiving liberal educations, they were, in order of their births, Daniel (1741–1799), Isaac (1743–1797), John (1744–1804), Benjamin (1746–1779) and Francis (1751–1811). The family retained the French pronunciation of its name, u'-GHEE.[1] Mary Chesnut in her famous diary recorded a pun on the name. Playing on the word refugee, social enemies of Isabella Johannes (Middleton) Huger, the widow of Judge Daniel Elliott Huger, called her "Rough Huger."[2]

Major General Benjamin Huger, C.S.A.

Frank Huger descended from Benjamin of the five Huger brothers. Before his death by friendly fire on May 11, 1779, Benjamin Huger became friends with the Marquis de Lafayette, a friendship that began when the young Frenchman landed from France in 1777 at the Huger plantation. Benjamin's son, Francis Kinloch Huger (1773–1855), educated as a doctor in England, succeeded in liberating Lafayette temporarily from his imprisonment at Olmütz, Austria. Francis married the daughter of Thomas Pinckney in 1802. Eight children issued from this marriage: Anna Isabella Huger, born about 1803; Elizabeth Huger, 1804; Thomas Pinckney Huger, about 1804 or 1805; Benjamin Huger, November 22, 1805; Francis Kinloch Huger, 1811; Cleland Kinloch Huger, 1818; Mary Ester Huger, 1820 and Harriott Horry Huger, 1822. From these children Benjamin Huger became the father of Frank Huger, the subject of this work.

Benjamin Huger, West Point class of 1825 and career army officer, married his cousin Elizabeth Celestine Pinckney on February 7, 1831. Their five children were: Benjamin Junior, Eustis, Francis Kinloch or Frank, Thomas Pinckney and Celestine Pinckney.

Benjamin Huger commanded at Fort Monroe with the rank of captain at the time of his son Frank's birth in nearby Norfolk.[3] Then before Frank was three years of age his father left for Europe as part of a four member board authorized by Secretary of War Joel R. Poinsett to tour and examine European artillery and ordnance facilities. Concern for his family's well-being prompted Benjamin Huger to write to Abram Eustis, his wife's uncle and an army officer, seeking protection for the family. Following are two letters Eustis wrote to Benjamin Huger which make clear that Ben's wife, Celestine, had been ill and outlined the nature of the board's mission. Captain Anderson was Robert Anderson who as a major commanded at Fort Sumter in April of 1861. The Paixhan whom Eustis mentioned was Henri Joseph Paixhans (1783–1854), a French artillery officer, who invented the shell gun and shells for use in it.

Tomettey 6th March—1840

My dear Sir,
I received your letter of the 28th ult. yesterday—What is the matter with Celestine, & what could have induced you to salivate her? [Salivation was a medical condition of excessive secretion of saliva often times brought on by the use of mercury and its compounds.] *We had not heard that she was ill, until Mrs. Pinckney wrote of the salivation. I trust she is quite well before this time. I am sorry you made any suggestion to the Secretary* [Joel R. Poinsett] *about sub-*

mitting the *Instructions for Artillery to me a second time. His vacillating conduct in relation to this, & some other matters, has utterly disgusted me, & I desire to have as little to do as possible with any matter under his immediate control. The translation of the French Instruction for Field Artillery was prepared by Capt. Anderson, under my supervision, at the special & immediate request of the Secretary of War. I submitted the manuscript & a thousand copies were ordered to be printed. Now he declines accepting it as the manual for our service. I have done my part, & now wash my hands of all further interest in it. Conflicting interests will in like manner prevent his adopting any system of material for Field Artillery. The iron founders have too much political weight to be slighted, & the West Point Foundry, not yet quite bankrupt, has its representatives at his elbow, in his personal friends Kemble & Fenwick, & Paulding—your labour I fear, is all in vain. Already the system of carriages has been violated to make a light piece for Horse Artillery, & the carriage for the service, which requires most strength, has been weakened. I like the idea of trying the effects of chambering all guns. It is at least worth an experiment. But has it not been already tried in Europe? & what was the result? I have no books here to refer to; but am under the impression that Paixhan [sic] treats of this matter.*

I have received a long & interesting letter from Major Mackay, describing the "dogs of war," & detailing operations in Florida [the Second Seminole War, 1835–1842]. *He say "I would recommend you to get, if you have not already* [unclear] *the Map lately drawn by Mackay, which is now being distributed to the Army by the War Dept. I pray you to ask Major Cooper to send me one of the Maps. Perhaps he can tell you whether the Secy is still bent on another attempt at a camp of instruction, & whether I am to be again victimized.*

Mr. Blake returned to [unclear word] *on the 1st inst. His* [unclear word] *& baby have gone to Pedee to patronize Ralph and Rose. I understand we may expect them here about the 1st April to pass the remainder of the season with us.*

"The Lord raineth (reigneth), let the earth rejoice." After the most excessive, long continuous draught, which I ever knew, we were refreshed three days ago with a bountiful rain. There was not enough to be of any essential benefit to the planters; but it refreshes the gardens, & has caused the planted shrubs to raise their drooping heads & "shout for joy." The country is now delightful. For three weeks we have not had a fire in the house, nor even a white frost without. The trees are all in blossom, & the yellow Jessamine hangs about them in golden festoons. Aunt Patia cannot be kept within doors; but is all day sauntering among the shrubbery & setting out more roses, gardenias, viburnums etc. etc. In the evening from two to three hours are devoted to backgammon, of which we never tire, & half past eleven usually finds us retiring to bed. All goes on now so [paper torn] *comfortably, that I do not even envy you your journey in Washington.*

With our cordial love for Celestine and kisses for the boys, accept the assurance of my sincere friendship—

Yours
Abram Eustis

Capt. B. Huger
I am directed to ask Celestine to enquire of Mrs. Gen. Macomb, about Mrs. Col. Pierce, & report her answer verbatim.

On March 15, 1840, Abram Eustis wrote the following letter to Benjamin Huger. The members of the board selected by Secretary of War Joel R. Poinsett consisted of Major Rufus L. Baker, Captains Benjamin Huger and Alfred Mordecai and foundry man and former ordnance officer William Wade.

Tomettey 15th March—1840

My dear Sir,
Your letter of the 8th & 9th inst. came here yesterday. This decisive action of the Secretary in sending your Board to Europe, looks as if he really intended ~~to~~ [the word to is crossed out] *finally to determine* [Eustis avoided splitting the infinitive] *on some system for Field Guns. He has made a capital selection of men to examinine* [sic] *the European founderies, & I think the business could not be in better hands.— But as you say what is to become of the wife & little boys? & what do I advise? Unhappily, I am so situated that I can neither advise nor assist. If I had a home or summer residence, I should say at once give them to me. But I am adrift, & have no information how I am to be employed during the summer. I wrote only yesterday to Captain Anderson to desire him to enquire of Genl. Scott to my destination. Be assured, if I can so arrange affairs as to afford comfort, countenance or protection to Celestine during your absence, I will not fail to do it, & I need not assure <u>her</u> how cordially her Aunt will unite with me for this purpose. If she determines to remain at Old Point,* [Virginia near Fort Monroe] *which but for the want of <u>suitable</u> society, would be the most comfortable arrangement; we will certainly make her a visit, which on the part of one or both of us may be more or less long according to my destination for the summer.—As you are not to leave this country for some weeks, I trust I shall hear from you again in time to reply, after you have more fully considered & determined your domestic arrangements. I appreciate the complicities of your wishing to put me at the head of your commission. But it is in better hands. Major Baker is better qualified, & in every way more suitable than I am; & besides*

I have had quite enough to do already with the Ordnance Board. I should like the voyage & the tour of Europe. But I wish to make it as my own master, untrammeled by official instructions. For three or four years past I have been saving money for this purpose, which I invested in stock of the U.S. Bank, as being available funds in Europe. What cost me $13000 is now worth $7000! Admirable encouragement for economy!

Where is "Finisburg." I suppose in Sweden, but I have neither Maps nor Gazetteer here. Do you take the Packet for England or France? If the latter, I wish you to take a letter to Williams for me.—

Tell my dear Celestine to be of good cheer, & give her a cordial kiss for <u>me.</u> Love to the boys, & believe me

Faithfully your friend
Abram Eustis

The letter was addressed to Capt. Benjm. Huger Ordnance Dept Old Point Comfort, Vir.

Abram Eustis was an old artillerist whose service began during the War of 1812. He saw action during the Black Hawk War and served in Florida, taking over from General Winfield Scott. The U.S. Bank, in which Eustis held stock, as well as its President Nicholas Biddle were always under attack from President Andrew Jackson. Jackson refused to renew the bank's charter and withdrew Treasury deposits. Of its demise Robert V. Remini wrote, "Soon smart investors sold its stock. With credit and reputation gone, the bank closed its doors in 1851, dragging down a number of other banks across the country."[4]

Young Frank Huger attended the Alexandria Boarding School run by Quaker Benjamin Hallowell. Although a Quaker, Hallowell had a number of associations with men in the military. Ordnance officer Lieutenant Stephen Vincent Benét, a future chief of ordnance, used his influence to obtain admission to the school for young Frank. The following letter established Frank's admission to the school.

Alexandria Boarding School
10 mon. 1st 1851

Esteemed Friend,

I wrote thee yesterday in reply to thy favour of the 26th ult. stating that we were unable to accommodate the son of thy frd [friend] Col. Hugher [sic] in con-

sequence of our School being full. I have just learned that one of the Students who was entered is so much indisposed as to render it improbable that he will able to [text blurred] *the present Term, and I write immediately to state that Col. Hugher's* [sic] *son, if of the required age etc., can fill the vacancy thus made.*

Col. Aberts' [sic] *and Col. Turnbull's sons are now with us.*

Please let me hear from thee on the subject by return mail.

In much haste,
Thy Sincere Frd
Benjm Hallowell
Lieut. S. V. Benét U.S.A.

Col. Aberts was Colonel John James Abert of the topographical engineers. Col. Turnbull was William Turnbull, also of the topographical engineers. Hallowell forgot to mention the most famous military figure to have attended his school, Robert E. Lee. In February 1825 Lee entered the school in preparation for his entry into West Point. "He was a most exemplary pupil in every respect," Hallowell wrote.[5]

The young scholar Frank, however, did not refer to the school by its proper name when he wrote home. Writing from the school to his mother on Saturday April 15, 1854, he addressed the letter as being from "Brimstone Castle." (There was no year on the letter. A perpetual calendar shows the only year in the 1850s where April 15 fell on a Saturday was 1854.) He also mentioned the letter arriving in Baltimore. In 1854 his father left his post at Harpers Ferry and assumed command of the Pikesville Arsenal in Maryland, just outside Baltimore in those days. The school enjoyed a good reputation. Hallowell (1799–1877) established the school in 1824. It was set up along the lines of Quaker schools, the students taking on the task of instructors. In 1859 Hallowell, also a noted scientist, became president of the Maryland Agriculture College. Frank wrote the following concerning his school and schoolmaster Ben Hallowell: "*He* [Ben Hallowell] *is so independent, from the fact, that with the reputation his school has, if every boy was dismissed tomorrow in a month he would be full again, so that gives him an independence that few school masters have.*"

Frank revealed in his letter what kind of student he was and also revealed his pragmatic side.

"*At the close of this session,*" Frank wrote his mother, "*he* [Ben Hallowell] *is going to give a certificate to those boys that study hard and behave themselves according to his rules, and his certificate will be of great assistance to a boy here-*

after, so I intend to get one of them this year if possible to shew (sic) what I can do if I try, but next year I don't care if I get one or not. I am now in his surveying class so have to study like <u>blazes</u> and for some time to come expect to get up at 5½ so as to have as much time to study as possible. It will take me just three weeks to get through his course, then I'll take it easy."

Frank wrote his mother he was nursing a sore throat and using Dr. Byrne's gargle. He described a lecture at the school delivered by Elihu Burritt. (Frank dropped the last "t" from Burritt's name). Burritt, "the Learned Blacksmith" (1810–1879) had a natural ability to learn languages, mastering ten of them while working at his forge. He became a linguist and philanthropist and was active in peace movements in Europe. The lecture he delivered at Frank's school concerned Burritt's efforts to reduce the ocean postage rates. Burritt argued that if we can send a letter three thousand miles over land for three cents, why should it cost fifty cents to send one across the seas? Frank wrote that he considered Burritt and enterprising man. "His ideas seem very liberal," Frank wrote.[6]

It was no accident that Burritt, an activist in the peace movement, spoke at Quaker Benjamin Hallowell's school. Neither was his topic chosen carelessly. In correspondence with such men as Massachusetts senator Charles Sumner, the Quaker John Greenleaf Whittier and poet Henry Wadsworth Longfellow over the years, he worked to reduce postage rates for overseas mail. Reducing these rates would encourage international correspondence, Burritt argued, and in turn promote peace. An 1876 letter from Longfellow congratulated Burritt for having virtually achieved his goal.[7]

Frank's older brother Benjamin Jr., five years his senior, wrote a brief account of himself in a letter requesting an appointment as first lieutenant in the Army of the Confederate States. Going right to the top, Ben Jr. wrote the following letter to Confederate secretary of war L. Pope Walker. The Cambridge Scientific School that Ben mentioned was associated with Harvard University.

Montgomery Ala. May 1st 1861

Hon. L. P. Walker
Secretary of War Confederate States
Sir,
    I am anxious to be appointed a First Lieutenant in the Army of the Con-

federate States either of Artillery Infantry or Cavalry, and hope that this application may be favorably considered by you.

I am twenty nine years old, a graduate of Princeton College then a student at the Cambridge Scientific School and for more than nine years have been in the service of the United States Coast Survey; the last five years of that have been in charge of party.

Very Respectfully
Your Obdt. Servant
Benj. Huger Jr.

I am a native of Virginia and I believe a native of South Carolina.[8]

Ben Jr.'s name along with that of his father and his younger brother Frank is listed in Regular Army Officers of the Confederate Regular Army.[9] The following letter, written to Ben Sr., indicates that Ben Jr. may have considered attending West Point.

Headqhs of the Army
N. York, March 13/50

My Dear Colonel:

I perceive that Ben's name is not included in the cadet's list of appointments "from at large," published in the Washington "National Intelligencer" of yesterday. I much regret this, less on account of Ben than that of the Academy. Indeed, I am not so sure that his ill-success is not greatly to his advantage, or will ultimately prove to be so. The General [Winfield Scott] regrets that Ben was not appointed, & is anxious that you should know of the steps he took to procure his appointment.

Early Feby last, the General wrote the Sec. of War on the subject, generally, of the appointments to the academy "from at large," & at the same time submitted a list of <u>ten</u> names as candidates for the present year. In that list Ben's name was included with the following recommendation:—

"<u>B. Huger,</u> son of Bvt. Col. Huger, a captain in the Ordnance, who served with highest distinction in Mexico."

Two only of the persons named by the General have been appointed, & two of the ten appointed are the sons of civilians. These, of course, were not recommended by the Genl.

Please present my best regards to Madame, the <u>young lady</u> & the boys.

I missed seeing you when you were in N. York by about <u>two</u> hours. I called but you had left.

If I can do anything for any of you, here, pray command me. Meanwhile, take care of yourselves, & remember me always as very sincerely
Your friend
Tom Williams

P.S. Frank Taylor's stables were burned at the <u>narrows</u> last-night. No horses lost. Col. Benjm Huger Old Pt. Comfort

---

Note that Army Headquarters were written in the heading as being located in New York. It was not until 1853 that Scott and his personal staff relocated to New York as Scott and the new secretary of war, Jefferson Davis, were at odds.[10]

None other than John C. Calhoun along with others that included Colonel George Talcott, chief of ordnance, Vice President George M. Dallas and former secretary of war and now senator from Michigan Lewis Cass signed the recommendation to President James K. Polk to appoint Benjamin Huger Jr. to West Point. The recommendation carried the date January 21, 1848.

A summary of Ben Huger Jr.'s military record appears in his compiled service record. May 20, 1861. Appointed from South Carolina as 1st Lieutenant, C. S. Infantry.

Huger's command

June 8, 1861. Ordered to report for duty to Gen. Huger at Norfolk, Va.

Aug. 14, & Sept. 19, 1861. Signs as 1st Lieut. & A.D.C. to Gen. Huger.

Jan. 14, 1862. Appointed Capt. A.G. Dept.; to rank Jan. 6, 1862; to report to Gen. Huger.

Jan. 31 & June–July, 1862. Returns & reports show him to be Capt. & A.A.G. to Ben Huger.

Nov. 17, 1863. Gen. Huger says Capt. Huger is now doing the duty of Chief Asst. in this Ord. Bureau of the Trans-Miss. Dept. Memo.— Gen. Huger was announced as Chief of Bureau of ordnance of Trans-Miss. Dept. July 17, 1863.

Nov. 25, 1864. Signs as Capt. & Asst. to Chief of Bureau of Ordnance Trans-Miss. Dept., and says he was assigned to duty by Gen. E. K. Smith.

General Benjamin Huger wrote the following two letters to General Samuel Cooper on behalf of his son, Benjamin Jr.

Headquarters Department of Norfolk
Norfolk, Va., January 3rd 1862

General S. Cooper
Adjt. & Inspector General
Sir,

    I reply to your endorsement on enclosed letter, I have to recommend that 1st Lieut. Benjm. Huger Jr. of the Confederate Army, now Aide de Camp, be appointed Asst. Adjt. Genl. and assigned to the special duties referred to in my letter.

    I have hesitated to name this gentleman on account of my personal relations towards him: but, believing that he is better qualified to perform the duties than any other I can think of who is available, I feel it my duty to recommend him to the War Dept. for the appointment.

Very Respectfully
Your Obet. Servt.
Benj Huger Maj. Genl.

Ordnance Bureau T. Miss Dept.
Marshall, Texas Nov. 17th 1863

Genl. S. Cooper
Adj. & Insp. General,
Sir,

    I request that Capt. B. Huger Jr. Asst. Adj. Genl. may receive the Commission of Major & A.A.G. As the Agj. Genl. or one A.D.C. to Major General are allowed the rank of Major, I ask the position for this Officer who has been performing the duties of A.A.G. since Lt. Col. Anderson, was detached in July 1862. Capt. Huger is now doing the duty of Chief Asst. in the Ordnance Bureau established for this Department and I have no Aides de Camp, not having appropriate duties for them in my present position.

I remain Very Respectfully
Your obt. Serv. Benj Huger Maj. Genl.

    The 1850 census for Elizabeth City County, Virginia, shows Eustis being two years older than Frank, making his birth year 1835. His brother Thomas Pinckney, three years younger, was born in 1838. Celestine Pinckney's dates are May 23, 1843, to September 17, 1878. She became Mrs. John Smith Preston in April 1863. In Frank's letters that follow his younger brother is referred to as Pinck and his sister as Cel or Cellie.

One — Frank and His Family

Other prominent Hugers rounded out Frank's extended family. Alfred Huger (1788–1872), Frank's father General Benjamin Huger's older cousin, was a planter and longtime postmaster at Charleston, South Carolina.[11] He was the son of John Huger (1744–1804) the third eldest of the five Huger brothers of Revolutionary War fame. In 1823 Alfred purchased Longwood Plantation in Berkeley County. His obituary, carried in the *New York Times* on May 15, 1872, described him as: *Hon. Alfred Huger, a well-known resident of Charleston, S.C., and conspicuous Unionist in the days of nullification and secession, died, yesterday in that city, of paralysis, in the eighty-fourth year of his age. He was Postmaster of Charleston from the time of President Jackson until 1865.*

Charleston, South Carolina, in the 1830s demanded more from its postmaster than other cities its size. Work started as ordinary on July 29, 1835, when Alfred Huger began the supervision of sorting the mail that had arrived on the steamboat *Columbia*. Thousands of antislavery tracts were among the delivery, addressed to leading members of the Charleston community including the clergy of all denominations. As William W. Freehling wrote, "The American Anti-Slavery Society had begun its intensive campaign to convince slaveholders that bondage should be abolished." Huger decided to keep this incendiary literature inside the post office until he could get some instructions from Postmaster General Amos Kendall. Before Huger received his instruction, which gave him sweeping power to suppress the tracts, locals broke into the Charleston post office and confiscated the abolitionist literature. The next evening it fueled a large bonfire on the Charleston parade grounds. Although a confirmed Unionist, Alfred Huger warned leaders in the North that he would not sit by while abolitionists inspired the Negroes to put a torch to his house and subject his family to brutality.[12]

In February 1861, diarist Mary Chesnut wrote of Alfred Huger: "I remember liking one speech so much — voice, tone, temper, sentiments, and all. I sent to ask the name of the orator and the answer came: Mr. Alfred Huger."[13]

An important insight into the character of Alfred Huger may be found in a letter he wrote to Robert Newman Gourdin February 6, 1861. Robert N. Gourdin and his brother Henry were Charleston merchants. The letter concerned a moral dilemma Gourdin faced by happening to know of some contingency plans of Major Robert Anderson, commanding Fort Sumter. Huger wrote:

> I was put in possession of your two letters one to myself, the other (Copy) to Major Anderson, both have my undivided attention, which their *source & subject* would equally command. The responsibility to whh [which] you allude

finds its solution in my own mind. Major Anderson's expressions clearly indicate his determination in certain contingencies to blow up fort Sumter! He has imparted this disposition to you, with no confidential restriction, therefore the matter is at your discretion, but had he exhausted the language in masking his communication "confidential" it wd [would] in my judgement [sic] be, *morally* impossible for you to recognize *his* right to enjoin secrecy upon you, *involuntarily* made the recipient of his intentions! There is manifestly a previous obligation to your country & to humanity which no compunction could justify you in disregarding — suppose for illustration, Major Anderson, had imparted to you his plan for "shelling" & destroying Charleston, could any *private* feelings be plead in your defense if you did not endeavor to save life by causing women & children to be secured and by throwing any obstacle in the way of his consummating such an act? Can it be doubted, that before you even saw Major Anderson, or knew of his existence this "*duty*" was imposed upon you by the instincts of Nature, & by the Ordinances of God?[14]

Alfred took in his infant nephew Thomas Bee Huger when the baby's mother died. Alfred raised him as his own son rather than as a nephew. Thomas was born about 1821. He was appointed as a midshipman in the U.S. Navy March 5, 1835, and made his first cruise in the ship of the line *North Carolina*. The Navy Register of 1861 gave Lieutenant Huger sixteen years sea service and three years shore duty. He was first lieutenant on the steam sloop *Iroquois* on the Mediterranean Station at the time he resigned (January 1861) and was one of the first to tender his resignation.[15]

"Tom Huger was my ideal of a dashing, devil-may-care sailor," Mary Chesnut confided to her diary. "And I felt certain if any chance came his way he would do something heroic."[16]

While still a midshipman in 1845, Thomas B. Huger married Mariamne Meade, younger sister of future Union general George Gordon Meade. Mariamne, born in Philadelphia on September 14, 1822, died in Charleston, South Carolina, on December 7, 1857. Five children were born to Thomas and Mariamne Huger.

Thomas B. Huger commanded the *McRae* at the Battle of New Orleans. A sea-going steamer mounting six thirty-two pounders and one nine-inch shell gun, it was a fast packet vessel confiscated by the state of Louisiana and converted to a warship in riverboat facilities in New Orleans. Admiral David D. Porter described the engagement of the *McRae* and the Union warship *Iroquois*.

> Above Fort Jackson, from which she did not receive a single shot, though passing its levee within fifty yards, the "Iroquois" was attacked by a ram and the gun boat "McRea" [sic], both of which were driven off, and the commander of the later (Lieut. Huger), mortally wounded.
> The "Iroquois" suffered much loss and was considerably cut up in her

actions with the gun-boats and Fort St. Philip.[17]

Mary Chesnut described the death bed scene of the mortally wounded Thomas Huger:

Lieutenant Thomas B. Huger, C.S.N.

> Tom Huger resigned his place in the U.S. Navy and come to us. The *Iroquois* was his ship in the old navy. They say as he stood in the rigging, after he was shot in the leg, his ship leading the attack upon the *Iroquois* &c &c, his old crew in the *Iroquois* cheered him. And when his body was borne in, the Federals took off their caps, in respect for his gallant conduct. When he was dying, Meta Huger said to him: "An officer wants to see you. He is one of the enemy." "Let him come in. I have no enemies now." But when he heard the man's name: "No, no. I do not want to see a Southern man who is now in Lincoln's navy." The officers of the U.S.N. attended his funeral.[18]

Following the death of Thomas Huger on May 20, 1862, mortally wounded at the Battle of New Orleans, his five children were raised by their great-uncle Alfred Huger. In a letter to his wife dated May 14, 1862, General Meade wrote about Thomas Huger, who died April 25, 1862, of wounds received the day before, "I have not seen the death of Huger positively announced in the papers; all I have seen was that he was badly wounded. But he does not seem to have been made prisoner."[19]

On May 3, 1865 General George G. Meade wrote the following account of his sister Mariamne's children:

> At Mrs. Garnett's I saw Mrs. Tully Wise, who was all last summer in Columbia, South Carolina, and there met Mrs. Alfred Huger with Mariamne's children. She says the children are all sweet, and that Mr. & Mrs. Huger are devoted to them, but that Mr. Huger has lost everything, and is now very poor, that he is old and infirm, and will not probably live long. She says Mr. Huger's house in Charleston was burned in the great fire of 1862, and everything in it destroyed, all the old pictures, and all the clothes, jewels and everything belonging to Mariamne's children. Mr. Huger at this time was Postmaster of Charleston, and used to come up and spend Sundays at Columbia. Mrs. Wise had not heard from them since Sherman's occupation.[20]

The destructive fire General Meade reported swept through 540 acres of Charleston and destroyed nearly 600 homes, Alfred Huger's among them. It erupted on December 11, 1861.[21]

Poor, old and infirm though he may well have been, Alfred Huger's mind was clearly made up as to his condition in the days following the war. He wrote the following letter to Robert Newman Gourdin on September 21, 1867.

The loss of property, the sudden transition from comparative wealth to almost *want, the total ruin of ancestral Estate, which* (you *know) produced many comforts, the burning of both Houses, town and country, are the least of the Trials we are dom'd to Contend with. Even the shedding of* that *precious blood, so much dearer to me than my own, being due to the State that gave Tom birth, seems like a Sacrifice to God, & the "agony & bloody sweat." God enables* us *to endure, it is the loss of Status as a Man & the loss of Liberty as an American, that I cannot patiently bear. There are "causes" of Sorrow which like ourselves are temporal, but there are other causes of Sorrow, which are* permanent *as they affect the well being of Humanity when we shall cease to Suffer. Tom's "Murder," for the enemy had ten guns to his one, was an injury to me, is too "foul" to be forgiven, but his "Mother" demanded his life and he gave it. I would not have it otherwise. The more heart rending and bitter is the "thought" that I have no "country" and that the glorious sensation of loving "One," is stricken from my bosom. If I were a Russian, it would be different, because I would have inherited "loyalty" to oppression, unfortunately I am an "American," and those who call themselves Americans have made me a Slave, if it were possible for me to Envy you, (which God be praised it is not), it might be because you are in a free atmosphere where "Right" meant something and where "Law" is not an obsolete and useless word. My prayer is that England's People may continue to appreciate the blessings of the Constitutional Monarchy, that they may never cease to remember what it cost; and that they may not be deluded by the political madness that is presented, on* our *side of the Atlantic, for* their *imitation. You know I am an old federalist with but little confidence in "majorities" and still less in "Equality," that foolish "legend," that claiming kin with* Liberty, *but is her deadliest foe. I read the debates in Parliament with deep interest. Especially on the question of Suffrage of which, an Englishman, happily for him, knows so little and by which an American feels his bitterest curse. In all matters of Jurisprudence, I look to England for wisdom as the world does for "Longitude" and I confess myself alarmed. I read Lord Shatford's speech and my alarm does not diminish. Well, may the country gentleman of the ancient Tiller to his Land, & ponder. Well, may every hearty son of that island "Set in* the Slaer-Sea" give his brave & manly mind to the Past, the Present, & the Future of his country; they are within hearing of the cataract, the Rapids are near, there is sublimity in Niagara, but & or was it Lord Shaftsbury?

There is death & desolation in the Whirlpool below; is the Ship on her true Course or where is she drifting to? There are questions which those who have stranded their own vessel may honestly ask here — it seems to my feeble vision, that some are there who do not! To me England has been as the "Light of the World" & as the "Salt of the Earth," and I, sincerely with that Every Lord & Every commoner, would read, learn, & inwardly digest Mr. Calhoun's [John C.] "'Disquisition on Government' and then study his Essay on the Constitution of the United States, thus clearly see & comprehend those incontrovertible truths which demagogues, who are Traitors to that constitution, call it Treason in the South, then, who (more wickedly than) foolishly, talk of the Union they have destroyed unmindful that a Vulgar consolidation can have no Union with itself, and Equally is mindful that God created the African & the Anglo-Saxton for different purposes and that the arrangements of Nature, and the Ordinances of Divine wisdom, are not to be disturbed with impunity, but a Yankee would change the multiplication table to defraud his neighbours & abolish the ten commandments to conceal his own iniquity."[22]

A final distinguished member of the Huger clan and active in South Carolina politics with his cousin Alfred, Daniel Huger, along with men like William Drayton and Joel R. Poinsett, was a respectable and conservative Unionist opposed to nullification. Known as a low-country or tidewater nationalist, Daniel Huger lost the 1826 U.S. Senate race in South Carolina by two votes to William Smith. He supported the political career of John C. Calhoun but broke with Calhoun later over nullification.[23] Described as a striking-looking man with swarthy complexion, bristling eyebrows and a sardonic grin, his appearance won for him the title of Milton's Satan. He was Charleston's typical gentleman of the old school.

In 1830, a debate occurred between South Carolina radicals led by William Preston and moderates led by Daniel Huger. A duel nearly took place between Huger and Robert Barnwell Rhett until the next day when their passions cooled. Three years later during a nullification convention Robert Barnwell Rhett openly defied any delegate to say that he loved the Union. Daniel Huger met the challenge. "It has been the pride of my life to submit to the laws of my country," he said.[24]

CHAPTER TWO

West Point

Frank followed in his father's footsteps, entering the United States Military Academy at West Point, New York, high above the scenic Hudson River, in 1855. He was eighteen years of age. The family lived in Baltimore since 1854 when Frank's father, Benjamin Huger, transferred from Harpers Ferry Armory to take command of Pikesville Arsenal outside Baltimore. Frank was enrolled in the class of 1860, the only class to have a five year course of study. A roster of the initial cadets appointed in 1855 appeared in the April 26, 1855, *New York Times*.

Out of the eighty-six cadets listed below, only thirty-six appear in Francis B. Heitman's *Historical Register and Dictionary of the U.S. Army from its Organization, September 29, 1798 to March 2, 1903*. The letter (H) appears after the name if listed in Heitman's register. An asterisk (*) before the name indicates a spelling difference between the *New York Times* entry and Heitman.

Cadet	State	Cadet	State
Abbott, Jacob	Miss.	Gleaves, Robert H.	Ill.
Allen, Wm. H.	Penn	Hazlett, Chas. E. (H)	Ohio
Andrews, John N. (H)	Del.	Hollister, Geo. L. (H)	N.Y.
Ashe, John G.	N.C.	Hook, Jr., Cornelius (H)	Ill.
Bacon, John	Texas	Hopkins, Edward (H)	N.Y.
Bates, Geo. W.	Mo.	Huger, Frank (H)	At large
Beck, Wm. B. (H)	Penn	Johnson, Richard Z.	Ohio
Berill, John M.	Ky.	Jones, Wm. G.(H)	Ohio
Birdsall, John	At large	Jordan, Wm. H. (H)	Ohio
Bonestreet, Jacob P.	Wis.	Kellogg, Josiah H. (H)	Penn
Bowen, Nicholas (H)	N.Y.	Kent, Francis S.	Penn
Boorman, Chas. S.	At large	Knox, L. Gilbert	Ohio
Burlosh, Fred. F.	Conn.	Laramee, Wm. H.	Neb'a
Butler, Pierce M.	At large	Livingston, Chas. E.	Penn
Chamberlain, W. W. (H)	N.Y.	Lewis, Martin	Ohio
Cushing, Sam'l F. (H)	R.I.	Lynn, Daniel D.	Ind.
Dean, John	Penn	Lyon, Chas. D.	Mich
Edson, Theodore (H)	Mass	Maitland, John A.	Penn
Embrich, Fred	Penn	Marbury, Horatio	Tenn
Edwards, Nicholas M.	Ky.	Marion, A. Wycough	Ark.
Gibbes, Wm. G.	S.C.	Mariott, Wm. H.	At large
Gilmer, John C.	N.C.	Marsh, Salem J. (H)	Mass

Cadet	State	Cadet	State
Martin, Jas. P. (H)	At large	Rugg, DeWitt C.	Ind.
Matteson, Merritt	N.Y.	Scott, Abel S.	Va.
Mills, Anson (H)	Ind.	Shoemaker, Ed. W.	N.M.
Mishler, Lyman (H)	Penn	Sloan, Jr., B. F. (H)	S.C.
Mitchell, Robert W. (H)	At large	Small, Randolph S.	Penn
Myers, Geo. A. (H)	N.Y.	Smith, Alfred T. (H)	Ill.
McCreery, Jr., W. W. (H)	At large	Sweet, John J.(H)	Ill.
McFarland, Walter (H)	N.Y.	Taber, Jas. M.	Miss.
McGowan, Jas. A.	Cal.	Talbot, Lycurgas	Kanses (sic)
McIntosh, A.J.D.	At large	Taylor, Richard	Fla.
McIntyre, Henry C.	La.	Tardy, Jr., John A. (H)	N.Y.
McNally, Robert	N.Y.	Thomas, Winfield S.	Ga.
Norris, Jas. B.	N.H.	Vanderbilt, Geo. W. (H)	N.Y.
Parker, James	N.C.	*Wesley, Merritt (H)	Ill.
Parker, Henry C.	La.	Williams, Rigdon	Ohio
Pennington, Jr., A.C.M. (H)	N.Y.	Wilson, John M. (H)	Wash
*Porter, Horatio (H)	Penn	Whittmore, Jas. M. (H)	Mass.
Potter, Carroll H. (H)	R.I.		
Porrell, Albert M.	Md.	**Total 86**	
*Ransour, Stephen D.(H)	N.C.		
*Randall, Alansom M. (H)	N.Y.	*Indicates misspelling of names. Porter's first name should be Horace; Ransour should be Ramseur; Randall, Alansom M. should be Randol, Alanson M. Wesley Merritt's name is reversed.	
Ricketts, Wm. W.	Penn		
Riley, B.B.D. (H)	At large		
Ritnour, Oliver P.	Ill.		
Robinson, Jas. A.	Cal.		

Those were significant years for the United States and for the U.S. Army. Under the authority of Secretary of War Jefferson Davis the rifle and rifle musket were adopted as the standard shoulder arm for the service. While in command of Harpers Ferry Armory Frank's father, Colonel Benjamin Huger, supervised the development of this arm. He also supervised the development of the new bullet, the Harpers Ferry bullet, to replace the inferior Minié ball. This new arm and its wartime modified models were to become the workhorse weapon for the American infantry during the coming Civil War.

Other significant events while Frank Huger was at West Point caused the strains that finally split the Union. In 1856 Southern congressman Preston Brooks beat Massachusetts senator Charles Sumner with a cane while Sumner was at his Senate desk. What prompted the caning, according to Brooks, were Sumner's unprovoked insults on South Carolina senator Andrew P. Butler and Sumner's "foul-mouthed denunciation of South Carolina."[1] The South supported Brooks, and the North supported Sumner. In 1857 the country was in the grip of an economic panic that strained North–South relations. The S.S. *Central America* sank during a hurricane 160 miles off the coast of South Carolina that year. Its cargo, a gold shipment from California, was lost. Many banks in the country were relying on the gold to prevent their collapse. The loss of the gold and the ensuing bank failures helped to bring on the Panic of 1857.

The question of slavery strained relations between North and South. An extreme abolitionist group, the Garrisonians, considered the dissolution of the Union. The more conservative antislavery National Compensation Emancipation Society, as its name implied, advocated payment to the South to free the slaves through purchasing their freedom. This organization was led by such men as wealthy philanthropist Gerrit Smith, Yale University scientist Benjamin Silliman, Williams College president Mark Hopkins and pacifist Elihu Burritt, the "Learned Blacksmith who spoke to Frank Huger's class at "Brimstone Castle."[2]

In August 1859 Edwin Drake drilled the first successful oil well in northwestern Pennsylvania. At the time few were prescient enough to see the far-reaching effects of that discovery. About six weeks later John Brown and his band raided the armory town of Harpers Ferry, Virginia. Few failed to realize the significance. Virginia reopened its state armory in Richmond following John Brown's raid.

The military academy that Frank entered in 1855 had undergone some extensive remodeling. Under the superintendence of Robert E. Lee (September 1, 1851 to April 1, 1855) new barracks were completed in 1851 at a cost of $186,000. A new mess hall was built in 1852 and a new riding hall in 1855. Improvements continued to include gas works to light the buildings and better accommodations for officers and professors. The gas lights also provided the cadets with the means to create a burner on which they made taffy while the pipes themselves, when tapped on with a knife blade, served as a warning system to alert cadets of an impromptu inspection.[3]

Still the new barracks were not too comfortable, particularly on the north side in winter. Cadets had to wear their overcoats to keep warm. Cadet Tully McCrea, class of 1862, described the rooms: "Our rooms are heated by means of hot air furnaces, situated in the basement, from which the air is conveyed to our rooms by means of flues in the walls. On the north side barracks the cold air generally manages to get in through the crevices about the door and window faster than it does through the flu, so that on a cold day our room is continually cold."[4]

These new barracks were long overdue. In 1840 Secretary of War Joel R. Poinsett described the West Point barracks as dilapidated. They were, he added, in a state of decay, badly constructed originally and "as unhealthy as they are inconvenient." Testimony from succeeding boards of visitors for several years prior to Poinsett's report advised the construction of new barracks. "Whenever the condition of the Treasury will permit," Poinsett wrote, "it is very desirable to erect new barracks at West Point.[5]

In a letter home after just three weeks at the academy Cadet McCrea described a day at his first encampment. Frank, of course, was at West Point too at this time. Reveille sounded at five A.M. and the drums beat for about ten minutes. During that time the cadets had to be up, dressed and on the parade field. Then post police for half an hour where all the cadets had to pick up debris from the parade grounds. Whether this phrase was used then Cadet McCrea did not say, but the bent over position to pick up paper and other assorted trash these cadets and soldiers ever after had to collect prompted one wag of an NCO to say that all he wanted to see during police call was "assholes and elbows."

After the policing detail came an hour-long drill. Then breakfast of bread, coffee and a hash of mostly potatoes and very little meat. After breakfast the cadets had nothing special to do until eleven A.M. when they drilled for another hour. The cadets had from noon until one P.M. (Cadet McCrea did not write 13:00) to prepare for the mid-day meal. The menu included soup, boiled beef, boiled potatoes, boiled greens and a dessert of bread pudding and molasses. They had nothing to do until four then post police, and drill at 5:30. At seven P.M. was dress parade and inspection.

At the end of August the cadets returned to barracks. "Friday evenings," Cadet Tully McCrea wrote, "we have to fire cartridges and it makes our guns very black and dirty inside so that we have to take them all to pieces and clean them out, and it generally takes up all of our Saturday afternoon. If we go to Sunday morning inspection with a dirty gun we are sure of being 'skinned' and a report for a dirty gun gives three demerits." The best way then and now to remove black powder fouling is with hot soapy water. But if the cadet did not thoroughly dry his weapon it would rust. Cadet McCrea twice had a dirty weapon.

Frank was not the student his father had been when he attended the academy. In June of 1856, at the end of his first year in a class of sixty-one cadets Frank ranked 33rd in mathematics and 27th in English. However he must have done well or at least better in some classes as he ranked overall academically 21st in the class. Seven of the sixty-one did not pass and advance.

Frank's conduct was another matter. During his first year at West Point Frank collected sixty demerits. While this number was far short of the two hundred needed for expulsion, fifty-one of the sixty he received in the last six months of the year. Perhaps the reader will remember Frank's letter to his mother from the Quaker Benjamin Hallowell's Alexandria Boarding School or "Brimstone Castle." Frank worked hard and diligently to a point and then took things easy. At West Point cadets were ranked academically by class but in conduct the academy tabulated standings across the entire institution.

Frank's sixty demerits gave him a standing of 49th among the 182 cadets. Readers may not be too surprised to learn who was at the bottom in conduct with 182 demerits, as many demerits as there were cadets at the Point. This apparently happy-go-lucky cadet was Marcus A. Reno. While Reno saw service in the Civil War, most readers know of him in connection with General George A. Custer and the Battle of Little Big Horn. Reno and his men were the first to engage the Indians and after an encounter along the stream, retreated to a defensive position on the high ground above. Reno and his men survived, Reno going on to face court-martial.[6]

Young Frank Huger may have been more interested in high jinks than high marks. The report for June 1857, Frank's second year, placed him 35th out of forty-two cadets who passed. Three more young men did not pass and were weeded out. This drop from number 21 out of 61 to 35 out of 45 meant that Frank slid from the top third to the bottom fourth. Records show that Frank stood 36th in mathematics, 24th in English and 38th in French. In conduct he did no better. In his second year his demerit count totaled 115. If there was a bright spot he collected only 52 in his last six months.

Frank did not perform for his teachers at West Point as well as he had for Benjamin Hallowell. Among the faculty charged with Frank's education at West Point were men destined to achieve fame in the coming Civil War, men like William J. Hardee or "Old Reliable," Oliver Otis Howard and "cool as a steel knife" John Gibbon. Frank declined yet again in his third year, falling to 36th in academic standing out of 41 passing cadets, another one of his classmates having failed. He ranked 37th, 39th and 33rd in natural philosophy, French and Spanish respectively. Only in drawing did Frank rank well. Being twelfth in the class saved him from falling to the bottom. For the modern reader to appreciate the importance West Point placed on drawing as part of an engineer's training, the following quote may help. "Before the development of photography circa 1840, the only way for an officer to quickly and accurately render a battlefield description was to sketch. The only way to direct the construction of a fort was to draw a diagram. And so it is that the fine arts have always been an integral part of West Point's academic program."[7]

One cadet, a budding artist if no soldier, was James McNeill Whistler who left West Point in 1854 just before Frank entered. The son of a soldier, George Washington Whistler, James McNeill Whistler had no stomach for the discipline. Nearsighted and in poor health, he should not have been accepted in the first place. The purpose of introducing him here is to show something of the drawing class at West Point, presided over by professor of drawing Robert W. Weir. Accurate observation was the emphasis in Weir's classes. Artistic license was frowned upon and not permitted. Young cadet Whistler drew a bridge from which two boys were fishing. When ordered to remove the boys, Whistler removed them to the riverbank where they continued to fish. Still not what Weir wanted, he ordered Whistler once again to remove them. Whistler did so but marked their place and passing with two crosses.[8]

Frank did better conduct-wise in the school year of 1857-58 collecting only ninety-seven demerits. Having only twenty-two going into his last six months of that academic year Frank kicked up his heels and earned seventy-five more. By June 1859, Frank's fourth year at the academy, he slid still further. Now he ranked 38th out of 41 passing classmates. Fortunately he held his twelfth place in drawing which helped him overcome his dismal standing in civil engineering, ethics and chemistry where he ranked 37th, 37th and 39th respectively. Neither was Frank's conduct very becoming. Of the 143 demerits he accumulated that year, eighty-four he received in the last six months. No wonder Frank wanted to graduate in four rather than five years.

Among the Huger Family Papers is a letter written by Secretary of War John B. Floyd, April 29, 1859, to Congressman John Mason, the same John Mason taken from the mail packet *Trent* early in the Civil War. Secretary Floyd wrote:

Sir,

I have had the honor to receive your letter of the 22d instant, with the enclosure from Cadet Frank Huger, of the United States Military Academy.

The question of allowing the second class of cadets to graduate next June has been already fully considered, but I have been unable consistently with my views of the interests of the service, to make any exceptions in their case, however much I might otherwise feel disposed to yield to the wishes of their friends in their behalf. The disappointment of these young men at the resumption of the five years course, is natural, but affords, certainly, no just grounds for complaint as they entered the academy with the distinct understanding that they were to remain five years.

When Frank graduated in 1860 he managed to work his way to 31st in a class of 41. Maybe his father, Benjamin Huger, had a talk with him. Maybe the John Brown raid in October 1859 of the armory his father had commanded had a sobering effect upon him. Frank could no longer rely on drawing to help keep him afloat as it was no longer part of his curriculum as a senior. While such courses as engineering, ethics and mineralogy and geology stimulated Frank to earn the modest standings of 28th, 29th and 33rd respectively and put him in the lower half of the class, he stood 18th in ordnance and gunnery. Perhaps artillerist John Gibbon, class of 1847 and author of *The Artillerist's Manual*, may have had something to do with Frank's improved standing. Frank would benefit from his association with John Gibbon later on when he was a prisoner of war. Tactics also made a claim on Frank's attention. He stood 25th in cavalry tactics, 16th in artillery tactics and an impressive 8th in infantry tactics. His demerits shrank as his standings improved. He finished his final year with a meager thirty-nine demerits, the fewest for all his years. To recap his demerit count over his five years at West Point, year by year, they amounted to, 60, 115, 97, 143 and finally 39.

Frank's classmate and close friend from North Carolina, Stephen Dodson Ramseur, destined to be a distinguished Confederate general, exhibited a fondness for tactics as did Frank. Ramseur finished 14th and stood 12th in all three tactics courses. Being at West Point for five years, Frank met with many young men who would take part in the forthcoming Civil War. In addition to Ramseur, Frank graduated with Pennsylvanian Horace Porter, a member of General Ulysses S. Grant's staff; Wade Hampton Gibbes of South Carolina, who served throughout the war and although seriously wounded at the Crater in July 1864 lived until 1903; and Wesley Merritt, a Union cavalry man who rose to the rank of general and whose service extended to the Spanish-American War. Senior to Frank were Edward Porter Alexander, Fitzhugh Lee, Marcus A. Reno, Richard Kidder Meade, Jr., Edwin H. Stoughton, John S. Marmaduke, George D. Bayard and Lundsford L. Lomax. Members of classes following Frank's class of 1860 that he knew were: Thomas L.

West Point cadets Stephen D. Ramseur, left, and Frank K. Huger (courtesy William A. Turner).

Rosser, John Pelham, Mathis W. Henry, Adelbert Ames, Henry A. DuPont, Orville A. Babcock, Morris Schaff, James Dearing, Emory Upton, Patrick H. O'Rorke, Alonzo H. Cushing, Pierce M. B. Young and the demerit magnate George A. Custer. Custer's record was worse than that of his Little Big Horn subordinate Marcus Reno. Custer hovered close to 200 demerits each year he attended the academy.

Among those who taught Frank at West Point in addition to Robert W. Weir and John Gibbon already mentioned were Cadmus M. Wilcox, William J. Hardee, John Pegram, Charles W. Field, George L. Hartsuff, Oliver O. Howard, Dennis Hart Mahan, John M. Schofield, Quincy A. Gilmore, Surgeon Samuel P. Moore, Gouverneur K. Warren, Alexander S. Webb and E. Porter Alexander. See appendix IV for short biographies of these men.

The source for Frank Huger's academic record is *Official Register of the Officers and Cadets of the U.S. Military Academy, West Point, New York, June, 1860*. Four earlier versions of the *Official Register* cover Huger's earlier years, each with identical title, except for the years 1856 through 1860.

Unfortunately no letters from Frank while he was at West Point exist among the Huger Family Papers. In fact there are no folders for the years 1856 through 1859. Yet among the family papers is one stating that Frank was a member of the Dialectic Society, United States Military Academy, June 1, 1860. The president was John Pelham and the secretary George S. Lovejoy. Frank's West Point diploma is contained within the family papers as well (Huger Family Papers 2006-0187, large folder). It is a beautiful document. Measuring eighteen inches long by twelve inches wide its borders are richly engraved. An eagle clutching American flags and banners in its talons is on top while the bottom is full of the instruments of a military education. A lone cadet, his musket by his side, points to a drawing of a fortification while all around him are books, a globe, drawing instruments, a telescope, chemical apparatus and a mortar. On the left margin classical implements of war are engraved—armor, a helmet, a shield and a short, Roman-type sword. On the right are flags, drums, sabers, a musket and pistol as well as a shako. The wording is as follows:

United States Military Academy
Be it known that Cadet Frank Huger of the State of Virginia having been carefully examined on all the Branches of the ARTS, SCIENCES and of LITERATURE taught at the United States Military Academy has been judged worthy to receive the Degree required by LAW preparatory to his advancement in the

U.S. Army. In testimony whereof and by Virtue of authority vested in the Academic Staff We do confer upon Him this Diploma and recommend him to the President for Promotion in Infantry, Dragoons, Mounted Rifles or Cavalry.

Given at West Point in the STATE of New York this fourteenth day of June in the Year of our Lord One thousand Eight Hundred and Sixty.

Frank's diploma was signed by the men listed below.

Richard Delafield, Colonel of Engineers and Superintendent of the Military Academy; D. H. Mahan, L.L.D., Prof. of Engineering; A. E. Church, L.L.D., Prof. of Mathematics; Robert W. Weir, N. A., Prof. of Drawing; J. W. French, M.A. Chaplin, Prof. of Ethics; P. de Janon, Prof. of Spanish Language; J. C. Duane, 1st Lieut. of Engineering Instruction; W.H.C. Bartlett, L.L.D., Prof of Natural Philosophy; W. H. Hardee, Maj. 2nd Cav., Instructor of Artillery, Infantry and Cavalry tactics; H. R. Agnel, Prof. of the French Language; H. L. Kendrick, Prof. of Chemistry; J. G. Benton, Captain, Ordnance Instructor.

Two cadets of the class of 1862, Morris Schaff and Tully McCrea, studied under the same faculty as did Frank Huger. They had definite opinions of these men. Schaff described Superintendent Delafield or "Old Dell" as "a pudgy man with heavy, sandy eyebrows, abundant grayish sandy hair, and a pronounced eagle nose. He wore glasses, and had the air of an officer and a man of cultivation, invested, furthermore, with the honor of a wide and well-earned distinction." When Delafield was relieved as superintendent in 1861 by Colonel Pierre G. T. Beauregard McCrea wrote, "Old Dell, our worthy Superintendent, has been relieved from duty here and his place is taken by Colonel Beauregard. You may be sure that this was a welcome change to the cadets who all detested 'Old Dell' for the manner in which he used his power over us."

Of the chaplain, John W. French, who also held the position of professor of English studies, Cadet McCrea wrote, "He is no more qualified to fill the place than the man in the moon." Tully McCrea's big objection was that Professor French made his classes study two works on grammar. Tully suffered under his French professor, Beekman Du Barry, and went to the head of the French Department, Hyacinth R. Agnel, who promised to look into Tully's charges. Tully also suffered under Dennis H. Mahan, professor of engineering. Mahan had a reputation for a cold eye and unbending manner. He was meticulous and irascible but at the same time known for unforgettable teaching. Tully described him this way: "Professor Mahan is the most particular, crabbed, exacting man I ever saw. He is a little slim skeleton of a man and is always nervous and cross." Tully did get along with W. H. C. Bartlett, professor of philosophy. "Old Bart," Tully wrote, "is an odd looking little man. He has a little sharp-pointed face and little eyes that are always dancing around and watching everything that is going on. His hair sticks out straight all over his head and he is so nervous that he cannot keep himself still for a minute.... Notwithstanding his looks, he is a very smart man and continues to make a very difficult subject interesting." McCrea got along with chemistry professor Henry L. Kendrick, an entertaining professor who had served on the plains and in Mexico. Another of McCrea's favorites was Captain Kenner Garrard, the riding instructor. Garrard, an old bachelor, took pains in teaching horsemanship to each cadet. The commandant, Colonel William H. Hardee, was not one of McCrea's favorites. Upon his replacement in 1860, McCrea wrote, "The Old Commandant [Hardee] who has been here ever since I have is ordered away and we have a new one who commenced his duties this morning. Colonel Hardee was disliked by all the cadets and they witness his departure without a feeling of regret. Major [John F.] Reynolds, the new one, has the reputation of being very strict and particular, and I expect that he will make the cadets toe the mark and behave themselves."

Cadet Schaff's opinion of Colonel Hardee was mixed and more flattering than McCrea's. Schaff described him as tall with large, solid gray eyes, a low forehead, heavy grizzled moustache and imperial and soldierly bearing. Hardee was, in Schaff's opinion, no ordinary man. Of the professors, Church, Mahan, Bartlett, French, Kendrick, Agnel, and Weir, Schaff described them as "beyond middle life; benignant, white locks softened the faces of most of them."[9]

Cadet Morris Schaff wrote a very moving description of what it meant to be a West Point graduate. Surely more cadets than he must have felt the same although they may not have had the ability of Schaff to describe it the way he did. Perhaps it was because of the time he spent in the library with various works of literature, a pastime not encouraged at West Point, that he could describe his feelings the way he did. He wrote:

> Among the immediate personal influences which are, so to speak, the initial processes of the spirit of West Point for transforming raw cadets into officers, are the stimulating effects which come with wearing the uniform, with the mastery of one's motions in walking, marching, or entering the presence of a superior, with the constant regard for neatness and the habit of scrupulous truth-telling. Moreover, there is something uplifting in finding one's self among high-minded equals, and in realizing that in your superiors is lodged one of the most important functions of government,— the right and power of command. Then, too, the cadet begins to be conscious of the exclusive and national distinction of the Military Academy. Very soon, the monuments, the

captured guns, and dreaming colors — which at the outset are mere interesting, historic relics — beckon to him; he feels that they have something to say. Before he leaves West Point they have given him their message, revealing from time to time to his vision that field from which lifts the radiant mist called glory.[10]

When Frank graduated, near the bottom of his class, he received an unusual graduation gift from his father, a pair of no ordinary spurs. The spurs had been given to Benjamin Huger by General Winfield Scott who came by them from Mexican General Antonio Lopez de Santa Anna. When the Mexican general surrendered to Scott in Mexico City in 1847 he offered his sword to Scott who promptly returned it. In a gesture of appreciation Santa Anna gave Scott his spurs. Soon after Scott presented the spurs to Benjamin Huger, Scott's chief of ordnance and artillery, for bravery at Vera Cruz, Molino del Rey and Chapultepec. Frank had the spurs all through the Civil War; however their interesting history did not end with Frank's ownership. The reader will learn more about them in Frank's letters that follow. See the following website — http://www.norfolkhistorical.org/insights/2002_spring/huger.html — for a picture of the remaining spur.

On July 2, 1860, Frank received a signed document from the War Department that the president appointed him a brevet second lieutenant in the Third Regiment of Infantry. It was signed by the secretary of war, John B. Floyd. On January 19, 1861, Frank received his commission to the Tenth Infantry Regiment but as late as April 15, 1861, he had not yet accepted it, preferring the Eighth Regiment instead. His indecision was recorded in a letter he wrote on April 15, 1861, to his friend "Legs." "Legs," the school name for Alfred Theophilus Smith, was a second lieutenant in the Eighth Infantry. A classmate of Frank's, Smith served the Union in the Civil War and made the army his career, retiring in June 1899. Dod may be Albert Baldwin Dod listed in Heitman's register as being a captain in the 15th Infantry as of May 14, 1861. Dod was from New Jersey. Frank mentioned a number of soon to be famous Civil War officers of both sides in his letter to "Legs": Fitzhugh Lee, Charles W. Field, Robert Anderson and Samuel P. Heintzelman. Frank mentioned meeting another classmate, Second Lieutenant George W. Vanderbilt "whiskers and all" is how Frank, now in the Tenth Infantry Regiment, described him. Vanderbilt, son of Commodore Vanderbilt, a good athlete but poor scholar, became a captain in the Tenth before dying January 1, 1864. Frank told "Legs" about a girl he did not name but wrote, "She is a nice girl — the more I see of her the better I like her, but Civil War and females don't go together." Frank's Civil War letters reveal it was hard for him to keep the two apart.

Fort Columbus, N.Y. H.[arbor] April 15, 1861

My dear Legs

Yours of the night of the 12th I recd yesterday.— and what a crowd of events to have transpired since. Sumpter taken, and civil war now on us. I've just read an article from the "Courier and Enquirer" of this morning, which made me so mad that I determined to write to you by way of appeasing my wrath. I'll cut it out and send it to you tho' probably you will see it in some of the papers. I suppose Bob Anderson will be here Wedy. Morning when we'll get some of the particulars. I'm glad you saw Dod. He no doubt gave you all the details of this part of the world. I was mighty sorry to see him resign, but it's likely he only anticipated what he would soon have to do by a very few days. Johnson has not resigned — he is here having just got back from leave. Major Heintzelman is here, took command today. A recruiting rendezvous has been opened in Phila. Woods is ordered there, will go this week, at the which Josh is cussing severely, as he is anxious to get away from...

... saw Warren and walking down the street met Vanderbilt.— whiskers and all.... Saw Charley Field, Fitz Lee and Owens. Got a good cursing from them for not going in the Cavalry. Had I done so I would now be the 2nd, 2nd Lieut. in the 2d Cavy., just where Sam Sweet is. I'm glad he had the luck anyhow. McMillan came over here last night, par consequence I got tight.... Everybody here is as usual. She is very well I believe. Saw her last Thursday. She is a nice girl, the more I see her the better I like her, but Civil War and females don't go together.... [Vertical note up the left margin of page one: *"If father hasn't seen this article show him the cursed slander."*]

This letter by Frank Huger was sold by Historical Collectible Auctions, then situated in Graham, North Carolina, in their sale of May 8, 2003. Historian Robert K. Krick produced this transcription for inclusion in this work, based on the original HCA catalogue page, which photographically reproduced the first page of the manuscript, and he also supplied a partial typed version of the second page. Mr. Krick also identified Sam Sweet as John Jay Sweet.

At some point Frank did become part of the Tenth Infantry. When he resigned from the U.S. Army the Adjutant General's Office wrote that his resignation had been accepted on May 21, 1861. It was addressed to him at Tenth Infantry, Fort Columbus, New York.

On June 6, 1861, Virginia governor John Letcher commissioned Frank Huger a captain in the Fourth Regiment of Artillery of the Ninth Brigade and Fourth Division of the Virginia Militia. Included among the papers comprising Frank's service record is an equipment list for his mounted battery.

Received at Norfolk July 23rd 1861 of Brig-Genl J. C. Pemberton Chief of Arty the following Articles for the equipment of my mounted Battery of Field Arty,

Fourteen	14 Sets Arty Harness for Livery
Nine	9 Sets Harness Caissons
Twelve	12 Saddles
Twenty Four	24 Yards Sheeps Gray for Saddle Blankets
Thirty Two	32 Leather Halters
Four	4 Bridles for Chiefs of Pieces
Eight	8 Leg Guards
Nine	9 Leather Pads
Eight	8 Leather Whips
One	1 Caisson
One	1 lb. Lamp Black
One	1 Iron Brace & Bit
One	1 Hand Saw [unclear]
One	1 Tenant Saw
Two	2 Bridles for Sample Harness
Six	6 S Hooks & Two Camp Stools

Frank Huger
Capt. Compy D
Light Arty Service

Frank acknowledged in July 1861 (day either not given or too badly faded) the receipt of thirty-three horses from General Pemberton "for the service of my Field Battery."[11]

On April 4, 1863, Frank took the rank of major of artillery in the Provisional Army in the service of the Confederate States to rank from March 2, 1863, the order signed by Confederate secretary of war James A. Seddon. Following is a letter written by E. P. Alexander requesting the promotion of two officers to higher rank, T. C. Jordon and Frank Huger.

Warrenton, Va. June 14, 1864

General
    I respectfully beg leave to renew an application for the promotion of Capt.

T. C. Jordon comdy Battery in my Battalion of Arty to the rank of Major of Arty to be assigned to duty with the Battalion. I made application for this promotion last August thru Gen Pendleton Chf Arty AnVa [Chief of Artillery, Army of Northern Virginia] *by whom it was approved but the Battalion being sent out to the Army of Ten. shortly after nothing more was heard of the application. My Battalion consists of six Batteries smooth bore & rifle& is always necessarily divided on the field sometimes by long distances & into many fragments & the assistance of two field officers is often seriously needed even when I am in personal command myself. At present & for sometime past I have been assigned as Chief of Arty of Gen. Longstreets Corps & thus removed from the immediate command of the Battn leaving but one field officer with it.*

Major F. Huger thru circumstances & the size of my command, I think warrant the appointment of another field officer & I repeatedly recommended Capt. T. C. Jordon for the promotion. Capt. Jordon has commanded his Battery since the commencement of this war on the Peninsula the first year & since then in all the campaigns & battles of Longstreets Corps in each & all of which he has won the praise & high opinion of every one of his commanders by his gallantry & efficiency & has been frequently recommended by them for promotion.

I most respectfully request at the same time the promotion to the grade of Lieut. Col. of Maj. <u>Frank Huger</u> (now & for the last year Major of my Battn.) both on the grounds above mentioned of the size of my command — (larger than any Regiment of Infantry) & my operation from it by other duties, as well as from his distinguished skill & gallantry in fighting it on the fields of Chancellorsville, Gettysburg & the recent Knoxville campaign in all of which it has been almost wholy [sic] under his control. I have always been assigned to command additional Battalions.

His promotion will be as beneficial to the service as it is well merited by his conduct.

I am General very respectfully
Your obdt. Servt. E. P. Alexander
Col. and Chf Arty Longstreets Corps

To
Gen. S. Cooper
Adgt. & Inspt. Genl C.S.A.

I most respectfully ask the reception of this paper without its reference thru Corps Hd Qrs which would require much delay. The promotions I feel confident will meet the approval of Gen. Longstreet.

E.P. Alexander
Col Arty[12]

Frank became colonel of artillery in the same service as of February 18, 1865, the order signed by Confederate secretary of war John C. Breckenridge. These documents are among the Huger Family Papers. Upon attaining the rank of colonel Frank had to take an oath of allegiance to the Confederate States of America. The document follows.

ACCEPTANCE AND OATH

Having been appointed Colonel in the Artillery of the P. A. C. S. [Provisional Army Confederates States] I do hereby accept the same and certify that I am aged 27 years 6 months, born in the state of Virginia appointed from the state Virginia and I Frank Huger Col. P.A.C.S. do solemnly swear or affirm that while I continue in the service I will bear true faith and yield obedience to the Confederate States of America, and that I will serve them honorably and faithfully against their enemies, and that I will observe and obey the orders of the President of the Confederate States and the orders of the Officers appointed over me, according to the Rules and Articles of War.

Frank Huger Col Arty

This was sworn to on March 22, 1865.

The last in the following series of Frank Huger's wartime letters describes in detail his capture and surrender. Shortly after his capture his West Point friend Brigadier General George A. Custer temporarily took charge of him. Custer offered to look after Frank's historic spurs. It may have been just as well. The Yankees he first encountered stole his watch. Some months after the war Custer asked to keep the spurs indefinitely and he did, wearing them at Little Big Horn. One of the spurs was recovered from Custer's remains and given to Custer's widow, Libby. She returned the spur to Frank. The spur remained in the Huger family until a family member presented it to the Virginia Historical Society. See the website: http://www.norfolkhistorical.org/insights/2002_spring/huger.html.

On April 12, 1865, Frank Huger took the oath of parole, granting him permission to pass within the Petersburg, Virginia, city limits. On June 25, 1865, Federal major general George S. Hartsuff, commanding the District of the Nottoway, signed an order extending the limits for Col. Frank Huger to include the entire extent of this command. On that very day Frank wrote to the U.S. secretary of war applying for restoration of his civil rights as a citizen of the United States. On September 2, 1865, the Office of the Commissary General of Prisoners, Washington, D.C., wrote to Major General John Gibbon, commanding the District of Nottoway that Frank Huger by direction of the lieutenant general commanding, in consequence of Frank's ill health, was to be "placed on the same footing as other officers of Lee's Army surrendered and paroled at Appomattox Court House." Finally on November 11, 1865, Frank received a final receipt of his parole granting him the right "to go to his home and there remain undisturbed."

CHAPTER THREE

The War Letters

1862

This letter, uncovered among the Huger Family Papers, Virginia Historical Society, Richmond, Virginia, was not among the set of letters in the transcribed set from Mr. Lloyd Smith. It begins with one written to Frank's mother by his older brother Ben Jr. An attachment from Frank follows. At Seven Pines, the battle described, the clouds began to gather that darkened Benjamin Huger's military reputation. Yet as Joseph T. Glatthaar explained, General Joseph E. Johnston issued two vague orders to Huger, neither of which informed him that a battle would take place. General James Longstreet, who was not clear in his understanding of Johnston's intentions, marched down a road that caused his troops to collide with those of Huger's. "To the south," Glatthaar wrote, "Longstreet completely mismanaged the attack, finally getting Huger in position to fight but with instructions to await further orders. None came."[1]

Letter Number 1

Moseley's battery, the 3rd Richmond Howitzers, fought under Edgar F. Moseley. Moseley rose to the rank of lieutenant colonel and commanded a battalion later in the war. He was killed at Petersburg December 16, 1864. Col. Anderson was George B. Anderson, in command of a brigade when killed at Antietam.

Here Frank first mentions his friend Tilghman, the first of several references to him in the letters that follow. Tilghman is never fully identified but the reader can make an inference that he was a close friend of Frank's. There are some data that indicates Tilghman's first name may have been Lee. Tilghman had a brother named Tench. Tench Tilghman, aide to General George Washington, was from Maryland and following the Revolutionary War established a business and a family in Baltimore. Tench Tilghman the younger and brother to the Tilghman Frank wrote about may certainly have been named for his famous ancestor.

The most detailed account of "Lee" Tilghman is in a letter to Frank from Frank's older brother Benjamin Huger, Jr. Written from Augusta, Georgia, on December 13, 1862, a Saturday, the letter told of Tilghman's death, two days before this letter's date. "We buried him yesterday morning ~~from the~~ [the two words "from the" were scratched out] in a private burying ground adjoining the Arsenal." The letter stated that Tilghman, sometime earlier, had been in Florida. He had just spent a few days at the arsenal when he died of natural causes. The possible cause of death, from the written description in the letter, was a ruptured appendix. Finally, Cel is Frank's sister, Celestine Pinckney Huger.

Head Qrs Huger's Division
Williams Farm May 31st 1862

My dear Mother
I am left here to keep shop while all the rest except Frank have gone to the vicinity of a pretty stiff skirmish which is going on not very far from here. Men have been pouring in through here all day, and we must have a very large force although [unclear].

Frank's attachment:

Ben has just stopped to make out a forage acquisition and as I have just happened in I'll say the scrimmage has commenced about three miles from here. Moseley's battery is here too. There are so many Guns and men that I'm afraid only a few will have a chance — Every thing (considering) is looking well — all in good spirits and determined to give the Yankees a good thrashing, which we will do tomorrow sure — if our advance don't do it all tonight. I got the clothes bag, much obliged. All well — except Col. Anderson, who has been slightly unwell but is out today and better. — We have all been busy as you may suppose — Love to darling Cel. — Don't be uneasy about us —, act now on any old rule, that is don't be alarmed until you hear for so many men are pouring out of Richmond, I hardly see how they will ever get organized again — and any men sent away for one time. Tilghman is well.
Your affect.[ionate] Boy,
Frank Huger

Before he commanded a division on the Peninsula Benjamin Huger commanded at Norfolk. His conduct there has been described as incompetent. Subordinate to Huger was General Henry A. Wise, commanding a force insufficient to withstand Union general Ambrose E. Burnside and his advance on Roanoke Island, of incalculable importance for the defense of Norfolk. "Men and supplies," wrote Craig M. Simpson, "were so scarce as to compel reflection on what motives the Confederate high command could possibly have had in sending Wise and his men to almost certain defeat. Huger offered nothing. His almost complete obliviousness to impending disaster indicates his gross incompetence."[2]

The Union advance was no surprise to Huger or to the Confederacy. Standing with a telescope on Sewell's Point Huger could pick out individual faces on the ships sailing to North Carolina. Huger cabled to Richmond accurately reporting every ship and he concluded they were sailing to North Carolina.[3]

General Wise pleaded constantly with Huger for engineers, gunners, powder, shot, entrenching tools and infantry, items that Huger had in relative abundance. Huger responded with encouraging advice but no substantial help.[4]

Letter Number 2

Huger presented his side in a letter written to Confederate general Samuel Cooper.

Headquarters Dept. Norfolk
Norfolk, Va. Febr. 16, 1862

General S. Cooper
Adjt. & Insp. Genl.
Sir

I submit for the consideration of the Secretary of War a proposed arrangement of the Brigades of this division, rendered necessary by the movement of the enemy.

I had sent the 6th Va. Regt. Col. [Thomas Jefferson] *Corprew to the Currituck bridge, with orders to hold that point and to prevent the enemy from passing through the South branch of the Chesapeake and Albemarle Canal.*

General [Henry A.] *Wise on his retreat from Nag's head came to Currituck Bridge, assumed command, removed the battery of three 32 pdrs. erected there and began abandoning the place before any enemy appeared. Soon after two or* three gunboats came up, fired a few rounds, which fell short, and our troops left. The enemy have not advanced since and our Cavalry pickets are still there.

I had no report from General Wise for two days, but heard he was falling back on Norfolk. I sent yesterday to establish batteries near Great Bridge, on the North branch of the Albemarle and Chesapeake Canal to block that passage and visited that place to day. I found General Wise there, with the five Companies of the 6th Va. Regt., five pieces of artillery under Col [Charles Frederick] Henningsen and about four companies of his [Wise's] Legion under Col [John Harvie] Richardson.

I enquired of Genl. Wise why he abandoned his position at Currituck bridge <u>without orders,</u> but could get no satisfactory answer. He said he intended to occupy a position N. W. River, but on reaching there in a snow storm found no quarters for his men he fell back to Great Bridge, twelve miles South of Norfolk where he is now.

I must be allowed to consider General Wise supernumerary with his army and relieve him from duty. His Legion has no doubt fine material, but I consider it entirely disorganized and I shall feel stronger if it is removed.

I am Sir
Very respectfully
Benj. Huger Maj Genl Commdg.

Back in May 1861, General Lee had to acquaint Henry A. Wise with the military facts of life. In reply to Wise's letter of May 3, Lee wrote from Richmond on May 24, 1861, explaining the difficulty of preparing defenses at the many threatened points in Virginia. "We are still engaged in making gun carriages for the river defenses and field service, preparing ammunition for all arms, constructing machines for the manufacture of caps, &c., ammunition wagons, &c., which must be continued," Lee wrote. "It seems to me, therefore," Lee continued, "impossible at this time to prepare a marine battery, such as you describe, which would be effective in carrying out your design, as desirable as it would be." Lee then went on to explain why some other of Wise's proposals was not within the means of the Confederacy at present.

"General B. Huger, formerly of the U.S. Army, an officer of great merit, has been assigned to the command at Norfolk, and I hope will be able to secure it against successful invasion," General Lee wrote. He replaced General Walter Gwynn at Norfolk with General Huger after Lee inspected Norfolk on May 16. Gwynn, drowning in detail, had not seen regular military service since 1832. Progress on the fortifications proceeded slowly.[5]

As of March 24, 1862, General Huger had 13,000 Confederate troops in the Department of Norfolk. This force covered the city, the navy yard and the south side of the lower James River. Huger was exposed to attack up the inland waterways from Albemarle Sound. Across Hampton Roads was Union general John Wool at Fort Monroe, in position to make a descent on Huger once the Confederate ironclad *Virginia* was silenced.[6]

The friendship between Generals Lee and Huger began at least as early as the 1830s, when the two were posted together at Fort Monroe. Although Huger was only little more than a year older than Lee, his was the West Point class of 1825, Lee's was the class of 1829. There is little chance their cadet years overlapped. Other companions at Fort Monroe in addition to Huger were James Barnes, Robert Parrott and Albert E. Church, "all of them brilliant."[7]

Letter Number 3

The following letter is one of the first of many complete letters Frank wrote to his mother, the former Elizabeth Celestine Pinckney. She married Frank's father, Benjamin Huger, on February 7, 1831. Frank misspelled Charles Town in this letter. His mention of Dick and the horses refers to his servant and the artillery horses that often traveled apart from the guns. His two references to General Lee are to General Robert E. Lee, commanding general of the Army of Northern Virginia. The Col. Waggerman Frank named may have been Eugene Waggaman. His rank of lieutenant colonel dated from Jan. 16, 1862. Although captured at Malvern Hill, Waggaman returned to duty following his exchange on August 5, 1862, time enough to have been in charge of the camp as Frank reported in the following letter.[8] The Rifle G[un] and Howitzer are artillery field pieces. The date of this letter puts it seven days before the battle of Antietam or Sharpsburg. This letter helps to confirm the heavy straggling in General Lee's army during this Maryland campaign.

Of this battle Joseph L. Harsh wrote, "For one brief coruscating moment Antietam stood as the undisputed turning point of the Civil War. The battle carried the war into wholly new dimensions. The man-made cyclone that engulfed the hills around Sharpsburg on September 17, 1862, scaled a fury previously unknown in the Civil War. It was as though the two days of Shiloh or the Seven Days around Richmond had been collapsed into a single bloody dawn to dusk."[9]

Oliver Wendell Holmes, Sr., described his feelings upon seeing the Antietam battlefield just days after the carnage. His son, the future jurist Oliver Wendell Holmes, Jr., received a neck wound serving as a captain in the Twentieth Massachusetts. Holmes Sr. searched for his wounded son to take him back to Boston to recover. "I picked up a Rebel canteen, and one of our own — but there was something repulsive about the trodden and stained relics on the stale battle-field. It was like the table of some hideous orgy left uncleared, and one turned away disgusted from its broken fragments and muddy heel-taps."[10]

Winchester,
Wednesday, Sept. 10th, 1862

My dear Mother:
After a rather long but pleasant ride, I arrived here this morning to find that the Yankees have possession of Charlestown [sic] & Harpers Ferry, and here we have to stay until we can get away. After I arrived at Gordonsville on Friday last, met Dick with the horses, and after kicking my heels, and trying to get something to eat at every place, I started in the cool of the evening for Orange C.[ourt] H.[ouse] eleven miles, where I got a good supper and a clean bed. The next day rode to Culpepper C.[ourt] H.[ouse], found very little for horse or man except wounded and sick men of both armies, and on Sunday rode to Warrenton where I arrived at 11 P.M. Could get nothing to eat for the horses, the place was crowded, sick, wounded and stragglers. The entire country from Orange C.H. to Warrenton is a desert, every thing destroyed and nothing to eat for horse or man. Beyond, in this direction, affairs seem better. At Warrenton we received orders from General Lee to join the army by Front Royal and this place, as his pickets were withdrawn and the usual road was not considered safe, so after two nights on the road here we are established at a Boarding house. We can't get to Maryland now but the road through Charlestown [sic] will be opened soon I think. Stragglers are pouring in and they have established a camp. Col. Waggerman is here, and is going to take charge of the camp. I shall report there for duty today (Thursday) and when we get five thousand men we should be able to march to H.[arpers] Ferry. Ten thousand will be here in a day or two; at all events I have so far obeyed Gen. Lee's order in coming here, and shall stay, until I can get away. I tried to get from Paris to Charlestown, [sic] but when I got near Berryville and found the Yankees were there, I started for this 'burg. The Yankees came within a few miles of this place last Sunday, and why they don't come here now and capture the five hundred wagons we have I don't see. I tried to cross the ridge and river near Paris, not coming by Front Royal. Tell Tilghman that I've seen men from the battery. They did well, at North Branch of the Rappahannock and Manassas. The Rifle G and Howitzer are lost, abandoned when they broke, between North —
    [Remainder of the letter is lost].

Letter Number 4

Frank wrote to his father just four days after the battle of Antietam or Sharpsburg telling him of the condition of his battery. The day here cited, Wednesday, was September 17, 1862, the day of the battle. The Jackson he referred to as having whipped the Yankees was, of course, Thomas J. "Stonewall" Jackson. Poor Grimes was Captain Cary F. Grimes of Grimes' [Portsmouth] Virginia Battery. Captain John Taylor was John S. Taylor of Tyler C. Jordan's [Bedford] Virginia Battery. General Anderson was Richard Heron Anderson. Anderson commanded a division of Lieutenant-General James Longstreet's 1st Corps to which Huger's battalion was attached.[11]

Winchester, Sunday, 21st Sept. 1862

My dear Father:

I left here last Sunday and I am again after the roughest week I've ever spent. I'm about 7 miles from here on the Martinsburg Pike, and am here today to get my two pieces changed for one 3 in. rifle and a light Napoleon gun. My Battery is very much crippled—nearly useless, for on Wednesday it was nearly used up—6 horses out of twelve killed. I only got in for a few minutes, found everything crippled and could hardly get off. I want two days now to fit up. I hear today that Jackson whipped the Yankees that crossed yesterday at Shepherdstown and that our army had recrossed.

I have not heard of you all since I left. Poor Grimes was killed—acted very gallantly. We brought his body and that of Capt. John Taylor and buried them in Virginia. Love to all—

I write very hurriedly—am well. General Anderson is here, not very badly hurt.

Your Affec. Boy
Frank Huger

Letter Number 5

On Sunday, September 28, one week after the letter above, Frank wrote again to his father, a major general under a cloud for poor performance on the Peninsula during the Seven Days.[12] He was, however, underutilized in his position of inspector of artillery and ordnance. The letters to Lieutenant General James Longstreet and the settlement with him that Frank mentioned in the following letter refers to the dispute between Longstreet and the elder Huger over confused troop movements at Seven Pines.[13]

Forden was the last name of Frank's prior sergeant and he now had become a hospital steward at General Hospital. Dr. Moore is probably Samuel Preston Moore, a former U.S. Army surgeon who was appointed Confederate surgeon general in 1861. Dr. Moore was at West Point when Frank was enrolled there as a cadet. Dr. Moore spent twenty-six years with the U.S. Army and served in Mexico under General Winfield Scott.[14]

Wilcox was General Cadmus Marcellus Wilcox (1826–1890), a division commander in the Army of Northern Virginia. He authored *Rifles and Rifle Practice* (1859) and *History of the Mexican War* (1892). A Lt. Gale is listed in Jennings C. Wise's book *The Long Arm of Lee* as commanding a section of Captain Valentine J. Clutter's Richmond Battery. Cellie was Frank's only sister. Jack was John Smith Preston, and future husband of Celestine Pinckney Huger. Sloan was Benjamin F. Sloan Jr. a member of General Benjamin Huger's staff and Ben was Frank's older brother.

Sunday, Sept. 28th, 1862
near Winchester

Dear father:

I have frequently written to you and to Mother within the last two weeks but as I have a good chance today I write again to tell you that the letters you gave me for Longstreet and your Bridg<u>rs</u> were all left in my bag which I have never seen since I left Gordonsville. One of my men who was coming on said he would bring it from Rapidan. He has never gotten here, and I understand has gone back to Richmond. Forden, at Dr. Moores Hospital would probably know his whereabouts. I had intended sending Lieut. Gale down but he can't go now. I believe I have written the above two or three times but I want you to know the facts.

Our army fell back yesterday from in front of Martinsburg to this position, viz. Jackson at Bunker Hill—12 miles from Winchester and the rest of the Army between the 6 mile post and Winchester. I don't know what caused the move, but it is evident this force can't subsist in this region where every thing is scarce and our Army must be clothed and shod this winter. Its pretty cold at night now. My horses have not had a bit of corn since I've been with the battery. Wilcox is in command of the division.

Have not heard a word from any of you since I left. If you direct to me and enclose to Maj. Walter Taylor, A.D.C. to General Lee, Hdqts. Army N.V., I would get it. I am anxious to hear how you all are. Tell Cellie Joe is still with the battery but that Ned was lost just after the fight at Warrenton. Lost my nigger Jim, that

I brought from Norfolk, the night we crossed from Maryland. He was a simple brute and is no doubt wandering around our army looking for me. Hope he will succeed in finding me. If I only had your letters and some papers which are very valuable, I wouldn't care to have my bag with me, for as we are hauled around, marching any time day or night, it is almost impossible to keep any thing—, a tooth brush and a pocket comb which is sufficient for active service. It appears to me that we must fall back to some point nearer Richmond, where we can get supplies and I do hope and trust that you can settle with Longstreet. You had better send it through General Lee.

What is Sloan doing and where is Ben and Tilghman? Love to all—Tell Cellie I once had hopes, not longer than two weeks ago, that I could bring her something handsome from Baltimore, but I must postpone it now. Where is Jack? It is very dry and the dust can't be described. I've only seen one paper in two weeks so if any thing important come out, do send it to me.

Your affect. Boy—
F. H.

Letter Number 6

General Huger was concerned with General Longstreet's characterization of him at the battle of Seven Pines. He wrote the following letter sometime in November 1862.

Charleston South Carolina
November [day is missing] 1862

Honl. G. W. Randolph
Sec. of War
Sir,

As I hear Genl. J. E. Johnston has reported for duty, I hope before he is assigned to any distant command the "exigencies of the service" may permit you to grant me the Court of Enquiry promised. As Genl. Johnston's published report of the battle of "Seven Pines" ignores the presence of the Division I there commanded at that battle, it is but justice to the whole of the Division as well as myself that the Court of Enquiry directed by the President should be assembled as soon as possible.

Very Respectfully Your Obt. Servt.
Benj. Huger Major General[15]

Fredericksburg

"The Fredericksburg Campaign wrought a remarkable season of change. The December encounter proved to be the last battle fought by the majestic full might of both armies. The Army of the Potomac and the Army of Northern Virginian never met in battle again with such immense, burgeoning legions. Fredericksburg was the final battle of the celebrated Confederate triumvirate of Lee, Jackson, and Longstreet."

"In terms of Confederate leadership, Fredericksburg may be summed up by the old saying, 'shooting fish in a barrel.'"[16]

Letter Number 7

Camped outside the town several weeks before the battle of Fredericksburg, Virginia, a battle Frank did not anticipate at the time, he wrote the following letter to his mother. Aunt Henderson, if she were an actual aunt and relative rather than someone the family held dear, was in all probability one of Frank's father's sisters. His mother's only sister, Rosetta Ella Pinckney, married Ralph Stead Izard, a wealthy South Carolina planter, who died in 1858. While there is no record of Frank's aunt Elizabeth Huger (1804–1882) in the online genealogical records of having been married, she may have been and may be the elusive "Aunt Henderson" who is mentioned in other letters as well. Her older sister, Anna Isabella Huger, married Edward Harleston in 1826. Another sister, Mary Ester Huger, married Joseph Alston Huger. Her youngest sister, Harriott Horry Huger, married Alfred Ford Ravenel. At the close of a letter dated November 27, 1863, from Marshall, Texas, Major General Benjamin Huger wrote to his wife that General John B. Magruder's impudence was astounding. He followed that revelation with "Need not tell Henderson." The census of 1860 for Fredericksburg, Virginia, lists a Mary Henderson, a possible candidate for the role of Aunt Henderson.

Mrs. Anderson may have been distressed because Ned and Joe might possibly have been slaves she rented to Frank. From other letters Frank makes clear that he had a manservant whom he rented and was concerned that he not get behind in his payments to the owner.

The "old Burnsides" he referred to was Union major general Ambrose E. Burnside, who replaced General George B. McClellan as commander of the Army of the Potomac in early November 1862.

Mrs. Huger, Frank's mother, was on her way to Richmond having been in Columbia, South Carolina, and now in Raleigh, North Carolina. Frank's concern was probably for his paternal grandmother's whereabouts, Harriot

Lucas Pinckney Huger. In a letter dated Dec. 13, 1862, from his brother Ben Frank learned of Tilghman's death, and that the rest of the family was in Charleston to read Grandmother's will.

Near Fredericksburg, Sunday Nov. 23rd, 1862

My dear Mother:

We arrived here yesterday evening after a very tough and never-to-be-forgotten march from Culpepper C.[ourt]*H.*[ouse] *having left there Wednesday evening. It had been raining for two or three days and during the entire march it poured down a miserable cold rain — the roads were awful. Thank Heavens that part of our Journey is over. I'm in camp about two miles from town. As soon as I got here I was ordered into town to report to General Longstreet and as I was there I went to Aunt Hendersons. Found her just about to leave the town as the Yankees said they would bombard it at 3 P.M. She had time enough tho' to give me a nice lunch and a bottle of brandy and a ham to bring to camp. Many persons think the town will be shelled. I do not and rather incline to the opinion that the Devils are now making a move in some other direction. I don't expect any fight here and rather look for the next one on the South side of the James River. I told you I had received my boots. They are worth ten times their value on this march. Mrs. Anderson will be distressed to hear that Joe* [unclear, looks as if something was enclosed in parentheses] *is lost. He had a custom of going into Culpepper every day and staying all day, so when we marched he was absent and had to be left to the great distress of us all. This ends the history of Ned and Joe. The Yanks are in immense force over the river. Their batteries command every street. They picket one end of the bridge, and we the other. Many persons are passing now from town carrying their valuables, I suppose, which apparently consists of old bedding, broken looking glasses & crockery. It is really distressing tho' to see women, old and young and little children, being carted out of town in all kinds of vehicles, this cold day. I hope we can drub old Burnsides well, the first chance we get. Your letter from Raleigh I received the day after I answered yours from Columbia. I'll send for the things as soon as I can get a chance. I have a great many men that want stockings and some few that are entirely barefooted. Any thing is useful and awfully appreciated now a days. I don't know when I'll have an opportunity to send this off — but will pocket it for the first chance I may have. Love to all. Where is Grandmother. I want to write to Tilghman as soon as I know where he is.— Turning very cold and feels like snow. Love to all —*

Your affect. Boy
Frank Huger.

1863

Letter Number 8

Frank's next letter to his mother was dated a full two months after his last. It contained little of the Battle of Fredericksburg. Frank's superior, Lieutenant Colonel Edward Porter Alexander, the battalion commander, wrote, "Fredericksburg was the most dramatic of all our battles; the opposing hills & intermediate plain affording some wonderful & magnificent scenes. And I expect few who heard those two cannon shot, that cold morning, and rose & ate & hastened to their posts by starlight ever forgot the occasion."[17] At the time of the letter below Frank was camped outside Fredericksburg near Banks Ford on the Rappahannock River about a mile and a quarter almost due north of famous Salem Church. Frank misspelled Massaponax Church, located a few miles south of Fredericksburg, as "Massahonax."

Getting letters from home was important to Frank and the Taylor he mentions to whom his mother's letters should be sent is the same Major Walter Herron Taylor, A.D.C. to General Lee, he identified in the letter above to his father dated September 28. Ruther Glen, site of the post office Frank mentions in his postscript, is in Caroline County on route 652, just east of present day I-95 and about half way between Fredericksburg and Richmond, Virginia. The Jones from whom he received a letter was probably Frank Freeman Jones as there was a Baltimore connection and that Jones was inspector of small arms for most of the war at the Richmond Armory. Frank referred to Jones in a letter to his father (letter number 10) while Huger senior was still arms inspector and before he was sent to Trans-Mississippi.[18] Anderson was Major General Richard H. Anderson, a division commander in Longstreet's corps. Aunt Rosey is probably Frank's mother's sister Rosetta Ella Pinckney (1817–1872) who married Ralph Stead Izard. She was a widow at this time. L. Moore may well be Lieutenant Joseph D. Moore of whom Frank wrote in a later letter. Lieutenant Moore was in Frank's battery.

In Camp — near Fredericksburg
Sunday night — January 25, 1863

My dear Mother:

Your letter of the 16th and one from Jones of the 13th reached me today. You see I've again moved since writing you, and now at 10 P.M. I've got through putting my battery in a new position perfectly masked within three hundred yards of the *enemy's pickets. The location is splendid and if the Yanks try to come over Banks ford I'll be in clover. At the last fight I thought I had the best position to do some work but didn't have much of an opportunity to do any thing except be shot at. Should they come again, I hope the fun will be reciprocal.*

On the evening of the 16th, we got orders to bring up all the artillery <u>at once</u> as a fight was momentarily expected. It was bitter cold. The next day by 12 o'clock I reported the batteries as nearly up and was ordered to halt, which I did at Massahonax [sic] church 8 miles from here. The day following moved two miles nearer and yesterday was moved again to near this point. Today I received orders to come to these works—and now I hope it is intended to let us stay here for I'm tired of moving this wet weather and my horses all nearly starved to death. I wouldn't mind all this trouble if I thought we should be used but I don't think there is the slightest prospect of a fight and I know that is Gen. Anderson's opinion. However, I've got good quarters—in a sheltered ravine and ought to be satisfied. I'm very sorry indeed to hear of little Claude Brownriggs death. She was a sweet little girl, very natural in most of her ways, and a very good friend of mine. I was very fond of her and used to be there a good deal when stationed in New York.

I suppose it would be charitable to consider Aunt Rosey crazy. I saw a published list of arrivals but she was not among them and I'll bet she will not come until the war is over which, by the way it appears from the general tone of the Northern press, is not an impossible thing in a short time. I'm ready for it I'm sure. I had intended asking you what arrangements Cel had made about getting married but you tell me none as yet. I declare I hate to think about her marrying but I suppose the sooner it is, the better satisfied they both be. Whenever it does happen, I'll surely be there, military necessities, tho' the contrary not withstanding. You'd better send your letters to Taylor—those to Ruther Glen I've received straight. L. Moore says the boxes have not yet arrived in Richmond, tho' he says

Wartime photograph of Frank Huger (courtesy Petersburg National Battlefield).

he expects them in a day or so — upon what he bases his expectations I don't know. I'm very well. Love to all —

> *Your affect. Boy*
> *Frank H.*

Monday Morning — 7 A.M.

Have just received orders to return to Caroline County forthwith. I was a member of a Gen. Court near there and hoped this move would get me clear of it for I expect it will be in session 'till March but now I'm ordered back. Better direct to Ruther Glen P.[ost] O.[ffice].

Letter Number 9

Less than two weeks before the battle of Chancellorsville, Frank wrote to his sister, "Celly." He was unsure if she had married yet. That April she married Jack, John Smith Preston, Jr., in Columbia, South Carolina. Jack's father made his money in sugar and was South Carolina's secession commissioner to Virginia. Jack volunteered as a private in the Confederate service at the very beginning of hostilities. Mary Chesnut described him in her diary as follows: "Jack Preston has not his father's imposing presence, but he understands as well all the acts of a gracious hospitality. Jack is such a good fellow, so kind, so witty himself, and so ready to make the most of other people's wit and humor."[19]

Little Seve is a reference to Frank and Celly's mother. Dr. Jno Bayler [sic] was Dr. John Capron Baylor (1835–1879) who earned the degree of M.D. from the University of Pennsylvania. He was appointed assistant surgeon, Provisional Army of Virginia, May 16, 1861, and then to Chimborazo Hospital, as Frank's letter makes clear. He was captured in Richmond April 3, 1865, when the city fell. Paroled at Richmond April 17, 1865, Baylor is mentioned in more of Frank's letters.

Frank named Guiney's Station as the place his mother sent a letter. This station on the railroad a few miles south of Fredericksburg would soon become a shrine to Stonewall Jackson, who died there on May 10, 1863, following his wounding at Chancellorsville. Pinck is the family name for Frank's younger brother, Thomas Pinckney Huger. His reference to Alexander's Battalion is the artillery battalion formerly commanded by Stephen D. Lee and now under the command of Edward Porter Alexander. Actually Frank had been serving under Alexander since autumn of 1862. Alexander was to write of Frank Huger, "But Joe Haskell & Frank Huger were the most loveable comrades that the Lord could make in the pattern of man." Frank's announcement that he achieved the rank of major as of March 2, 1863, is confirmed by a document in the Huger Family Papers.[20]

Miss Buck is Sally Buchanan Preston. The American sculptor Hiram Powers carved her portrait bust. She was romantically involved with General John Bell Hood. Of Sally, Mary Chesnut wrote: "Buck, the very sweetest woman I ever knew, had a knack of being 'fallen in love with' at sight and of never being 'fallen out of love' with. But then, there seemed a spell upon her lovers — so many were killed or died of the effects of wounds."

Hooker is Union general Joseph Hooker, who was now in command of the Army of the Potomac, having replaced Ambrose E. Burnside after the Union loss at Fredericksburg. Mrs. Martin, who had Frank's trunk, was very possibly Mrs. William Martin. William Martin was a Methodist minister from Columbia, South Carolina. He ran a clothing depository for soldiers. The Martins were the parents of Isabella Martin, a good friend of Mary Chesnut. Mary Garnett of South Carolina was one of the young women in the circle of young women the bachelor soldiers of Frank's association admired. Another Mary Garnett was related to Mary Chesnut's husband James Chestnut. Her maiden name was Mary Stevens; she married Congressman Muscoe Garnett of Virginia in 1860. Fannie Kerr may have been the daughter of John B. Kerr, a Baltimore lawyer and member of Congress from Maryland from 1848 to 1851. Frank and his brother Ben wrote to her. Lt. Moore, of whom Frank had a poor opinion, was probably Joseph D. Moore who took command of the Norfolk battery and rose to the rank of captain at least.[21]

In Camp — Tuesday, April 19th, 1863
Near Fredericksburg

My dear Celly:

I was just wondering if you were a married woman this morning, and if I should carry out my intention of writing to you whether to direct it to Miss or not, and that set me speculating as to whether this horrid war, about the only thing I know of in the world that could have produced such uncertainty, will ever end or not, and so I'll just write you for a solution of all my difficulties.

Yesterday I received Mother's letter dated not at all — and directed to Guiney's Station, but it came direct here. Don't you think the little Seve must have some Irish blood in her? Pinck's letter of the 13th arrived this morning. I'm sorry he has been under the weather, but I hope it was only temporary. He must take care of himself this summer, for I fear Columbia is a very warm place.

My appointment as Major has arrived, dates March 2nd and I'm ordered to report to General Lee — shall go to Headquarters tomorrow — expect to be assigned to Alexander's Battalion which is camped about three miles from here.

Longstreet is evidently doing something at Suffolk but we have heard nothing positively as yet—hope he'll get lots of provisions. Dr. Jno Bayler has obtained his transfer to Chimborazo Hospital and went down yesterday morning. He is very devoted to Miss Mary Garnett and now he will have it all his own way—he flatters himself he is going to cut me out, but he'll find himself mistaken. By the way Jack never gave me that photograph he promised. You must send it on to me as soon as you can, and do tell Miss Buck I shall have mine taken for her as soon as I get to Baltimore. You must remember me most kindly to all the young ladies. Dr. Bayler's brother Bob, to the astonishment of everybody, got a ten days leave a few days ago, went to Louisa C.[ourt] H.[ouse] and married a <u>widow.</u> That will astonish some of the confiding girls in Norfolk. I spent a morning with Mrs. Camp in Richmond. She was not look—very well tho' very pretty indeed. Tell Ben I received a long letter from Miss Fannie Kerr yesterday, dated 31st March. She desired to be recommended to him. She is a great girl and writes a mighty good letter.

My mess chest has not arrived yet. I instructed Forden to take your shoes to Mrs. Chesenetts [probably Mary Chesnut, the diarist] *to whom I gave your directions. I told Forden if the box had not got to Richmond to telegraph to Pinck, that he might see if it had started. I'm very glad to hear that Mrs. Martin has my trunk. Recon she had better keep it. Stringent orders have been issued about baggage and transportation, and inspections have been ordered to see that no officers even, carry more than fifty lbs. We are to march light and I rather fancy that if Hooker sends his forces to the South side we will cross over and catch him on the move. The weather is now delightful, and if it continues we must move before long as the wads* [wet lands] *are drying rapidly. I must get to work to settle my papers with this company. I feel sorry to leave the old company for if Lt. Moore is promoted (which he never shall be with my consent), I fear he can't hold it together long, and as the largest and as good a company that represents Norfolk, I feel proud of it. Give my love to Aunt H. and all the rest. You must write me soon. I wish you all the happiness in the world. God bless you.*

Your affect. Bro.
Frank Huger

Letter Number 10

Several days following the letter above, Frank wrote to his father, who appears to have been in Charleston. Preparing to move to the Trans-Mississippi Department, the elder Huger helped establish the arsenal at Tyler, Texas.[22] Frank was concerned over this move west and hoped his father could have resolved his differences with General James Longstreet before departing.

G. W. Smith was Gustavus Woodson Smith, a former New York City street commissioner and former army engineer. A West Point graduate, class of 1842, Smith commanded a wing of General Joseph E. Johnston's army at the battle of Seven Pines, May 31, 1862. There he seemed to have abdicated his position and acted as a mere observer. The Charleston affair Frank alluded to was the Union naval attack of ironclads on April 6, 1862, under the command of Admiral Samuel Francis DuPont.

The Whitworth gun that ruptured belonged to James H. Lane. Lane had been colonel of the Twenty-eighth North Carolina regiment and was promoted to brigadier in the 2nd Corps of the Army of Northern Virginia following the death of L. O'Brien Branch, killed at Antietam. He was described as "a Two-fisted, vigorously human commander.[23] His Whitworth gun was an imported breechloading piece of artillery designed by the famous British mechanical engineer Joseph Whitworth. The screw that blew out and the hinge that tore off were the fundamentals of the gun's breechloading ability. The round breechblock was supported within a circular ring of iron that permitted the block to rotate within it. The ring was hinged to the gun so the block could be swung out for breech loading. On the circumference of the circular breechblock were interrupted threads. Once the block was swung on the hinges and placed into the breech of the gun, a cannoneer turned a handle on the block and rotated it a partial turn to engage the interrupted threads on the block with similar interrupted threads cut into the breech end of the gun barrel. Now the breech was secure and could withstand the pressure of the charge. Once fired the handle was turned in the opposite direction to disengage the threads and the block swung out for reloading. Indeed the gun should always be fired with large sized powder. To begin to appreciate the granular size difference between cannon, rifle and musket powder the following data are taken from *Introduction for Field Artillery* by Major Wm. H. French, Captain William F. Barry and Major Henry J. Hunt. The number of grains (granules) of powder in 10 grains Troy were: cannon, 159; musket, 1,100; rifle, 6,000.

The McCreery who sent Frank a Confederate shell section was William W. McCreery Jr., a West Point graduate. He attained the rank of captain and was acting assistant adjutant and inspector general to James Johnston Pettigrew as of January 8, 1863. McCreery was killed at Gettysburg July 1, 1863. At Gettysburg Pettigrew commanded a brigade in Henry Heth's division in A. P. Hill's corps. Pettigrew was mortally wounded on the retreat from Gettysburg at Falling Waters July 14, 1863, and died July 17.

The expression $ab = 2cd$ is best explained by the diagram Frank sketched in his letter. The diagram shows the hollow cavity to be way off center causing the thickness of the shell wall to be unequal. In his cross sectional diagram of the shell the thicker wall, labeled "ab" is twice the thickness of the thinner wall labeled "cd." This disproportionate wall thickness would cause the shell to fly erratically and when it burst to break into a few pieces only and therefore reducing its potential for inflicting wounds and destruction. Poor artillery ammunition plagued the Confederacy throughout the war. During the winter of 1861-62 after First Manassas E. P. Alexander wrote about the quality of Confederate artillery ammunition. In *Fighting for the Confederacy* Alexander wrote, "I felt some doubt about the quality of the artillery ammunition & made an early opportunity to try some at target practice, & I found it in really dreadful shape." He reported that shells exploded prematurely, and rifle shot and shell would tumble rather than go point first. "The enemy were always far ahead of us in artillery ammunition of all kinds both in quality and quantity." At the Battle of Fredericksburg Alexander was ordered to move his guns to replace those of the Washington Artillery. Alexander requested that Rhett's battery, firing directly over the route Alexander had to take to move his guns, cease firing because, as he wrote in *Fighting for the Confederacy*, "its shells sometimes exploded prematurely." Later in the war things had not improved. Alexander wrote, "I also made an attempt to cut down one of the enemy's tall signal towers, at a mile range, with captain Parker's light rifles, but our ammunition was not reliable enough for such nice work, & we gave it up after a short trial."

Frank's promotion was to major and is mentioned in his letter to his sister above.

Port Royal is on the right bank of the Rappahannock River about twenty-five miles below Fredericksburg as the crow flies. Guiney's Depot is the same place as Guiney's Station located several miles south of Fredericksburg on the Richmond, Fredericksburg and Potomac Railroad. Jones, to whom Frank's father is to report about Rusty, was identified above in letter 5 as ordnance officer Frank Freeman Jones.

In Camp — Friday, April 24th, 1863
Ruther Glen, Caroline Co; Virginia

My dear Father:

I was surprised to find my Mother's letter of the 20th received today that none of my letters home had been received but I reckon by this time that they have piled up sufficiently to satisfy you all of my welfare. My last was to Celly written three or four days ago. I regret so much that you have to go West before you get your court. It has set me to thinking if it could not be avoided and one thing has suggested itself, that is, that as your business will require time and research, could you not apply for at least two or three competent persons as your aids and send them ahead to examine and report on localities etc. and that would at least save a great deal of labour for you and in the mean time write to Mr. Davis and tell him in the plainest language that you've now waited nearly a year for an opportunity to refute officially a charge against yourself, affecting your reputation as a soldier, dearer to you and your children, than all the world besides — that if you await your return from the West you can not possibly have the opportunity you desire 'till the fall and that you are not willing to delay that long. Johnston is doing nothing now, and the few witnesses you desire could be spared even during active operations, and that you demand an immediate investigation. You can depend on it that they will never allow you a hearing as long as you leave their [paper of the letter is torn out and missing] *alone. G. W. Smith I believe is aware that Longstreet knew you ranked him, and I think moreover that he knows something concerning some of the movements at Seven Pines in which Longstreet failed to comply and that he used you to escape. Longstreet is a politician and nothing else, and I would like him to be shewn up. As soon as you have cleared up that matter, I hope you'll apply for active service for I think it would suit your health better than travelling nowadays—. This has suggested itself to me. I only hope it is practicable. The sequel has proved that I was right in my opinion concerning the Charleston affair, for I felt pretty well satisfied that when they did not return the morning after the attack, that they had been sufficiently amused.*

I heard that Lane had burst his Whitworth gun in N. C. or rather that the screw blew out and the hinge was torn off. Should not that gun always be fired with large sized powder? A few days since the gun boats on the Nansemond dismounted his two 20 pd. Parrotts but I don't reckon that is much of a loss, as I have mighty little confidence in guns of that caliber, made here and especially in the projectiles. They either burst in, or [paper torn and missing] *the gun, or else they don't go straight. Found on my return an old letter here from McCreery who is now with General Pettigrew in N. C. He sent me a section of a shell that had burst near the gun, something this fashion.* [Here Frank drew a diagram of the shell with the cavity way off center]. *No wonder they don't go straight. $\underline{ab = 2cd}$, and from all such the Lord deliver us. I don't know where it was made.*

We are now having a terrible storm, in fact it has rained all the time since I got back. I have received my promotion and reported to Alexander. There is a rumor this morning that the enemy are trying to cross at Port Royal. We've received no orders yet, but I should not be surprised if Hooker attempted something as soon as the weather favored. It's a fact that we have been furnished with pontoons, expected to be used when we cross the Potomac, but I doubt if we do anything until the foraging parties return. My mess chest that Pinck shipped for me has not arrived yet or rather has not got to Richmond. Tell Jones I believe I'll sell Rusty as soon as I get a good chance as Tilghmans mare and Jessie are about as much as I want. Mules can not be bought at all around here, that is [paper torn out and missing] *I saw a very indifferent pair sell for* [paper torn out and missing] a few days since. I hope Jones has [paper torn out and missing] *for my chest for I'll make the rascal* [paper torn out and missing] *for it if it don't come.*

So Celly is to be married the 29th, I had supposed that she was on the 11th but probably you staid in Charleston 'till all the iron clads left.

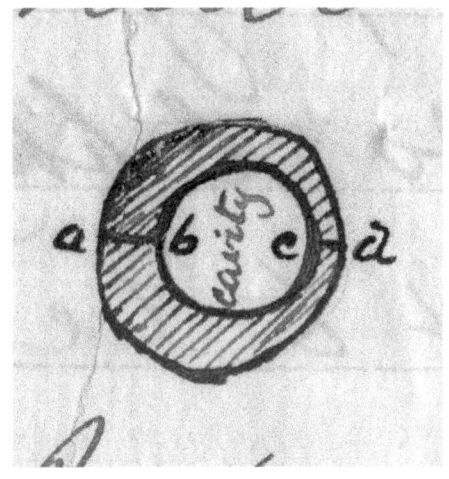

Enlarged diagram from Frank Huger's letter to his father dated April 10, 1863. Frank drew this illustration to show a poorly cast Confederate artillery shell with varying wall thickness (courtesy Virginia Historical Society).

It's a great disappointment to me not to be at her wedding, but under the circumstances I ought to be satisfied that I got my leave. Goodbye, love to all—Mother writes me to Guineys Depot, why I don't know, unless it is that I've never been there but the letter cam [sic] quicker than any yet received. The proper way is Alexanders Battalion, Ruther Glen P.O. Caroline Co. Va.

Your affect. Boy
Frank Huger

Chancellorsville

"R.E. Lee's stunning tactical victory at Chancellorsville capped a remarkable eleven-month period during which he built the Army of Northern Virginia into a self-confident and formidable weapon.... Their triumph at Chancellorsville cemented a bond with Lee unrivaled on either side during the Civil War."[24]

Letter Number 11

This letter below described the battle of Chancellorsville. Frank mentioned Confederate major general Richard H. Anderson, a division commander in the First Corps, Union major general John Sedgewick, commander of the Sixth Corps of the Army of the Potomac, and Stephen D. Ramseur, Frank's close friend and West Point classmate. Frank was misinformed concerning the wounding of General A. P. Hill.[25]

Friday, May 8th, 1863
near Fredericksburg, Va.

My dear Mother:

 I hope by this time you have received a telegram I sent to Forden to send to you on Tuesday 5th after the Chancellorsville fight. We were engaged again on Wednesday but thanks to a kind Providence, I've passed through the hardest fight I ever was in untouched. On Wednesday, the 29th, Col. Alexander being absent from the Battalion, I was ordered to bring it up. It was raining very hard but I made a quick march and got here before I was expected. Found the enemy threatening General Andersons front on the plank road, 6 or 7 miles above Fredericksburg. The enemy had thrown their heaviest force about 5 corps, on our left flank while John Sedgewick with two corps threatened our front. On Friday, the 1st May, General Jackson was ordered to move to the left and outflank the enemy. We drove them that day about 4 miles up the plank road. Our battalion being the only artillery engaged. Alexander had joined us when we got there. Saturday, we marched around the enemy's right and by 5 P.M. had gotten in their rear, and at 6 o'clock attacked. They were strongly fortified but we did not come on their front. This will give you an idea of how we worked it, Jackson's old game—(drawing inserted here) Sunday, we fought the battle of Chancellorsville—a hard fight in which the enemy were completely whipped. They fell back in the U.S. ford and were strongly fortified. That evening we were sent back to Anderson who was behind the enemy that had gotten to Fredericksburg and Monday evening we whipped them away from here. Tuesday night and Wednesday we shelled them all the time. All the artillery did a great deal to insure success and was handled well. During the fight it rained hard and after 7 days I got my boots off with my foot so swelled they'll fill a bushel bag today—but I'm very well. Have not heard a word of you all since I left Caroline County, not a word of darling Cel's wedding. Ramseur, who was slightly hit on the foot, told me he received an invitation. Jackson and A. P. Hill were wounded by our own men. The former has had his arm amputated.

  Love to all—Saw Mr. and Mrs. Guest a few days ago—they were well—
       Your affect. boy—
       Frank Huger

Letter Number 12

Frank's letter below, written to his mother about two weeks after the battle of Chancellorsville, hides most of the horrors from her except to say how hot it was for his battalion. As always he was concerned for the mail and instructed his mother to send it in care of Major Walter H. Taylor, identified in an earlier letter. At this time Frank was anxious to hear the details of his sister's wedding. The Caroline he mentioned leaving was Caroline County, Virginia. Frank made reference to White Oak Swamp, a dismal spot on the Peninsula, scene of maneuvering during the Seven Days battle in 1862. Ramseur saw much active service with the Army of Northern Virginia and attained the rank of major general. He was mortally wounded at Cedar Creek on October 19, 1864, and died in captivity. General Rhodes was Robert E. Rodes, who commanded a brigade in D. H. Hill's division of General T. J. Jackson's 2nd Corps at the start of the Chancellorsville battle. He was promoted to major general and commanded Hill's division during the battle. Rodes died during the battle of Third Winchester, September 18, 1864.

Camp near Milford, Va.
May 17, 1863 — Sunday night

My dear Mother —

I this evening received two letters from home, Pinck dated the 12th and one from Celly, from Charleston of the 8th. They are my first letters since we left Caroline before —, but I suppose the intermediate ones will come to hand one of these days. I hope so at all events, for I haven't heard any thing of Cel's wedding yet.

I had an opportunity on the 5th to ride to Richmond, so I wrote Forden to telegraph you that I was well which by Pinck's letter I see you received. I sent that on Tuesday, and on the next day, altho' the enemy had crossed, our battalion was in the hottest place I've any desire to be in again, and I'd almost made up my mind that I'd send you a fib, but fortunately it turned out all right. I hope by this time you have received my letters. We will probably be in this neighborhood until the next fight, until then direct here, but when active operations commence, enclose your letters to Maj. W. H. Taylor and I'll get them direct. So father and Ben have started. Now that Jackson Miss. has fallen, I reckon he will have to come back or wait until we whip them out there, which I don't humbly believe Joe Johnston is capable of doing. I haven't a bit of confidence in him. I hope I'm wrong and that we may soon win a victory there, for its discouraging to the army here, always to hear of disaster there. Had it not been for the storm of Tuesday eve. The 5th, I think our army would have been over the Rappahannock but we did all we could considering the marching, and the weather and the miserable country we had to fight in. The White Oak Swamp was a treat to it. Wonder if Ramseur has gone to N C [North Carolina] *If so he will get married before he returns. I met him several times during the fight. On Sunday, he appeared quite unwell, and had been struck on the foot, but he wouldn't leave and I understand he didn't go until General Rhodes sent him off.*

You will have seen by this time accounts which will give you a pretty good idea of the battle. The enemy abandoned all their baggage, but as I was very busy all the time, I did not have an opportunity to collect any trophies.

Tell Celly I will answer her letter soon. I am on an examining Board which will take me off for a few days and am still on a Gen[eral] *Court*[s martial]*, so am very busy. I am anxious to go to Richmond, but I don't see any chance just now.*

Tell Jones I will look about, and if I see any opening for him I'll let him know right off.

Goodnight—I'll keep this open 'till tomorrow, when I hope to hear.

Frank Huger

Monday morning—Nothing doing today. No news in any directions. Love to all—

Letter Number 13

Leading up to the battle of Gettysburg Frank wrote the following letter on June 15, 1863, to his younger brother Thomas Pinckney. Frank had no idea what lay ahead but was sure General Robert E. Lee and Confederate president Jefferson Davis were working up a plan. A better prophet of the fate of Vicksburg, Frank missed the date of its fall by only three days. Frank's reference to Stephen D. Ramseur not using his right hand at all was the result of his being seriously wounded in the right arm at Malvern Hill, July 1, 1862.

One has to wonder what kind of wedding cake Celly and Jack served their guests. Frank wrote that a letter might have had Celly's wedding cake and to have it kept for him until next winter. His final reference to the "Hascalls" were John Cheves Haskell and Joseph Cheves Haskell both of whom were staff officers in the First Corps or with E. Porter Alexander. John lost his right arm at Gaines's Mill. Both survived the war and lived into the twentieth century.[26]

Camp near Culpepper C.[ourt] H.[ouse]
June 15th, 1863, Monday morning

My dear Pinck:

    You have heard by this time of our whereabouts, and I've now to tell you orders have just come to move at 3 O'clock on the Winchester Road. I am completely at a loss to know what Lee is driving at— Ewells Corps moved up to Front Royal several days ago and we are following today. A. P. Hill is before Fredericksburg and I have no doubt we are developing some plan, hashed by Gen. Lee and Jeff. I only hope we can get at Hooker in a fair field fight when we will drub him soundly. I don't know as I am anxious to go into Maryland, for although we have a fine force now, still a battle and a victory would cost 20 or 25,000 men which would so cripple us that we couldn't take advantage of it. It appears to me that we ought to watch Hooker, and reinforce Vicksburg. You must know I feel very blue about that place and I firmly expect to hear of its fall any day. I don't believe Johnston can relieve it, and I rather think by the 1st July the Yanks will have it. If we are "a going a raiding," I only hope we will get into Pennsylvania. Tell Celly I saw Jack on Thursday. His horse (and a fine one it was) got hit in the leg and quick took the opportunity to lose him. Jack was very well and received while I was there a note from Mother of the 6th. Last night I got Mother's letter of 4th— it had been to Milford.

    I saw Ramseur a few days ago. He said he had received Mothers letter and would answer it as soon as he could do so. He doesn't use his right hand at all, and it is very difficult for him to write to a lady especially with his left, however, I believe he makes out very well as far as his sweetheart is concerned.

    Jno. Bayler writes me word that he's gotten two bundles, and a box for me. I suppose the letter has Cellys wedding cake. I'm going to write Jno. word this morning to keep it till next winter for its impossible to ask anyone to take a package to Winchester, it being a hundred miles to the nearest R. R.

    Its very warm today, think we are going to have a hot spell. I'm satisfied we can't stay a day in the valley, its all eat up. We must go straight through. I don't know where I'll next write from but just you direct to Alexanders Battalion, Longstreets Corps. A. N. Va., and we leave word with the P. ill's where to send them. I'm mighty sorry to hear that Celly has been sick. I hope she is well before this. Give her my best love and tell her I shall kiss all her Baltimore friends for _prehaps_.

    Saw Jno. and Joe Hascall, (that ain't the way to spell it I don't believe) a few days since— both prime.

    Love to all. Are you a —————? [Frank wrote a long dash after the letter a] This is written in <u>no time</u>.

Your affect bro.
Frank Huger

Gettysburg

"The campaign and battle of Gettysburg have great significance in themselves, but they gain in dimension when viewed in the overall context of the American Civil War. The campaign of many weeks duration occurred almost midway in the course of the war. It began with a period of preparation in the middle of May, 1863, and ... ended when the last Confederate brigade slipped across the Potomac River on July 14."[27]

Letter Number 14

On the day that Union general George Gordon Meade replaced General Joseph Hooker as commander of the Army of the Potomac, June 28, 1863, Frank wrote the brief letter that follows to his mother. His hopes were high, expecting to capture either Harrisburg, Pennsylvania, or Baltimore, Maryland. Frank made a humorous reference to vinegar as if it were a fine wine with the designation SP for special product. Apple cider vinegar was and still is a vital product in the Pennsylvania Dutch country of Pennsylvania.[28]

Camp 1½ Miles north of Chambersburg, Pa.
Sunday, June 28th, 1863

My dear Mother:

You will perceive I'm in "furin" parts — a most delightful country, abounding in the sourest looking women, with big feet and no manners — and horses, vainly endeavoring to hide themselves. I wrote you while at Millfords — Events, in the way of marches, all alike, have crowded so rapidly that I hardly can tell one day from another, makes me forget dates, but I think it was about a week ago. Jack will give you an account of me, and now that we are in the enemys country and I suppose will lose soon our line of communications, which won't make much difference since we haven't got much to get from home; you must not expect to hear from me anymore 'till Xmas, unless the letter is there. I'm very well and flourishing. The country abounds in everything we want. We will live well. May have some hard fighting to do but probably not worse than we have had. I have no idea what we'll do except that our troops are d— here, so that we are threatening Harrisburg and Baltimore, — one of the places we will have sure — I expect in the morning we will start for the former. I suppose Jack will get home in a day or so — hope his wound may not be any more serious that it promised. Tell him the "Sp Vini Gal" flows in abundance, we buy and have for everything. Have taken nothing and destroyed nothing, *but when we go back through this country it will be different I hope. Love to all. I hope darling Cel is better. I haven't heard from you all for a long time; our letters will come along some day I hope. Tell Celly I'm going to fill my saddle bags with shoes. I did so wish for you yesterday, I got into a millinery shop where they had nice bonnets for $8.00 with about 20 yards of ribbon on them. Goodbye.*

Your affect. Boy—
F. H.

Letter Number 15

Five days after the battle of Gettysburg Frank wrote a more detailed letter to his mother describing to some extent the difficult fighting he had experienced. Frank could not bring himself to grant any fighting qualities to the enemy, explaining Yankee success in their being strongly entrenched and to "having many natural advantages." He admitted that it was the hardest fighting of the war, worse than Malvern Hill.

Lt. Heyward may have been Barnwell "Barny" Heyward.[29] Rhett's old company was that commanded by Captain Andrew B. Rhett of South Carolina. He left the battery to return to serve in a South Carolina regiment. Lt. William W. Fickling took command of the battery.[30] McCreery, identified in an earlier letter, was William Westwood McCreery, Jr. The two generals killed that Frank mentioned were Brigadier General Richard B. Garnett of Major General George E. Pickett's division and Brigadier General William Barksdale of Major General Lafayette McLaws' division, both in Lieutenant General James Longstreet's First Army Corps. While Frank's classmate Stephen D. Ramseur was unhurt this time, Brigadier General Wade Hampton of South Carolina was wounded. Despite the serious nature of Hampton's wound, he was too important to be left behind and was taken away by ambulance.[31] E. P. Alexander's horse Dixie, that Frank reported wounded, was treated by a real surgeon and not a veterinarian. Alexander himself wrote that the wound his horse received at Gettysburg, a gash in the mare's hip, had not healed. "A great excrescence of proud flesh had grown projecting several inches, & looking very badly." Captain William Watts Parker of Parker's Virginia Battery was a surgeon and performed the required surgery.[32]

Camp near Hagerstown Maryland
July 8, 1863

My dear Mother:
I have an opportunity of sending you a line today, which I'll improve and

hope it may get thro' safe. We fought a terrible battle on the 2nd and 3rd of July. On the evening of the 3rd, we endeavored to dislodge the enemy by a charge, but we failed to do it, they being strongly entrenched, and having many natural advantages. It was the hardest fight of the war, the fire worse than Malvern Hill. This Battalion lost several, Rhetts old company (losing in killed and wounded 37 men.) Lt. Heyward of S.C. who had just joined was not touched and altho' I never thought any one could get thro' such a fire untouched, still most Providentially I was not struck. We have had nothing but rain since we crossed the Potomac, and it is now pouring. We have inflicted a severe blow on the enemy, and if any thing could ever make these people make peace, this campaign would, by demonstrating that the party that attempts invasion generally speaking does not make much, but from my observation, I see no signs of a stop being put to the war until Lincoln's term expires. While in Pennsylvania, the people did not appear very happy to see us back in the Union. Poor McCreery died gallantly carrying the colors of the 26th N. C. on the evening of 1st July. He was killed outright—shot through the head with a Minnie ball. Gen. Garnett was killed, as also Gen. Barksdale. Ramseur was not hurt this time.

Tell Celly that I received the package of wedding cake just as I was going in the fight, and if we don't move today, I'll unpack the wagon and get it out today. I suppose Jack is home by this time. Sorry to learn that Gen. Hampton was wounded. I'm very well and quite busy. Col. Alexander escaped unhurt tho' his horse was wounded and he got a bullet through his pantaloons at the knee. I hope you are all well and that I may hear from you soon. Haven't heard for a long time.

Your affect. Boy
Frank Huger

Letter Number 16

The battle was over but not the campaign when Frank wrote a short letter to his mother on July 12, 1863, from Maryland. He was concerned for the health of one of his two horses, Jessie. He also expressed concern for his father getting across the Mississippi River to his post in Trans-Mississippi. Mrs. Hampton was probably Mary Cantey Hampton, third wife of Wade Hampton I, a Continental Army officer, U.S. congressman and reported to have been the wealthiest planter in South Carolina at his death in 1835. Mrs. Hampton was Willie Preston's grandmother and she congratulated him on his cannon shot at Fort Sumter.[33]

Near Downsville, Md. July 12, P.M. 1863

Dear Mother:

Today we received our first mail since leaving Millwood, and I was most glad to get several from home, tho' of old dates. One came from father from Mobile of June 15, and three from Pinck of June 22nd, 25th and 30th.

My letter written you a few days since was sent by a wounded officer, but he returned it to me this morning as he could not cross the river, so I tried another opportunity today. Hope you may receive it one of these days. Jack is I suppose at home ere now and I hope is rapidly recovering and darling Celly's anxiety is over. We have had a very severe campaign so far — nothing but hard work. We are now awaiting the enemy and expect the attack tomorrow. Before you've received this you will know the result of the fight. I keep very well indeed, but Jessie is very sick and I'm afraid I'll lose her. We hear tonight of the fall of Vicksburg, sad news, but I've expected it. Love to all. I write very hurriedly.

Monday morning, July 13, 9 A.M.

I wrote this very hastily last night— today it is raining; the enemy have not made any advance as yet. The courier starts now for Winchester, so I hope this will be there by night. I have not been able to procure anything since we got in foreign parts. The people have not been forced to sell to us, so we have not been able to get a thing. We have destroyed no property and only taken what was necessary for our subsistence and horses. I can't understand why such has been our policy. It seems to me a very mistaken one, and I can't reconcile it to my wishes. I hope when the courier returns, which he'll probably do on Wednesday, I may get some late dates from you all. I was sorry to hear of Mrs. Hamptons death, but I suppose it's a happy release to the poor old lady. I hope that Father has not succeeded in getting across the River. Now that the Yankees have Vicksburg, he will have a hard time getting back. Much love to all.

Frank Huger.

Letter Number 17

Frank's following letter to his mother needs few explanations. He continued to be concerned about mail delivery and for his father's safety on the Mississippi River now that Vicksburg had fallen to the Union. S. D. Lee was Stephen Dill Lee who commanded Frank's battalion at Antietam before E. Porter Alexander. Jno. Taylor was identified in an earlier letter. Gilmore, who Frank called one of the Union's ablest men was Major General Quincy Adams Gilmore, an engineer and commander of the Department of the South.

Camp Bunker Hill — 12 miles from
Winchester, July 16th, 1863

My dear Mother:

I hope by this time you have received some of my letters, or have heard of me, especially as I wrote a note on the 8th to John Bayler to telegraph you at once that I was safe. Last night's mail brought me five letters, some of yours a month old, and one from Pinck of 5th July, my latest date, telling me Jack had arrived home. I do hope Father did not succeed in crossing the river, now that Vicksburg has fallen, tho' it has always been my opinion that the place must go sooner or later, so was not at all surprised. The place has already been of little practical use to us for some time, and if Johnston can only now keep Grant from overrunning the state, he will do all I ever thought he could. Well you perceive we have been to Pennsylvania to get apple butter, but as the Union people did not give us the welcome we expected, after all the fuss they have made concerning our leaving them, and our ammunition being very low, we had to recross the river, thereby performing the greatest military feat we have performed; for to tell the truth for two or three days I thought we were in a very precarious position. It commenced raining the evening we crossed into Maryland at the ford at Williamsport, on 24th June, and today is the *first* day since that it has not rained — consequently the ford was soon impassable and has been so ever since. At Falling Waters we had a pontoon bridge, but the enemy destroyed about half of it, so after we failed to dislodge the Yanks on the 3rd day, and our ammunition being very short, we were compelled on the night of the 3rd to fall back to our position of the 1st. The enemy did not attempt to follow us and the following night we withdrew to near Hagerstown, in a pouring rain — then you see we were backed nearly on to the river with little ammunition, and no chance of escape if we were over powered nor of receiving supplies. Here we took up and fortified a strong line and held it in front of the enemy for three days until we completed our bridge when we fell back, over a horrid wad, [wet swamp] on the night of the 14th and I got across yesterday about 8 A.M. having been in the saddle 17 hours in a pouring rain. The rear guard under Gen. Pettigrew was attacked, and he poor man, received it is supposed a mortal wound, tho' he was not dead this evening. I do not think we can stay here long —, the country not affording sufficient supplies to maintain us. Of the battle of Gettysburg I've got so much to say I hardly know where to commence. We made a mistake I think in attacking them in their strong position for it was indeed most powerful. The evening of the 2nd and on the 3rd we were actively engaged and lost 131 men killed and wounded — that is one in four, and 101 horses. I was not touched. The Battalion behaved most nobly and I have the satisfaction of knowing that it is as distinguished as any other in service. I'm always proud to know I serve where such men as S. D. Lee and Maj. Jno. Taylor have before me.

I'm glad to hear Cel is getting better. So the enemy are trying Charlestown again—May they soon fail. Gilmore is, I think, one of their ablest men.

Love to all—

Your affect. boy—Frank Huger

General Longstreet Moves West

On August 24, 1863, President Jefferson Davis called General Robert E. Lee to Richmond for discussion. In July Union general William S. Rosecrans forced Confederate general Braxton Bragg to fall back on Chattanooga. Meanwhile Union general Ambrose E. Burnside was at Knoxville, entering the city on September 2, 1863. President Davis decided to reinforce Bragg with elements from the Army of Northern Virginia.

The plan called for General Longstreet and his two divisions under Generals Lafayette McLaws and John B. Hood to move to Chattanooga by way of the Virginia and Tennessee Railroad. Longstreet was to join with Bragg, attack Rosecrans and return promptly to Virginia.[34]

General Burnside's capture of Knoxville severed the main rail line to Virginia, helping to create the crisis in Tennessee for the Confederacy. The transfer of Longstreet's two divisions strained the transportation resources of the South as nothing had before. Fully sixteen railroad companies labored to bring about the transfer, altering schedules. The rerouting of trains stranded passengers and halted freight delivery. Had the main line from Virginia not been severed the trip would have been one of 540 miles. The long alternate route was one of 775 miles instead. Frank Huger traveled with Longstreet's troops as part of Colonel E. P. Alexander's Twenty-sixth Artillery Battalion.[35]

General Longstreet described the circuitous railroad route his divisions had to take to arrive at Chattanooga. They were required to go through the Carolinas to Augusta, Georgia, go to Atlanta, then north to Dalton and Ringgold. "There were two routes between Richmond and Augusta," Longstreet wrote, "one via Wilmington, the other through Charlotte, North Carolina, but only a single track from Augusta to Chattanooga. The gauges of the roads were not uniform, nor did the roads connect at the cities (except by drays and other such conveyances). The roads had not been heavily worked before the war, so that their rolling stock was light and limited."[36]

Letter Number 18

A package from home was always a special treat for service men and women of all ages and in all times. The one Frank acknowledged receiving in his September 4, 1863, letter to his mother was especially appreciated. The General Gilmer he mentioned should not be confused with General Gilmore of the letter above. This was Confederate major general Jeremy Francis Gilmer (1818–1883), who had been engineering officer to Albert Sidney Johnston.[37]

Near Orange C.[ourt] H.[ouse] Sept. 4, 1863

My dear Mother:

Yours of the 29th came last evening. I can't imagine why you don't get my letters for I write every five or six days but they'll all turn up one of these days. I went to a little "shindig" last night where I made a great many inquiries about getting some place for you and Celly to stay but the army has been here so long that every place is full and some holes not fit to be lived in are occupied by a half dozen ladies — I sent Aunt H's letter, received last Friday to Mrs. Taylor. I'll try and pay her a visit tomorrow, and get her messages for Aunt Henderson, which I will transmit at once.

Now that Gen. Gilmer is sent to Charleston, we will have more engineering than ever. I expect the Yankees will have a hard time making much further progress. See the enemy are advancing in Tennessee. I wish they would send a corps of this Army to the West and beat those devils — it appears feasible to me, for Meade is in no condition to advance on us. The box arrived last Sunday and that eve we had splendid ochre soup — a perfect success. The other good things we enjoyed tremendously especially the grog. To give you a correct but at the same time a rather incomprehensible idea of our society, I can say that previous to the arrival of that black bottle, I had only taken one drink during the month of August.

I'm on a horse board today, so must hurry off. I'll try today to secure you a place at some of these houses for I think that by Sept. 1st some of these folk will be tired.

Its regular September weather now. Love to darling Cel.

Your affect. boy —
F. H.

Letter Number 19

Between the time Frank wrote from Culpepper Court House on September 4, 1863, and the letter below dated September 30, 1863, from a camp on the Chickamauga Creek outside of Chattanooga, Tennessee, his artillery battalion and the two divisions of Longstreet's corps moved into north Georgia and Tennessee. As of September 1, 1863, Longstreet's corps comprised Lafayette

McLaws' and John B. Hood's divisions as well as E. P. Alexander's artillery battalion. The first troops began to leave from Culpepper Court House on September 9, 1863. The artillery arrived near Chattanooga on September 25, five days after the battle of Chickamauga, September 19–20, 1863. Longstreet, under General Braxton Bragg, commanded the Western District, took a position on the Confederate left. Taking advantage of a gap in the Union lines on their right, Longstreet drove that portion of Union major general William Starke Rosecrans' Army of the Cumberland back into the defenses of Chattanooga. Only General George Thomas holding the Union left prevented the defeat from becoming a complete rout. For that Thomas earned *nom de guerre* The Rock of Chickamauga.

Frank, disappointed that Bragg failed to do more, told his mother that Bragg had as many men as Rosecrans. Actually he had more. Troop strengths were 70,000 to 55,000 in the Confederates' favor. Generally Frank expressed little concern or remorse over Union deaths and losses. He did however inform his mother that a classmate of his, Bill Jones, fighting for the Union, had been killed. Bill Jones was William Graham Jones, a cadet at West Point in 1855. At the time of his death, September 19, he was colonel of the Thirty-sixth Ohio Regiment. The Col. Wright Frank saw in Atlanta just before the colonel's wedding was Moses Hannibal Wright, commander of the Atlanta arsenal. About Frank's age, Wright graduated from West Point in 1859. Among his accomplishments, Wright suggested a manufacturing improvement to strengthen the brass frame of the Confederate-made Spiller and Burr revolver.[38]

The *Inquirer* [sic] and *Examiner* were two of Richmond's five newspapers. Editorially they took opposite sides. Edited by John Moncure Daniel the *Examiner* was anti-administration and opposed Jefferson Davis. The *Enquirer* was more neutral and most of the government pronouncements, general orders and circulars were printed in this paper. The *Dispatch* had by far the largest circulation (e-mail correspondence between the editor and Robert E. L. Krick). Galt owned Frank's servant Dick.

Camp on Chickamauga, near
Chattanooga, Sept. 30th, 1863

My dear Mother,
    I wrote you a few days since to report myself and altho' I have not yet been to the front, I've heard enough of the affairs out here to satisfy me that we have made nothing by our transfer to this army. The Battery was moved here yesterday

where we will await our horses. The enemy are in Chattanooga, strongly fortified and how we are to get them out I don't see, nor from what I hear, do I believe General Bragg has any plan for doing so. What we are waiting for God only knows. The enemy are in our front, fortifying and reinforcing daily, and here we are in front doing nothing. If any thing could atone for the stupid criminality that allowed the enemy to escape after the most thorough rout since Manassas, it would be an attempt to crush them at once but Gen. Bragg seems to have no plan; his course is the subject of open and loud-mouthed criticism on the part of everyone and I'm sorry to say I think justly. I have always believed Bragg to have been abused — that he never had the men to cope with Rosecrans and that in Rosecrans, he had a superior man to cope with. I wanted to like him and expected to do so but after what has just occurred, I give it up. With his reinforcements, he had as many men as the enemy. After a loss of 14000 men he [unclear, maybe united] *the enemy and then let them go, capturing about 15000 and 40 pieces of arty. not half enough to pay for Hoods leg, and by the way, last night Gen. Hood was very low and scarcely expected to recover. He will be a tremendous loss if every one holds him as I do and that is as the first Major General in the country and next to Jackson the man best calculated to lead our troops. I doubt much if we get our horses, and are ready to take the field for a march. There has been no rain since 1st July. The entire country is dust, all the grass burnt up and very little vegetation left. It is coming on to rain now and I hope the reign of dust is over. You may recollect my class-mate Bill Jones from Ohio. He was a Colonel in the Yankee army and was killed in the last fight.*

We are all anxiously expecting news from the A. N. V. [Army of Northern Virginia]—*The papers seem to anticipate a battle on the Rapidan, its a strong line and one we have never yet lost on. I was sorry I did not stay long enough in Augusta to visit poor Tilghman's grave, but I passed right through. I saw Col Wright in Atlanta. He was married the day after we left. Tell Pinck to send me a paper occasionally, as we seldom see one here, or what better ask him to subscribe for me for three months to either the "Inquirer" or the "Examiner" and to direct to me "Alexander's Battalion, Longstreets Corps, Army of Tennessee. As soon as I can procure a check I'll send him one on the Treasury as I want to get him to send Galt some money. The month is up tonight, and it leaves me a year older, celebrated yesterday, by a tip-top ochre soup which was fully appreciated. Tell Celly I'm cutting out some work for her to do of which I'll write her when I've finished. My love to all, Goodnight—*

Oct. 1st— Its raining hard this morning so theres an end to the nasty dust. Every thing is quiet. I hope you are comfortably fixed in Richmond. I suppose Jack has gone back to the Division— Our cavalry out here doesn't compare with that in Va. but the Yankees are a great deal worse than ours even. This army is fully twelve months behind the Army of Virginia in every thing that relates to organization, and then the want of experience in marching and fighting. This is emphatically a war letter.

F. H.

Letter Number 20

From the letter below, dated Sunday, October 18, 1863, we learn that Frank used, to some extent at least, his younger brother Thomas Pinckney Huger as his commissary. Frank seems to have given little thought to what he wanted and composed his list of wants as the items came to mind. This time the go-between was Lieutenant J. Thompson Brown, instrumental in the formation of William Watts Parker's Virginia Battery. Lt. Brown enjoyed creditable service with Parker's Battery throughout the war and commanded it near the war's end. He is not to be confused with Colonel J. Thompson Brown who commanded a reserve artillery battalion in the 2nd Corps. Colonel Brown was killed by a Union sniper in the Battle of the Wilderness.[39] Mr. Robert K. Krick explained to this editor why there were so many Browns who used just their first initial and full middle names. After John Brown's raid at Harpers Ferry in 1859, few Southern men named John Brown cared to be known by that name any longer.

Mrs. Galt owned Dick, whom she must have rented or loaned out to Frank Huger as his manservant. Stephen Dill Lee, the first commander of Frank's artillery battalion, rose to the rank of lieutenant general. D.[aniel] H.[arvey] Hill had been with the Army of Northern Virginia, having served at South Mountain and Antietam. As of July 1863, Hill was in charge of the Department of North Carolina and responsible for the defenses of Richmond and Petersburg. On July 13, 1863, President Jefferson Davis promoted Hill to the rank of lieutenant general and sent him west to command a corps, face Union general William S. Rosecrans and defend Mississippi and Alabama. Hill was "Stonewall" Jackson's brother-in-law.[40] Hugo's work referred to the French writer and poet Victor Hugo (1802–1885). His *Les Misérables* was published in 1862 and immediately appeared in ten languages. Popular in this country it appeared in serialized form. Frank was anxious to read the next parts of the work, "St. Denis," and "Jean Valjean." The work was well known to soldiers on both sides and some Confederate soldiers referred to themselves as "Lee's Miserables."

The Prestons were a prominent family in the South and now related to the Hugers through the marriage of Celly to Jack—John Smith Preston, Jr. "B" is Frank's older brother Benjamin. Pinck—Thomas Pinckney Huger—

was evidently in the Confederate service at this time at least if he stood a chance of becoming a captain. His father wrote from Augusta, Georgia, to General Pierre G. T. Beauregard in Charleston, South Carolina, on Thomas Pinckney's behalf. The letter is faded but there appears to be no year in the date, only Dec. 28. The letter begins, "My son Pinckney has made application to the War Dept. for a commission in the 7th Regt. S.C. Infy. and sent it through Col. Baker Comdg. the Regt. and begged he would forward it through your office. I beg the favor of you to forward it with your endorsement."[41]

Benjamin Huger may have had old and inaccurate information. There was no Colonel Baker of the 7th S.C. Infantry. Colonel Thomas G. Bacon commanded this unit until May 4, 1862, and was replaced by Colonel David W. Aiken.

Col. Preston most probably was Col. William Campbell Preston (1816–1887) who had been a volunteer aide-de-camp to General Albert Sidney Johnston, who was killed at Shiloh.[42]

Near Chattanooga, Tenn. Sunday Oct. 18th, 1863

Dear Pinck:

Lieut. J. Thompson Brown goes to Richmond in the morning to attend to some business and I will get him to deliver this to you, enclosing $40. Of which I asked you in a previous letter to send $36. By a check if you can, to Mrs. Galt, as Dicks hire for the months of August & September. I asked you to do this in a previous letter which I hope you have received. I'll just mention here that I wrote to Celly on the 9th and to Mother on the 14th. We have had very heavy rains lately and the Bridges on the Chickamauga about 25 miles in our rear have been carried away, so we have had no mail for five days. My latest dates are the 4th, but I hope for letters in the morning when the courier returns. This is the hardest old country I ever saw. We can get nothing to eat except what the commissary furnishes, and that is very little. I want to get you to send me a few things by Lt. Brown who will stay in Richmond about five or six days as he is going to bring on lots of baggage, a little transportation more or less makes no difference. In the first place on my way here from Columbia, I lost my old blue overcoat. An English officer has kindly given me a light one that will answer very well if I can have it lined with some thick warm goods. If you can get me such an article, please send me five (5) yds. The coat is a kind of talena affair that has a good deal of cloth in it. If you can send the cloth, get Mother to put a skein of black cotton to sew with. Then if you can send me some sugar, and fill up with a few potatoes or any-

Three—The War Letters 73

thing that will keep, spirits for instance! why so much the better. Excepting a little rice and that very seldom, I haven't had any vegetables since I've been in this cussed place. Mother's ochra holds out very well but we can only hold out on soup once a week and live on remembrances and anticipation for the other six days. There is absolutely nothing here, not even decent water. Today is a very busy time. We are just issuing our horses and now have enough to equip five batteries. I think if I can make a good swap, I'll let old Rusty slide. I wrote to Father a few days ago and sent it to Stephen D. Lee—hope he may get it. General D. H. Hill has been relieved from command here and ordered to report to Richmond. He with many others, signed a paper to the President saying he had no confidence in Bragg, and for that was relieved, tho' the other generals have not been. If Bragg relieves all the army that have no confidence in him, he won't even have many privates in his army. Another thing I've just thought of. Do send me the last copies of the Literary Messenger—I've seen the Sept. No. you can get now Oct. and Nov. and if the last of Hugo's work is out, do send that. I've read the three first and now I want "St. Denis" and "Jean Valjean" and by the way we can't read at night without candles. Do send some of them. I reckon you have made friends with the commissary. I would send you more funds, but I'm dead broke as usual—the A. V. N. [Army of Northern Virginia] ditto. Give my love to Mother and Celly and also to the Prestons. Feeling very sentimental today and would send Miss Buck a piece of poetry if I could find it and had time. I begged her father to have B made a Major and I want you to get your Captaincy. I hope Col. Preston will do it for you before long.

Your affect. bro.
Frank Huger

Letter Number 21

Lieutenant General John C. Pemberton commanded the Department of Mississippi and East Louisiana. He was in charge of the defenses of Vicksburg when the city fell to Union General Ulysses S. Grant on July 4, 1863. After Vicksburg Pemberton requested a reduction in rank and served as a lieutenant-colonel of artillery in Virginia and South Carolina.

Camp near Chattanooga Nov. 4th, 1863—P.M.

My dear Mother:
Your letter of the 26th received a few days ago and was much disappointed to find that Lieut. Brown of this Battalion who had been sent on to Richmond

on duty and who carried a letter to Pinck had not yet arrived. I suppose by this time you have heard through him and I've written since. If you have received any of my letters, you will find that most, if not all of yours, and Jones letters have reached me. I write this hurriedly tonight to let you know that some move is going on. What it is exactly I don't know. I only know the part we are playing. For some days past we have had our rifles on Lookout Mountain, and have been shelling the Yankees in Chattanooga. The position was a beautiful one, the view grand, especially at night when the camp fires of both armies are apparently burning at your feet. I should have been satisfied to have stayed there a week, but last night at dark we received marching orders and today moved about twelve miles over the worst road you ever saw, from the extreme left, to our right, and beyond it. My impression is that there will be a move in a few days, so if you don't hear you mayn't feel uneasy for we may not have the chance to send to a depot. I'm delighted to hear Pinckney went to Ramseur's wedding and I only wish I could have been there too. Doubtless he had a pleasant time and you must tell him to give me the minuti. I hope he got back in time to see Lieut. Brown. I saw Gen. Pemberton when he was out here and he told me he was offered a command here but was anxious to get with the Virginia Army. Do tell me how you send your letters to go to the Trans-Miss Dept? I have written to father once since I got here and will do so again as soon as I get a chance. I'm very well. Love to all—

Your affect. boy
Frank Huger

Letter Number 22

Union General Ambrose E. Burnside, former commander of the Army of the Potomac during the Battle of Fredericksburg, was now operating in east Tennessee. He occupied Knoxville since early September 1863. General James Longstreet and his forces were moving on Knoxville to face Burnside when Frank wrote the following letter to his sister, Celly. Gen. B. is Braxton Bragg and Col. An is E. P. Alexander.

Camp near Tyness Stip. Tenn.
Saturday, November 7th, 1863

My dear Celly:

I only wrote to Mother a couple of days ago, but while waiting for the cars to come upon which we are to load our guns, I'll fire you a shot for I don't know when I'll have the ammunition at hand again. A part of Braggs Army under

Longstreet are going up this R.R. towards Knoxville. We sent our horses off by Road yesterday morning, and this evening we follow with the guns on the cars. It is evidently intended to make a diversion on Burnside. Whether it means a fight or not I cannot say, but I doubt if we have men enough. I hope we may be able to occupy Knoxville, and have good winter quarters on the R.R. to Virginia. I rejoice at anything that takes me away from Bragg. I've served a great deal longer in his Army that I ever want to again and now that the bad weather has apparently passed, I'd rather be "passing around" than laying in Camp, especially near Chattanooga. I hope we are going to have a pleasant trip and accomplish glorious results but I fear that Gen. B. hasn't done the things right, so far. They ain't very partial to us in this Army and they wouldn't care if we didn't come off first best. At least that's the estimate I mean enough to hold some of them in. If this move hasn't been made public in Richmond when you receive this of course you won't mention it. By the way, I've been thinking about getting you to press some of your friends into service and have some work done for our flag. Col. An and myself are both anxious to have the battles put on it, that is those in which the Battalion was engaged as such, tho' many of the companies have been in more, before they were put in this command. You had better have them done on strips of white stuff to be sewed on the white part of the flag. No word should be over two feet long. The letters had better be of blue 1 or 2" long, block letters are best but if any others are easier made, they'll do as well. Here's the list:

Second Manassas
Sharpsburg
Fredericksburg
Chancellorsville
Gettysburg

and by the time you get those done, I hope to have one or two more to go down. After due consultation, and much consideration, it is concluded that block letters of 1" is the proper length. Now there is some work to do and I know you will do it if you have time. Theres no hurry. The strips of white had better be 2" wide so the tailor can turn them down when he goes to put them on. You haven't answered my last letter yet, which Mother says you received. Every time you don't do so promptly, I'll send some such letter as this with a <u>reminder.</u> So Ramseur has gotten married at last. I shall expect a full account from Pinck, who I hope got home in time to see Lieut. Brown (no relation of his tho' to my knowledge) who went on from here some time ago with a letter full of wants. My "Examiner" comes pretty regularly now. Where is Jack? With the Army I suppose. Please give him my love and do the same to Miss Bucky and tell her I'm waiting anxiously for that bag, tho' just between you and I, I'll expect it when I see it. The best information from *a reliable gentlemen, in fact, the "oldest inhabitant," leads me to the above conclusion. I hope you are all comfortable in your new domicile. Our cars have come but I hardly expect to get away before midnight.*

Your affect. bro.
Frank Huger

Letter Number 23

Longstreet was besieging Knoxville when Frank wrote his November 23 letter to his brother Pinck. The Brown he mentioned was of course Lieutenant J. Thompson Brown, who had been in Richmond and was bringing numerous items back to Frank and the battalion. Frank suspected Lt. Brown was delayed at Dalton, Georgia, near the Georgia–Tennessee border. Cap. Winthrop was Stephen Winthrop, acting assistant adjutant and inspector general to E. P. Alexander. Winthrop, an Englishman, served in the British Army from 1855 to 1862. He had been on Longstreet's staff before coming on Alexander's. Winthrop committed suicide in England on March 13, 1879.[43] Eustis is Frank's other older brother and served for a time on his father's staff.[44] Freemantle was British Lieutenant-Colonel Arthur J. L. Freemantle of the Cold Stream Guards. He visited Army Headquarters and Longstreet's First Corps and was with Longstreet at Gettysburg. It is unlikely that Freemantle was the officer who gave Frank the coat as Freemantle was not in America that long.[45] The coat may have come from Winthrop. Frank's "examiners" were copies of the Richmond newspaper. Finally Butler was Union political General Benjamin Butler, famous for his occupation of New Orleans.

Near Knoxville, Tenn. November 23rd, 1863

My dear Pinck:

Your letter of the 3rd and Mother's of the 6th came up a day or so ago. I also received one from Brown on the 5th saying he would leave in a few days, and I suppose by this time he is at Dalton but he should not come across the river until the result of this expedition is apparent. I wish I could write you something satisfactory but I cannot. The enemy are closely hemmed in Knoxville, strongly fortified on commanding heights and our lines are all armed about 1500 yds. in front.— No attempt to assault has yet been made and I hope none will be. We can't afford to lose men that way now. We have been living very well — turkeys, chickens, and vegetables are quite common but when we go back to Chattanooga, our hard time will commence and Brown's stores will come in splendidly. I'm very much obliged for the things, and will be more so when I get them which I hope will be before long. I've conceived an original idea of using Celly's cloak as a lining—tell Mother—viz; putting Cellys on first, and mine over it—, I think that will answer and save work too. I wrote Mother last Wednesday and mentioned that Cap. Winthrop was wounded on the 18th. He was behaving very gallantly—leading a charge of Kershaw's Brigade, when he was shot through the shoulder. A few months will put him in the field again and I hope at the head of a regiment. I was glad to see Eustis' letter of 4th Oct. but I don't understand his allusions to comments by "a private of Cavalry." Does he mean to say he has joined, or how do you understand it? I hope you will hear from father soon. Ain't there some mail out in this direction that purports to go to the "Trans-Miss," if so tell me when, where from and for how much and I'll profit by the information.

I think when Brown comes with all those things I'll open a store. You can't imagine the prices out here. Atlanta beats Richmond all to pieces. An ordinary grey uniform coat costs $550., boots $250 &etc.——. Like Freemantle I always sleep in mine now to secure them against theft, my spurs too—especially as there is a <u>great deal of warmth in them.</u> Did you ever try it? I'll ride over now and take a few shots at the Yanks. If I could regulate it each shot should kill a thousand. This is the meanest country I ever saw, the majority of the people are union—few truly southern people—most of them blow N. & S. [North and South]*according as to which party are occupying the country. Its "O, Lord" & then "O, Devil" with them. Confed. money is at a very low estimate with them; it ain't (<u>worth the paper its printed on</u>) 10,000 = to how much?

If you see Jno. Bayler tell him to take my advice and quit flirting with the girls and attend to his legitimate business. A few more old "examiners" have come up, I've got about ten in all. I'm perfectly satisfied with the attempt to get Richmond Dailys. I've desires to be kindly remembered to you all. I pity the people of Norfolk now that Butler is going there. Someone should go down and shoot him. Love to all—

Your affect. Brother Frank Huger

1864

Letter Number 24

By the first of the year 1864, Frank Huger was still unsure about his letters reaching his father and brothers in Trans-Mississippi. So the following letter, written on New Year's Day, Frank entrusted to a man going on furlough to Mississippi. What Frank meant by his "dabbing" was to fill the cracks and chinks in the unfinished fireplace to make it and his lodgings more air-tight.

Frank wrote that he was alone, several of his fellow officers being either on leave or in the hospital. That surely made the absence of mail all the more melancholy. Colonel E. P. Alexander became the father of twins on September 21, 1863. Their names were Edward Porter II and Lucy Roy.[46] Lookout Mountain and Moccasin Ridge are landmarks around Chattanooga.

Frank Huger reported some of the problems with Confederate ordnance in his letters to his father, a long time ordnance officer, now associated with the arsenal at Tyler, Texas. Confederate artillery shells failed, bursting at an unacceptable rate of one in ten. The McEvoy attachment made no difference. This attachment resembled a paper-wrapped musket cartridge and was intended to improve the ignition of the paper fuse by catching the flame from the burning charge that engulfed the shell when the charge was fired.[47] The old principle was an impact fuse. The jumper was a metal piece that fit inside the fuse and floated freely. When its inertia was overcome by the shell slamming into a hard surface, the jumper hit a percussion cap with enough force to explode the cap. This fuse was least effective when the ground was turned to mud by rains or spring thaws. Then the shell buried into the mud where it failed to go off. What Frank wanted were shells filled with scrap iron or iron balls that would scatter when the shell exploded over the heads of advancing troops. Frank informed his father of very poor results at Knoxville when only two shells out of twenty burst. A shell that failed to burst usually sailed over the target and hit someplace of little consequence. The damage, if any, would be much like a hit from solid shot. The two 20-pounder Confederate-made Parrott guns burst. Not only was the ammunition unreliable but guns cast in the Confederacy were inferior to those cast in northern foundries. Wright has been identified in a letter above as Moses H. Wright of the Atlanta arsenal.

Frank's reference to Ransom and to R. referred to Major General Robert Ransom, Jr., of North Carolina. General Bragg's chief engineer was General Danville Leadbetter, an old engineer from the West Point class of 1836. He had been stationed at Knoxville for months and had built Fort Sanders.[48] Fort Loudon was in east Tennessee. Brigadier General Archibald Gracie, Jr., was wounded by a ball passing through his forearm. Gracie was killed on December 2, 1864, in the trenches around Petersburg. The term "little Swee" is a reference to Frank's mother and was first used as a term of endearment by his father. Frank's last reference was to Joseph B. Kershaw. Frank got his wish, Kershaw did gain the rank of major general. Kershaw commanded a brigade and later a division in Longstreet's First Corps.

Camp Alexanders Battalion
Near Russelville, Tenn. Jan. 1st, 1864

My dear father:

As one of our men is about to start on a furlough to Mississippi, and tells me he expects to communicate across the River. I will start you a letter by him and by the time it reaches you I reckon it will require a pretty long retrospective scope to wish you and Ben the Happy New Year I do today. It is bitter cold today and I crouching over a few embers in an unfinished fire place to a big tent, but its hard work keeping warm. However, when the weather moderates, and I can finish my dabbing, I'll be very snug for the winter. It has been so long since I have heard from any one that I can give you no news except as to my own "operations" since I last wrote you, which was from camp near Chattanooga about the middle of Oct. I don't know if you ever received it. We have been cut off from all communication ever since we left Bragg to go to Knoxville, and I have not heard a word from home in any way since Nov.5th now nearly two months, nor do I think they will have the bridges west of Bristol done for two weeks yet. I am all alone here now. Col Alexander having gone home on a sixty days leave to see his twins and Joe Haskell has ridden over to Abbeville to see his parents on a thirty days leave, and as Capt. Winthrop was badly shot at Knoxville and is still absent, it leaves me the sole representation of our mess. You have of course seen an account of our failure at Knoxville. An attack on the place was what Bragg should have done ten days after the battle of Chickamauga, and after a long delay he finally concluded to send Longstreet after it. We left Lookout Mountain on the night of 3rd Nov.—While there we had a good deal of practice at long range at the enemys battery on Moccasin Ridge, and their camps. I don't think we succeeded in bursting ten shells out of every hundred fired. (from the rifled guns), either with or without the McElvoy [sic] attachment. I believe the McElvoy [sic] attachment is radically defective in its mode of attachment to the fuse, for I think it breaks off the part of the fuse projecting out of shell. Alexander got Wright to make him some models at Atlanta on the old principle of the jumper and percussion cap, but we came away before they were finished. Until we get a good igniter, I don't think we ought to make any shell at all, except percussion—and few of them—for I think they ought to make us shrapnel for the rifles. The Yankees use it almost entirely, and I know its very demoralizing. Scrap iron would answer the place of bullets, or better still iron balls. At Knoxville on the south side of the River, I got a chance at some Yankees in a ravine and fired on them with a 10 pd. parrott [sic]— 40 rounds with 2 and 3" fuses. <u>Two</u> burst. One of our companies had 4 20 pdr. Parrotts—two U.S. captured at Harpers Ferry, and two C.S.— one of the later we burst at Fredericksburg, and the other on this trip. I don't want any more "sich like"—But this ain't getting up to Knoxville. We crossed the Holston River at

Loudon on the 15th without opposition, and on the evening of the next day we marched to within two miles of Knoxville, skirmishing all the way; the place was invested on every side except across the river. The mistake here was not assaulting the place next— instead of which we awaited the arrival of Ransom who Bragg told Longstreet would be ordered to cooperate with him from Bristol. After waiting several days, Longstreet sent a courier to Ransom, who found him at Bristol, which was the <u>first information</u> R. had that we were at Knoxville. Finding that R. was not coming it was determined to assault the enemys right on the morning of the 26th. Here Braggs evil genius interfered again, for the evening previous Gen. Leadbetter, Braggs Ch. Engineer arrived and without positively advising discountenanded the plan of attack, and argued in favor of our trying the left of their lines— so the attack was postponed. The 25th & 27th were spent reconnoitering the left, which was found to be the strongest part of the line—, so the original plan was reverted to. In the mean time we had been reinforced by two Brigades and two Batteries. The 28th it rained hard and was very cold. That night it cleared, and the next morning at day-break it was made. The troops were not well handled tho' and didn't show their usual spirit. The attack was made directly on Fort Loudon—, and was a failure, being repulsed with a loss of about 650, about 50 killed in the ditch and some on the parapet. Six or eight got in and were taken prisoners. Just as we were preparing to renew the assault, a courier arrived from the President ordering us back to Knoxville. Our pontoons and the heavy trains were started that evening when in a few hours a courier came from Bragg to say he had been whipped and had fallen back. Consequently our communications were cut off and we were left out in the cold. We soon heard that two or three columns were moving on us, so the night of 4th Dec. we raised the siege and after a very hard march camped near Rogersville on the 9th. The enemy cautiously to Bean Station where the road to Cumberland Gap comes in to the main Road from Knoxville to Bristol. On the 14th, we started back, and that evening had a heavy skirmish at Bean Station. Here Archie Gracie got wounded— not seriously tho'. The next day we pushed them to within 20 miles of Knoxville when it was evident we could not bring on a general engagement, so we halted. A few days after we crossed the River, and camped here 47 miles from K. and 86 from Bristol. We are building winter quarters. The R.R. to Bristol is much damaged and it will be sometime before we have any communication I'm afraid. Longstreet missed his chance when he let the enemy get away at Campbells Station. Bragg should never have sent such a small force against that strong place— it was sending a boy on a man's errand. We accomplished nothing and have suffered a great deal, supplies of all kinds being very much needed. If everything remains quiet this winter, I will go in and see the little Swee in March. I wish I could write you some news of them all but I have nothing from them, but I saw at Hdqtrs. yesterday an *endorsement from the conscript bureau of the 11th Dec. in Pinck's handwriting. A few days will I hope bring me some letters. McLaws has been relieved because I believe he did not cooperate in some of Longstreets plans, Kershaw is temporarily commanding the Div. I wish they'd make him a Major General.*

Letter Number 25

Major General Simon Bolivar Buckner's East Tennessee Department was united with General Bragg's command and became the third corps of the Army of Tennessee. Along with generals Leonidas Polk, James Longstreet and D. H. Hill, Buckner too became one of the anti–Bragg critics. Yet out of all the confusion Buckner got command of a division. Earlier in 1862, Buckner, abandoned by his superior officers John B. Floyd and Gideon Pillow, surrendered Fort Donelson to his friend Ulysses S. Grant. Among the social circles in Richmond Buckner was known as "the Poet."[49] His son, Lieutenant General Simon Bolivar Buckner, Jr., was killed in World War II on Okinawa. Major General Charles W. Field commanded a brigade in A. P. Hill's division during the Seven Days, Cedar Mountain and Second Manassas, where he was seriously wounded. Frank was correct; Field was promoted to major general and sent to Tennessee to command John Bell Hood's old division. Field traveled to Tennessee with E. P. Alexander after Alexander came back from his leave.[50] Lieutenant General Leonidas Polk commanded the right wing of Bragg's army at Chickamauga. Kerr, along with Taz Taylor and Camp was possibly John Bozman Kerr (1809–1878), a lawyer from Baltimore.

Frank's description of lovely young ladies partially undraped ties into Mary Chesnut's description of elaborate charades played in wartime Richmond.[51] The naked foot has parallels to the desires of John Chestnut IV or Johnny as his aunt Mary Chesnut called him.

Mary Chesnut recorded seeing Frank in Richmond on March 24, 1864. Frank was at the capitol grounds in company with Robert A. Dobbins, a Baltimore publisher and lawyer before the war. They were there to see some returned Southern prisoners and walked away in the company of a young woman, Susan Frances Hampton Preston or Trudy.[52]

Added to this letter was the announcement of his promotion to lieutenant colonel, coming through on March 14, 1864, to rank from February 27. Of his promotion Robert K. Krick wrote,

> Major Frank Huger, who had served admirably as the second ranking officer in the battalion for almost a year, succeeded Alexander as battalion commander. Huger had commanded the battalion in action for months during the periods when Alexander acted as corps artillery commander—which was

almost every time there was fighting.... Although Huger proved to be an extremely competent battalion commander, he never displayed the brilliance that characterized Alexander's actions. Perhaps this was because Huger did not have an opportunity to exercise command until the Confederate cause was on the decline, or perhaps it was the inevitable result of succeeding Porter Alexander, who was a virtually impossible act to follow.[53]

Camp at Bulls Gap, E. Tenn.
March 6th, 1864

My dear Ben:
With my usual procrastination in reference to such affairs, I have delayed answering a letter received from you about six weeks ago.— but our constant moving must serve as my excuse. Altho, we were nominally in winter quarters at Russelsville, we were moving all the time, and have had the hardest winter of the war. About the middle of February, this army commenced moving towards Knoxville—and I certainly thought we would reduce the place this time—but this day after crossing the river at Strawberry Plains, 16 miles from Va [Virginia] we suddenly pulled up stakes and fell back to this point—about 50 miles from Knoxville—Army Headquarters being at Greenville, 15 miles to the rear. Hoods old Division is immediately at this Gap, Gen. Buckner temporarily commanding, who is a great favorite with the Division, but I understand that Field has been made a Major General and ordered to it. Probably our advance was intended to have cooperated with Joe Johnston, who wanted to attack Grant, but being obliged to send off reinforcements to Polk, he could not carry out his part of the programme, and as he recalled all his cavalry, probably he, Longstreet, thought he could not maintain his long line of communication with his flanks exposed—and no cavalry to watch them, so dropped back here behind these mountains where we are in just as good a position for a forward move. The transportation is being cut down, and everything betokens a move—to Kentucky probably. If I can after that see a little service in the Trans-Miss Dept, I'll feel at home anywheres in the Confederacy. Alexander went home early in the winter and has not yet returned, but is expected back this evening. Should he get back, I'll probably go to Richmond this week and pay the little a visit—besides I feel like indulging myself in a little rest. General Johnston has applied to have Alex made a Brigd. and assigned to him as his Chief Arty.—I hope he won't get it tho' until I get off, and when it does come, I hope they may assign him to this Army for I shall miss him terribly. I am busy refitting the Battalion which has been pulled down very much by our continuous marching during the winter. Bully Alex has just returned with the big star in the middle and has been assigned to duty with this Army. General Lee refused to let him go

to the West—and we are considered a part of his Army yet, why his objection [to] send him there. I have applied for a 30 days leave and expect to be in Richmond this time next week. It is so late in the season tho', that I hardly expect more than 20 days, but that will be sufficient. I feel more at home in the field than anywheres else, and besides I rather pride myself on the fact that few men have been more with their commands or have asked less of the authorities. I have been again recommended for a grade—to have the command of this Battalion which I expect very soon, virtually I have been in command since Gettysburg, and Alex promises to urge my appointment to a full Colonel as soon as he thinks I can get it. From Norfolk we have sad news, the Beast Butler has scared the people out of their wits. They have taken the oath to a man, old Taz Taylor leading off. Kerr did not take the oath, but moved his family to Baltimore. Camp has done the same thing to New York, so our friends there are lost to us forever. Richmond went crazy I hear just before Lent—parties—starvation of the reverse, theatricals, tableaux, pantomime, charades etc, etc were the order of the day. I have been told of some curious doings—young lady—beautiful creature—represents piece of statuary—very little drapery, pretty naked foot—naked shoulders etc, etc. Thats the style. I confess tho' I feel as much shocked at the display, as my informant appeared to be, at least not until I had an opportunity of judging for myself. I'll put this away, until I hear something of my leave, and if I get it, will take this to Richmond with me.

Richmond, March 14, 1864

My furlough has been a military success—as I arrived here on the 10th, find them pretty well here. Mother is giving you all the news. I'm just starting for Petersburg—Love to father and My appointment as Lt. Colonel is out.

Letter Number 26

The letter below was from another affectionate boy, Eustis, writing from Marshall, Texas. The movements of General William T. Sherman are of concern to Eustis at this time. On February 3, 1864, Sherman left Vicksburg and marched to Meridian, Mississippi, to break up railroads and to make an experiment in terror.[54] Things were going smoothly for the Trans-Mississippi Hugers. The garden and the weather were their major concerns. Major Alexander was George D. Alexander in charge of the Confederate States Arsenal in Marshall, Texas, which was different from the Confederate States Depot also located at Marshall, Texas.

Marshall, Texas Mch 9, 1864

My dear Mother—

Ben started a letter last week and I will send this off today in hopes that some of them will reach you. As I hear the mail is going regularly now. We have dates by it to the 16 Janry but nothing from you. But I hope a letter will come along before very long. I hope Sherman's expedition will not stop them. All are very anxious to know what he has gone after. We hear that he has 20 days rations & has left his rear open.—If such is the case we ought to make very short work of him. We now hear the rumors that he is in full retreat towards Jackson. I trust we may capture him yet. It seems almost impossible to hear the truth now. It is getting very warm now and the garden is doing very well.—Last week we had a Northern and great fears were felt for the fruit, but very little injury was done to anything, and I think it bids fair to be a good season. Which is the great event we have to look for—Col Stockton who commands the San Antonio Arsenal got here yesterday from Shreveport & with father and Ben spent the day at the Arsenal and in the evening rode out to Mrs. Gaines. The Arsenal is I think the largest on this side of the river and Maj. Alexander deserves great credit for he has had an immense amount of work to do. Six months ago this spot was a wilderness and now it is quite a large place nearly as large as this great city.—Which by the way is as about a dull a spot as can be well found. All places are very poor now but this I think is a little the worse and now we are to have seven long summer months. With plenty of sand & all kinds of varmints is not a pleasant prospect.—but something may turn up in the meantime by which we may have to leave. The Yankees can never drive us away.

I suppose next month Mr. Dunwoody will come out again, don't forget to send out the cards by him. Mrs. Anderson gave father a pack but they will not last for ever and it is very hard to get any here and then they are $30 a pack and the meanest possible kind. Ben has entirely recovered from his attack. Father keeps well and now is busy with the gardenwhich is some occupation for him—he speaks of visiting the iron works in Davis County very soon and the sooner he gets off the better for it will soon be too hot to travel for pleasure. I think I will go with him.

Tell Jones no one has heard from him for a long time. Love to him and Cel.
Your affect. Boy Eustis

Letter Number 27

Tableaux—on stage when actors freeze in position before resuming the action of the play—used here as a comment on how slow the train was. Cary St. was a fashionable street in Richmond at this time. Smike was Major John

S. Saunders, chief of artillery in General Richard H. Anderson's division, Army of Northern Virginia. Saunders made a perfect Smike, a character from Charles Dickens' novel *Nicholas Nickleby*, in a performance in Richmond society during the winter of 1864.[55]

Charlottesville, Va.
Thursday, 14th April, 1864

Dear Mother:

    I went to Lynchburg on Tuesday and not being able to learn anything definitely there, I started for Bristol [Tennessee] yesterday, went about half way and met the down train, with General Longstreet and all his staff, so I changed trains, and returned to Lynchburg last night, witnessed the slowest specimen of a "tableaux" I ever saw and we all came over here in this morning's train. Battalion will be here by Saturday, and the horses in a week. I have my two here, both looking badly. Haskell is now riding around trying to find some resting place and if he don't get back soon I'll pitch a tent in the street. Dick did not stop at Farmville being asleep when the cars passed through, so he went on to Bristol. He says he left your shoes at a shop on Cary St. not one square from Mrs. Moores, and that Joe knows where it is, having shown him the place. I hope you are comfortably fixed in your new house, and that your cold is better. Had I known the exact state of affairs I would have staid in Richmond today and have joined them here this evening. Do ask Jack if he wants to use Tilghmans horse for Smike this summer.

I forgot to mention it to him. The horse is about 15 miles from here and if he don't want him I'll let Haskell use it, as he hasn't succeeded in finding the one he lost. Haskell is I'm afraid most too heavy. Celly must tell Miss Lillie McDowell that I shall have an opportunity to pay that visit now and do let me know what day she is coming up. I'll meet her at the depot with an escort. Love to all —
    Your affect. boy
    Frank Huger

Wartime photograph of Frank Huger in a porkpie hat (courtesy William A. Turner).

Letter Number 28

The abode of peace and Happiness
University of Virginia
No 3 Rue de Dawson
Sunday April 17, 1864

My dear Celly,
    I have told you where I am and how situated, above, and undersign my name just here, but I want to tell U something else so I'll [unclear] or rather you will I hope—which is to say and I said so once before in my letter to Mother on Thursday that when I got nearly to Bristol I met [unclear, may be all the big] guns with its appendages, on the down train, into which I deposited myself and got back here Thursday morning. That evening Alexander got possession of this house. As [unclear] and I are staying with him until my Battn. comes up, not one gun having yet arrived. It will be the 1st of May before I can get ready to move— bah, and I have met a great number of friends here and find the place not as utterly destitute as it looks. I manage to pass my time very pleasantly. For neighbors we have some friends of yours. Miss Sue and Emily Voss from Baltimore and also little Miss Gordon, who says she is a friend of Mary Mannings. Mrs. Fr[unclear] is here in one of the University buildings and Mrs. Rhodes and a great many ladies I have met at Orange last summer are in town—about a mile from this house. I intended to have gone to Church this morning but we had breakfast so late that I couldn't go down so I lost that chance of seeing the concentrated beauty of the "burg." However when Miss Sallie comes up and fulfills on Sugagsamuch [actual spelling] I'll have the opportunity. Miss Judy might come with her and I <u>really think</u> this mountain air will do Miss Buck good. Do give them my love and tell Miss Mary [unclear] like to have a <u>war talk</u> with her this evening. You must let me know where Miss Tillie is going to stay—that is if I'm right in my conjectures that she is going to stop here, and if she ain't, be certain to let me hear what day she is going to pass through. Tell Mother if she has found my sash to send it to me by the first person she knows that is coming—and give the enclosed letter to Bill Jones and ask him how the mischief he enacted it to get to Montreal via Bristol. He must be spooney. I have found no place yet that I think would suit Pinck if he comes to the field unless indeed he would like to be Chief Commig of the Arty 1st captain on Alexanders staff. I may create some vacancies on the Battalion when I get my hand on it. Love to all. I hope Jack hasn't gone back yet—but that he is free from that pain in his face.
                    Love, affect. F. H.

Letter Number 29

The following letter was written less than two weeks before the Battle of the Wilderness, the start of General Grant's bitter Overland Campaign. Gibbes was probably Wade Hampton Gibbes who took command of the 13th Battalion of Virginia Light Artillery in April 1864.[56] Perhaps Frank was able to find a young man's enjoyment with Miss Lillie and the dance he mentioned. The fighting of 1864 was unlike any that preceded it. "Eleanor[']s Victory" by Mary Elizabeth Braddon was published in 1863 and serialized in the weekly magazine *Once a Week*, March 7 through October 3, 1863. It was illustrated by George Du Maurier. Mary Braddon (1837–1915) was a prolific British novelist producing some 75 novels. Mary Chesnut, too, read this work.[57]

Camp near Cobham Station — 8 miles from Gordonsville. Sunday morning 24th April '64

My dear Pinck:

I wrote you a hurried note yesterday morning and didn't even tell you that the blanks enclosed were for the cloth that Joe Haskell wants you to get for him. We hear that there is cloth in Richmond now. Fields Division is coming up so slowly that I hardly expect the Review I wrote you of will come off at all or not for a week or ten days and in the mean time I am going to move as soon as I get my horses, which I hope to do this week. The neighborhood is gay and you must come up any day you can. Let me know before hand if possible but if not, it don't make any difference for I'm about 400 yds. from the depot on the right hand side of the road. Gibbes told me yesterday that he had opened a dispatch that had come to Charlottesville after I left which arrived Fri. morning and had answered it. This depot you understand is on the road from Gordonsville to Charlottesville.

I saw Miss Lillie yesterday and she gave me your note with the money enclosed, much obliged. I was flat broke. If you can, do bring my <u>store</u> clothes and my shoes for we will probably have a dance and you'd better bring some grub. lb. of hard old bacon and 1 tb. Of flour are our entire stock of luxuries per diem.

Come up as soon as you can and with love to all—
   Your affect. brother—
   Frank Huger

Do bring me "Eleanors Victory"

The Wilderness

One year, almost to the day, after the two eastern armies clashed at Chancellorsville in May of 1863, they were at it again in virtually the same place. Now the Union Army of the Potomac, under the nominal command of Major General George G. Meade, was in fact directed by the newly-minted Lieutenant General Ulysses S. Grant. General Robert E. Lee of course remained in command of the Army of Northern Virginia. On May 5 and 6, 1864, the preeminent commanders of the Civil War fought each other in the scrubby, second growth known as the Wilderness. At the end of the day, May 6, 1864, Grant and especially Lee and Meade, who had been fighting in this part of Virginia, knew the war had become even more severe.[58]

Edward Steere described the Wilderness as "a dreary wasteland fringing the south bank of the Rapidan River ... the primeval forest of stately pine and sturdy oak was felled by white invaders to provide fuel for smelting the iron torn from shallow pits. In later days a second growth of scrub trees, interlaced with dense underbrush and thorny vines, rudely covered the ugly scars left by the robbery of the subsoil. Casting eternal shadows over stagnant pools and marshy creek bottoms, this brooding jungle not only inspired the name but imposed the conditions of combat in its gloomy depths."[59]

It was here then, in these gloomy depths that General Grant began his overland campaign to defeat General Lee and his Army of Northern Virginia, "if it takes all summer."[60]

General Andrew A. Humphreys, chief of staff, Army of the Potomac, described the general locations of both the Union and Confederate armies prior to the 1864 Virginia Campaign. It is helpful to understand the general locations of the armies and the tactics of the Federals to place Frank Huger's letters in proper context. General Humphreys wrote that the Army of the Potomac lay between the Rapidan and the Rappahannock rivers with army headquarters near Brandy Station. The Army of Northern Virginia lay along the Rapidan River in its entrenchments along a line of some twenty miles. General Longstreet returned from the west with two divisions and was in the vicinity of Gordonsville. "Lee's army being the objective [of the Army of the Potomac]," Humphreys wrote, "the first question was, by which flank should the Army of the Potomac move." Humphreys explained the pros and cons of moving by his left and right flanks. The decision to move by the left flank was adopted for the following reasons. Moving by the left flank would put the army in close contact with the coast and the rivers for supply and removal of the wounded. But the left flank forced the Yankees to negotiate the Wilderness, an area the Union officers calculated they could clear before General Lee could react.[61]

Letter Number 30

The following letter was not dated. Frank reported on the Battle of the Wilderness.

On the Plank Road Friday 6 P.M.

Dr Mother,
I will send you a line this evening, and get some of these men to mail it in Orange City tonight. I was ordered to march suddenly from Cobham on Wednesday evening, march 6 m, that evening, yesterday marched 25m. halted three hours last night and reached the field after going 9m. at 7 this morning. Found the fight pretty general, and our Corps the only engaged. Brig. Genl. Jones (Rum) is killed, Benning and Stafford severely, and just now Longstreet was it is feared mortally wounded. He was Lee's best officer.— No Arty has been engaged from our Corps— and very little from the others. The country is not adapted to the use of Arty being right in the Wilderness. Gen. Jenkins is killed. There is much to be done, and the Arty can't be used only when we get in other country.—With full ranks here and the prayers of the people at home we will I trust end the war here.— I am well. Love to P & C.
Your affect. Boy F. H.
Box arrived this morning and we have just eaten the herring. They came in very well.

Letter Number 31

The following letter, written to his mother on May 18, 1864, was the day, according to Gordon C. Rhea, that marked the end of General U.S. Grant's failed policy of assaulting Lee's army in its entrenched line.[62] The day before, Grant gave up his intention of attacking Lee's right and proposed to attack the left. The left of Lee's line was held by General Richard S. Ewell. The Union command believed Ewell to be weak as his troops had been shattered on May 12 at the Mule Shoe. Frank's claim that the enemy did not charge with any spirit may be open to question. Union general George G. Meade, commander of the Army of the Potomac, observed that the several days prior had given his men a rest and the arrival of reinforcements put them in good spirits.[63]

Alexander of course was Edward Porter Alexander, Haskell was Joseph C. Haskell, Alexander's adjutant, and Grattan was Lieutenant James F. Grattan who replaced Joe Haskell as battalion adjutant when Alexander became 1st Corps chief of artillery.[64]

Frank corrected for his mother the newspaper account of the captured artillery pieces. According to Frank, Majors Wilfred E. Cutshaw and Richard C. M. Page, artillery subordinates to 2nd Corps artillery chief Brigadier General Armistead L. Long, had some of their guns captured at the Mule Shoe on May 12. E. P. Alexander stated Cutshaw lost eight and Page twelve.[65] Stephen D. Ramseur was wounded once again in his maimed arm at the Mule Shoe along with brigadier generals James A. Walker and Junius Daniel, the latter mortally. P. and C. are Frank's brother and sister Pinck and Celly. Frank must have received a wound because he wrote his hand was entirely well.

On the right of the line Near Spottsylvania Cth.
Wednesday, May 18, 1864

Dear Mother:

I sent a courier after the mail on Sunday. He has just returned without any, so I'll start him back and certainly expect to hear tomorrow. I have written to you very frequently and hope you have received some of my notes. We are delighted at the good news we are receiving from all quarters and our army is most enthusiastic. The enemy made an attack on our left this morning—they had masses there and evidently intended to make a great effort, but the men <u>wouldn't charge</u> with any spirit and were easily driven back. A few more days will I trust frustrate this great effort of the enemy to get to Richmond and if successes are as represented, peace will come this fall. I am very well. Alexander, Haskell, Grattem—and in fact all our crowd the same.

The papers I see state that some of Alexanders Arty. was captured, It's a mistake, it was taken from the 2nd, Ewells, Corps from Cutshaws & Pages' Battalions, commanded by General Long. The 1st corps is the only one that has held its own without ever once being broken. The 3rd was broken at the Wilderness fight and only saved by the timely arrival of Longstreet, and the 2nd was pierced in Thursday's fight. Ramseurs Brigade has done gallantly. He was hit in his wounded arm but is still on duty, not much hurt. My hand is entirely well. Love to P. & C. I saw Jack yesterday—very well indeed. Love to the Prestons.

Your affect. boy—
Frank Huger

Letter Number 32

The next letter, also to his mother, Frank wrote on May 30, 1864, after having withdrawn from the North Anna River. Dick was his servant, the one he rented from Mrs. Galt. The fight of the "new issue" of South Carolina Cavalry — the 4th, 5th, 6th and 7th regiments — took place on the Matadequin Creek and the Bottoms Bridge Road. At first the Union cavalry was outnumbered until General George A. Custer arrived with his Michigan troopers to turn the tide.

Pres. Hampton was Preston Hampton, the son of Confederate cavalry general Wade Hampton or Wade Hampton III. At Burkittsville, Maryland, in 1862, just prior to the Battle of Antietam, Wade Hampton passed his overcoat to Preston to take care of before he rode into the fray. The high-spirited boy threw the coat onto a fence and followed his father into battle. "I've come to Maryland to fight Yankees," Preston declared, "and not to carry Father's overcoat."[66] Preston, temporarily assigned to his father's staff, was killed in late October 1864 fighting in the defenses of Petersburg. Preston was not yet twenty. Wade Hampton IV received a wound as he rode out to his brother Preston. Their father, Wade Hampton III, rode out to them, kissed his dead son and asked aides to care for Wade. He then rode back to his place and fought the remainder of the day.[67]

---

9 miles from Richmond Sunday evening
May 30, 1864

Dear Mother:

On Thursday night, the enemy withdrew from our front on the N. Anna River, after looking at our position for two days and started in this direction. At sunrise on Tuesday, we moved in this direction via the Telegraph road and after a terrible march, we reached this place near Mr. Wingfields, on the Rd. from the Mechanicsville Road to old Church about 4 P.M. yesterday.

The enemy are in our front— across the Pamunkey [River] and we now have orders to be ready to move. I hope Gen. Lee feels himself able to attack them and will give them battle and a defeat tomorrow —, the 31st is the anniversary of Seven Pines, and I trust we may smite them again by that time. I'll send this in by my courier, who goes after the mail, and as soon as we get at all quiet, I'll send Dick in and you may be sure I'll come myself just as soon as I can.

The "new issue" of So. Ca. [South Carolina] Cavalry got into a fight yesterday — did very well I believe but got a little beaten, if report speaks truly, initiated rather roughly.

I heard of Jack this morning through Pres. Hampton whom I met on the road. He was well. Love to P. & Celly.

Frank Huger

Letter Number 33

Letter 33 was one of the longer of Frank's letters. Written to his father on June 28, 1864, it outlined the major battles of General Grant's Overland Campaign to the siege of Petersburg. Frank also included some reports on actions in the Shenandoah Valley. More names requiring explanation appear in this letter than any other. These names and the identifying data are listed in the order they appear in the letter. Some names are in error because of Frank's spelling.

Breckenridge was Confederate major general John C. Breckenridge and Hunter was Union major general David Hunter. Major General John C. Breckenridge was sent into the Shenandoah Valley to unite with forces there under Brigadier General John D. Imboden to face Union general Franz Sigel. Breckenridge had been vice-president under U. S. president James Buchanan. Major General David Hunter replaced Franz Sigel after the battle of New Market. He burned Virginia Military Institute and Virginia governor John Letcher's residence in Lexington, Virginia.

Lieutenant James N. Stubbs (1839–1919) was a signal officer to General John Bankhead Magruder. The river Stubbs was to cross was the Mississippi so Frank's letter and one from his mother would have a chance to reach Benjamin Huger, Sr. Ben and Eus. were Frank's older brothers Benjamin, Jr., and Eustis. Major General Henry Heth, was a division commander in A. P. Hill's 3rd Corps. Soldiers from Heth's division clashed with Federal cavalry west of Gettysburg on July 1, 1863, to start that three days battle. Brigadier General John Gregg commanded a brigade in Joseph Kershaw's division of Longstreet's 1st Corps. The brigade comprised the 1st, 4th and 5th Texas regiments plus the 3rd Arkansas. It was Gregg's Texans who cried out, "Lee to the rear," during the Battle of the Wilderness. Kershaw was newly appointed to division command but had been a brigade commander with the First Corps in McLaw's Division.

Major General Gouverneur K. Warren commanded the Union 5th Corps. He had been an engineering officer with the Army of the Potomac and is credited with placing troops of the 5th Corps on Little Round Top during the Battle of Gettysburg. He was given command of the 5th Corps during army reorganization in March 1864 and replaced Major General George Sykes.

Ned Johnson was Major General Edward "Old Allegheny" Johnson. He commanded a division in Ewell's 2nd Corps. Frank failed to mention Brigadier General George H. "Maryland Steuart" Steuart, a brigade commander in Johnson's division, as being captured as well. Major General Benjamin F. Butler was in command of the Union Army of the James.

Confederate General Pierre Gustave Toutant Beauregard, a long time engineering officer and Confederate commander at First Manassas, was at this time in command of the Richmond and Petersburg lines. Beauregard had been summoned from Charleston. Jessie was one of Frank Huger's war horses.

Major General Robert F. Hoke was a Confederate division commander under Beauregard. Hoke defended Drury's Bluff overlooking the James River below Richmond against Union general Benjamin F. Butler. At Cold Harbor Hoke's division was on the right of the Confederate line. Major General Jubal Early commanded a division in his close friend Richard S. Ewell's Second Corps. He was sent to the Shenandoah Valley in the summer of 1864; he won the battles of Second Kernstown and the Monocacy. Early went on to threaten Washington, D.C.

Major General William Mahone fought throughout the war in A. P. Hill's Third Corps. He rose to command a division. Mahone commanded of troops from the First and Third Corps that made the flank attack on Union major general Winfield S. Hancock's corps in the Battle of the Wilderness.

Major General August Kautz's cavalry operated with General Benjamin Butler's 10th and 18th corps. He burned three important railroad bridges between Petersburg and Weldon. Fitz Lee was nephew to General Robert E. Lee. Fitz was colonel of the 9th Virginia Cavalry and brigade commander under J.E.B. Stuart. After Stuart's death on May 12, 1864, following his mortal wound at Yellow Tavern, Lee commanded a division under Wade Hampton. In later life he was governor of Virginia.

Major Carr was probably Charles Edward Carr. Carr was assistant quartermaster in the Mexican War and the same to General Benjamin Huger in 1861. He served as quartermaster and paymaster in the Trans-Mississippi Department. Mrs. Anderson and Col. were probably Colonel and Mrs. Samuel Smith Anderson. An artillery officer in the Mexican War, Anderson is on the list of original members of the Aztec Club. He served on Huger's staff during the Civil War and later in the west with General Edmund Kirby Smith.[68]

Frank wrote that he had three guns disabled by Yankee artillery fire. Two of them were struck in the face and one on the chase. The face is the very muzzle of the piece into which data about the tube were frequently cast, such as the foundry, tube weight, date of casting and gun number. The chase is that part of the gun barrel between the reinforce and the astragal and fillets, narrow bands that circle the barrel and mark the beginning of the muzzle. On ordnance rifles without the muzzle-swell the chase is the forward part of the tube.

E. P. Alexander described his wounding on page 445 in *Fighting for the Confederacy*. He also gave the location of the Howlett house. It was on the left flank of the Confederate Bermuda lines. Uncle John Preston was chief of the Conscript Bureau.[69]

Mr. Stringfellow mentioned in this letter and the next one may have been the Reverend Thornton Stringfellow. He believed heartily in slavery and delivered a strong defense of it from his pulpit. Frank's father mentions a Mr. Stringfellow in his letter to his wife written from Marshall, Texas, on November 27, 1863. Stringfellow had a brother in ordnance at San Antonio.[70]

Another Stringfellow worthy of mention but hardly the man Frank named is Franklin Stringfellow (1840–1913). Small and wiry and weighing only ninety-four pounds, Stringfellow was a member of the 4th Virginia Cavalry. Later he was on the staffs of both J.E.B. Stuart and Robert E. Lee. He was a scout and had many close calls, entering the enemy lines in disguise. After the war he became a noted clergyman and popular speaker.

Chesterfield Co. Virginia
June 28th, 1864

My dear father:
The day we started from Cobham Station, I had commenced a letter to you, when orders were received to move at once to the front as the enemy had crossed the Rapidan, at Germana, and Ely's fords, so I had to close my letter hurriedly to save the opportunity by Lieut Stubbs who was going across the River. He promised to send my letter at once, and Mother wrote by him also. I hope the letters have been received — If this attempt don't bring another order to move I will try and write for you a sketch of our work since then; or at least of the part in which I have participated which will give you some idea of the amount done, and more remains to be accomplished yet. Mother sent me last night dates from Ben and Eus. 27–31st May, and yours of 2nd June. I was glad to hear of you all so recently, and can appreciate your anxiety to learn results. I have only been able to get to Richmond once since we have been operating around here, then I got in at 11 P.M. and returned at 7 next morning. Mother and Pinck were very well, darling Celly looked a little pale, but I hope the cool weather has benefitted her. Until within the last few days we have had excessively hot weather, which has been very trying to the men in the works. I have been so tied down to the Battalion that I know very little of what is going on except immediately around us, but that embraces now all the men in the Confederacy except those in the Trans. Miss. and immediately in our front is the consolidated Yankee nation — may the devil catch them all.
On the evening of 4th May we left Cobham Station about 7 miles from Gordonsville on the Central Road and reached Parkers Store in the Wilderness on

the morning of 6th. *This section of country is not at all adapted for the use of Artillery and very little was used by us. I was not engaged at all. Heavy fighting occurred here on the 5th, 6th & 7th. Longstreets Corps just got up in time on the morning of the 6th to save us from disaster — our centre had been pierced, Heth's Division giving way after hard fighting. Greggs Texans happened to be leading our corps & went in like devils. The tide was soon turned and we drove the Yankees handsomely. Just at this moment Longstreet was wounded, about 9:30 A.M., we didn't know what we had done for the enemy have since admitted that they couldn't reform until 2 P.M.! The night of the 7th, the enemy moved off to our right and we had a race for Spottsylvania C.[ourt]H.[ouse]. Our cavalry disputed their advance stubbornly, but had to give back before their infantry and their cavalry had occupied the place, but Kershaw came up with his Division and drove them out. Warren, commanding the 5th Corps, sent it in, telling them we were only cavalry and to bayonet us in the trenches. They came up gallantly, and actually did as they were told, but were driven back with great loss. The rest of the army came up in the course of the day, and we formed our line that evening. I was on Kershaw's line. We staid here until the evening of the 14th when the enemy withdrew from our immediate front, apparently massing on our right. During this week, we had a miserable time in the trenches, constantly under their Artillery fire, the lines not more than 600 yds. from our front, and constant rains. The dark nights, and the proximity of their skirmish line, gave them every opportunity of massing against us and attempting a surprise and well calculated to make one uncomfortable with twenty-five guns at stake. They assaulted several times but were repulsed, the steady fire of the infantry and double doses of canister, repeated as rapidly as possible during the business. They broke through Ewell's line capturing Ned Johnson, with about 400 men and 20 pieces of Artillery. Grant fought desperately, massing his men against certain points and then crowding in line after line. I had three guns disabled here by their artillery fire — two of them struck in the face, and one on the chase. They fired a 12 pdr. Solid shot plum into a 24 pdr. Howitzer. Several carriages were cut to pieces, or rendered unserviceable by being injured by bullets. In the meantime, Butler had made his demonstration on Richmond, was to [sic] slow and had been thrashed by Beauregard. Was driven down what the Yankees call "Bermuda Neck" and sheltered by his gun boats fortified. We followed suit, with our left resting at Howlitts* [sic, should be Howlett] *House and our right on Swift Creek. (map sketched in here) Breckenridge had defeated Sigel who was advancing down the valley, and then we made the fatal mistake, in sending for him to join us, thereby leaving the valley open to Hunter, who succeeded Sigel, and he destroyed that section of country and advanced rapidly on Lynchburg. When the enemy abandoned our front, we moved to the right of our Army, and took a position resting on the Po River. The enemy demonstrated a good deal, and felt us pretty strongly, when on the 21st he slipped off to the left again apparently for Hanover Junction. We moved at once and crossed the South Anna the evening of 22nd. I had a couple of Batteries near the river, but our line was weak there, inasmuch as the ground on the opposite side was much higher. The next day they massed a large* [unclear, may be assortment] *of Arty. and under its fire advanced on our on , and took it. Only one regiment was holding it, and they escaped. Jessie was here wounded twice by a mile from the Junction, and about the same distance from the river. The enemy crossed and fortified, skirmished a little until the night of 26th when they recrossed , and we at once moved down the Telegraph Road, thro' the "Slashes of Hanover" to a point on the old Church Road south of the Pamunkey, near Tapapohomey* [Totopotomoy] *Cr., on the 30th the enemy felt our left in force. On the morning of the 1st June, I was ordered to report to Gen. Hoke on our extreme right near new Cold Harbor I found him in position and supplied with Artillery, so I reported to Pickett and went in position on our centre. The enemy assaulted several times while we were here, endeavoring especially to carry Cold Harbor and Turkey Hill. They were repulsed with heavy loss. The night of the 12th, Grant again moved to our right and we moved on the 13th across the Chicahominy* [Chickahominy] *to the vicinity of Malvern Hill. The enemy demonstrated in this direction whilst his main force was crossing the James lower down. While at Cold Harbor, Breckenridge's Division was withdrawn and sent to the valley, but was too late to prevent immense destruction. About the 12th, Gen. Lee sent Early, commanding 2nd (Ewells) Corps. in which is Ramseur now commanding a Division, to the valley to check Hunter, who was threatening Lynchburg and to save the So. Side & Danville Roads* [railroads]. *When he attacked Lynchburg he quickly discerned that there was something of heavy caliber behind the works, and at once he fell back. We persued but haven't caught him yet, although he has been so hardly pressed that he had to destroy his ordinance* [sic] *and other trains. We laid near Malvern Hill until the morning of the 16th when we started towards Petersburg. Picketts Division with my Battery being in advance. On the eve of the 15th, Beauregard anticipating an attack on Petersburg was compelled to evacuate the line in front of Butler who at once took possession, and pushed forward to the turnpike, which he picketed and commenced to destroy the R.R. where it crosses the Road. As we marched up about 12 o'clock we discovered their pickets by receiving a volley from them—formed at once and cleared the road. Between the "Pike" and Beauregards line there were numerous intermediate lines and it was not until the 18th that we succeeded in regaining our old lines, after considerable fighting. We have a Battery of 8 heavy guns near Howlitts* [sic] *house. Since then we have been comparatively quiet—"observing our front." Grant attacked Petersburg carrying our outer line, reinforcements arrived in time to check him, and we hold the 2nd line. The enemy occasionally* throw a shot into a town and are near enough to damage it very badly. Before he crossed the Pamunkey Grant started Sheridan on a raid to destroy the R.R. between Charlottesville and Lynchburg—, then to cross the Danville Rd. and join him south of Petersburg. That expedition has come to grief. Hampton smote him severely near Gordonsville and again on the Peninsular, so he has returned. The enemy tapped the Weldon road about 6 miles from Petersburg, but Mahone drove them off. However, their left rests so near it, that they can shell it. Another lot of raiders under [August] Kautz reached Burkeville, and did a deal of damage to the Danville Rd. there. Fitz Lee's cavalry is after them and our prospects of destroying them is good. The enemy have assaulted our lines at Petersburg, but were repulsed. I was there last night for a few moments, and saw Mr. Stringfellow, What is to come next God only knows. Northern papers of 26th have been received. Under the pressure of Grants *successes* — gold has gone from 172 to 244, and they hadn't heard of Hunters defeat. The enemy's losses must be tremendous. I don't think 100,000 would more than cover their killed, wounded and prisoners. As the Yankees term it, Grant principle of "attrition" wouldn't work — it wasn't philosophical—, the reaction was greater than the action and very *direct*. The war is becoming more barbarous, the enemy destroy everything, rob, pillage and burn all the houses — steal all the horses, destroy all the crops, insult and outrage women in the most cold blooded fashion.

I have been most fortunate in losing so few men thus far, having only had one officer killed, one taken prisoner, and about 40 men killed and wounded. I hope soon to have my Battir [battalion] equipped according to my ideas. I want to have two batteries of 3" rifles, two of Napoleons and one of 24 and the other of 12 pdr. Howitzers. It is at present equipped nearly as I desire except that one of the Batteries that I should like to have all Napoleons, has 2 20 pdrs. I am out with the rifled guns, my 24 pdrs. are my pet toys, and if Grant will continue to attack in mass I'd prefer nothing else. Uncle John Preston has been made a Brigadier. I hope it will give Jones a lift, and make him a Captain. I had the misfortune to have Jessie shot again, but she promises to get well in a few days. Give my best love to Ben and Eustis. I would write them, but I think this is enough for all, and tell Eustis I received about two weeks ago a letter from him dated in April. I never hear anything from Norfolk now. I was glad to hear of Mrs. Anderson. You must remember me very kindly to her, as well as to the Col. and Maj. Carr and tell the latter I hope the time is not very distant when with combined forces we can destroy 80 "drops"—

Petersburg— Sunday, July 3rd, 1864
General Alexander unfortunately got shot in the arm near the shoulder on the 30th and has gone off, I have been temporarily assigned to duty on this side

of the river, and now am engaged putting up some mortar Batteries. Many persons expect a general shelling by the Yankees tomorrow. They are damaging the town very much by their constant shelling. This state of things can not last much longer— Our movements will probably cause Grant to change his base before long. Both John and Joe Haskell are here, very well— Goodbye—
>Your affect. son.
>Frank Huger

Letter Number 34

Concerning artillery ammunition Frank wrote the following report to General William Nelson Pendleton.

>July 7, 1864

General Pendleton,
Chief of Artillery, Army of Northern Virginia
General: Your directions in reference to collecting shells I will have carried out at once. We have procured some suitable for the mortars. I write principally to call your attention to the fact that there are a large number in the vicinity of General Pickett's line, and as all is reported quiet there there would be no difficulty in collecting them. I had some gathered while there; many of them 30-pounder Parrotts, which would be especially valuable.
>Very respectfully, your obedient servant,
>Frank Huger Lieutenant-Colonel, Artillery

The Siege of Petersburg

"The Siege of Petersburg," Richard J. Sommers wrote, "proved the longest campaign of the Civil War. It pitted the greatest general of each side, Ulysses S. Grant for the North and Robert E. Lee for the South, directly against each other. Lee's masterful defense of Petersburg and Richmond prolonged the life of his army, of his capital, and of his country for nine-and-a-half months. Yet Grant's characteristic ability to learn from experience and his successful application of the Federals' many potential advantages eventually doomed those two cities and, along with them, the Army of Northern Virginia and the Confederacy itself."[71]

Letter Number 35

Mrs. Meade and the young ladies of her family are difficult to identify precisely. One is tempted to find a connection to Union general George G. Meade. General Meade had relations in the Confederacy. He was related to Henry Wise, the former governor of Virginia who had been married to General Meade's wife's sister. Meade's sister Elizabeth Mary and her husband Alfred Ingraham moved to Mississippi and were completely ruined by the Civil War. Another of General Meade's sisters, Mariamne, married Midshipman Thomas B. Huger, who sided with the Confederacy. Neither of the general's two brothers could be the husband of Frank's Mrs. Meade.

Second Lieutenant Richard Kidder Meade Jr. of Virginia was one of the men serving under Major Robert Anderson at Fort Sumter when it was fired upon. He joined the Confederacy but died July 31, 1862. Richard graduated from West Point in 1857. It is possible that Mrs. Meade could have been his widow and the ladies in her family, sisters perhaps, old enough to be of interest to Frank. Maybe they were Richard's sisters.

Mrs. Paul may have been Sophronia W. (Pickerell) Paul, wife of Samuel Buckner Paul. He was volunteer aide-de-camp to General G.P.T. Beauregard in 1864 and 1865 and a lawyer in Petersburg. Another possibility is the wife of D'Arcy W. Paul a prominent citizen of Petersburg.[72]

Mrs. Johnson is also difficult to identify correctly. Certainly a Confederate officer's wife could reside somewhere far from where her husband was serving. General Bushrod Johnson was in the Petersburg area at this time but his wife died in 1858. Another possible candidate was Mrs. Bradley T. Johnson whose husband had been colonel of the First Maryland and at this time was in command of cavalry with Jubal Early in the Shenandoah Valley. However the sentence "Mr. J. has been quite sick but is improving now" makes that identification questionable.

Petersburg Monday July 11th 1864

My dear Mother

Before I start out this morning I must send you a line. There is nothing to report except Dick's safe arrival with clothes and vegetables. The Bottle of spirits leaked, but the catsup was saved and is very useful now that we have beef. Every thing is as usual here, the enemy fire in to town just enough to keep every body there miserable. Nearly all females have left. Mrs. Paul goes back to Richmond today. Mrs. Johnson has stuck it out bravely and is going to keep on staying. Mr.

J has been quite sick but is improving now. I took my tea here last, or rather my buttermilk . All the young ladies of Mrs. Meades family are out in the country. [The remainder of the letter is so badly faded as to be illegible].

Letter Number 36

Sunday night July 17th 1864

My dear Mother

Yesterday morning I had a visit from Mr. Stringfellow who said he should probably go to Richmond in the evening and would see you all, so I suppose you have heard of me lately. We have the usual [unclear] of Sunday rumors, among them that Grant was killed on Friday evening — to good to be true I fancy. It seems positive tho' that we have sunken a couple of transports on the James River. I have been expecting to see Pinck every evening on my return to Headquarters but I haven't seen him yet. In fact I have only had one letter from you in the two weeks I have been here. Jones would be interested here. I think, and I should like him to come, and see the state of affairs — Joe Haskell sends his love and says if P [Pinck] can do so without trouble, to keep us advised about Ar Nva [Army of Northern Virginia] cloth. I haven't had a thing for more than a year and as a consequence losing time on the Government. I spent a very pleasant eve at Mrs. Johnsons and saw the beautiful Miss Giles. She failed tho' to strike me all of a heap. —

Nearly every body is out of town. I've been only to the Meades and Johnsons, both pleasant houses to visit. Love to Celly and Pinck — I hope [unclear] Smith still continues [unclear].

I have just gotten Jessie up again — she is looking very well. Have you heard any thing lately from father.

Your affect. Boy F. H.

Letter Number 37

Actually E. P. Alexander did not return to the Petersburg defenses until August 15. While recovering from his shoulder wound in Georgia, Alexander learned that General Joseph E. Johnston was relieved of command of the Army and Department of Tennessee. This, to Alexander, was a nail driven into the Confederate coffin by President Jefferson Davis under political pressure from Georgia's governor Joseph E. Brown and Senator Benjamin H. Hill.[73]

Willie Preston was William Campbell Preston, Jr., a first cousin to Jack, Celly's husband. Jack's and Willie's fathers were brothers. Willie was killed on or about July 20, his heart literally shot away while he was getting his battery into position. At Fort Sumter Willie reportedly fired the shot that broke the Federal flagstaff.[74]

Frank Huger writing that he saw Frank Huger is a bit confusing. The other Frank may have been a cousin. Our Frank Huger's father was one of eight children and the Huger family liked to name offspring after their famous forebears. Frank, the writer of this letter, had an Uncle Cleland Huger who named one of his sons Francis Kinloch Huger, named for his grandfather. Frank's cousin Francis, however, was killed in April 1863, while in the Confederate service, so he could not be the Frank Huger who our Frank Huger saw. Cleland Huger and his first wife, Mary Dunkin, had eight children, two of whom were named Francis, Francis Kinloch and Francis Motte. Cousin Francis Motte Huger, on his way to Charleston, may have been the one. Adding to the confusion is the thumbnail biography of Frank K. Huger in "Who's Who in Railroading, North America, 1893." This Frank Huger was listed as having been born in the Clydesdale Beaufort District, S.C., on December 5, 1845. He entered railroad service in September 1865. Hugh Rose remains a puzzle.

Petersburg, July 26th, 1864 Sunday night

My dear Mother:

I'll wind up a hard days work by taking my pipe and sending you a few lines by way of consolation. This will probably be my last week here, as from letters received from Alexander today we hear that he will leave home tomorrow and report here by 1st August, when I will go back to the Clay House with much satisfaction and only wish he was coming tomorrow. For my part I am very well satisfied to attend to my legitimate duties, as I don't appreciate these temporary positions. If everything should be as it is now, I'll then have an opportunity of nosing in and saying howdye (sub-rosa). Can't tell you how distressed I was to hear of Willie Preston's death, my! What a sad blow to his family—I do sympathize with them most sincerely. Ned I saw a few days ago. He was detained here 'till 11 o'clock the night he came over and spent the day with me. Frank Huger came to see me the same day—he had just heard of his appointment and expected to go to Charleston in a few days. I was sorry to hear of Hugh Roses death—not that I recollect him so well, but that his name used to be a household word in Grandmother's time. I received today a letter from Ben dated Feb. 5th 5 months and 20 days! When you write do mention the fact and tell him I say hurrah for the C. F. Mails—

I think I'll send Dick over on Friday evening to come back on Saturday as about next Sunday I expect to depart hence. We have been very quiet here for the last few days, all very quiet—I rather suspect the enemy are mounting heavy guns and that when they next open, it will be a heavy fire —. We again have a Sunday evening rumor that Grant is dead. Haven't seen Mr. Stringfellow for several days. I believe he is going to South Carolina in a few days. Goodnight—

Frank Huger

Letter Number 38

The lieutenant general commanding, Richard H. Anderson, also suspected the enemy would open with a heavy fire. The next day after Frank wrote the above letter, Frank received the following one.

Headquarters First Army Corps
Near Petersburg, Va. July 27, 1864

Lieut. Col F. Huger,

An examination of the line yesterday by the lieutenant general commanding led to the belief that the protection for your guns is not sufficiently strong. They are much too thin to resist the effect of the heavy guns that we may expect will be brought to bear on them. The lieutenant-general commanding desires, therefore, that you will at once proceed to have more earth thrown up, and the parapet made thicker. At present the infantry are too closely and incessantly occupied to give you any assistance. You must put every available artillerist at work on the gun-pits, and make your positions ready for a stubborn and successful defense. General Anderson [Richard H.] desires that you will make to him every morning a written report of the condition of affairs on the line with reference to the artillery. You will note the progress of work in these reports, any changes or movement in the enemy's position or intentions, and such work as you may discover in progress with him. Report also such casualties or desertions as may occur, and give generally any information that may be useful or of interest.

I am, colonel, very respectfully, your obedient servant.

G. M. Sorrel

Lieutenant-Colonel and Assistant Adjutant-General[75]

The Crater, "The Greatest Fizzle of the War"

Frustrated by the strong Confederate redoubt a short distance below the crest of Cemetery Hill, Lt. Col. Henry Pleasants considered a plan unorthodox by military engineering standards but right down the alley for Pleasants' Forty-eighth Pennsylvania Volunteer Infantry Regiment. Recruited entirely from Schuylkill County, some companies from the county seat of Pottsville alone, most of the men in this regiment worked in the anthracite coal mines scattered throughout this part of Pennsylvania. Henry Pleasant himself was a mining engineer.

As early as June 21, 1864, Lt. Col. Pleasants conceived the idea of excavating a mine underneath the fort and opening the enemy lines by an explosion. However General Burnside's biographer William Marvel credits Pleasants' division commander General Robert Potter with the idea on June 19. To carry the works by direct assault would require a terrible sacrifice of life. As things stood Confederate sharpshooters or snipers picked off three dozen men per day in the Ninth Corps alone.

None of the officers of the high rank in the Army of the Potomac had any faith in the endeavor except for the division commander General Robert Potter and Ninth Corps commander General Burnside. General Meade and his chief engineer Major James Duane believed the undertaking to be impossible. Pleasants and the men of the Forty-eighth were on their own. They had to make their own tools. The 18,000 cubic feet of dirt and soil excavated had to be removed by men carrying handbarrows made from hardtack boxes. To keep the fresh-dug soil from forming a pile and being observed by Confederates, it was carried far and wide to be deposited out of sight. A bridge was torn down to provide timber for shoring up the tunnel. Work was halted from time to time when Confederates began to probe, expecting the Yankees might be tunneling. Edward P. Alexander, as the following letter reveals, suspected the Yankees were digging but he could not fully convince General Lee that they were.

The experienced miners overcame all obstacles be they lack of support, shortage of tools, enemy counter tunneling or engineering problems. To solve the ventilation problem they dug a vertical shaft to act as a chimney. Then they built a long square wooden box that they extended as the tunnel lengthened and ran from the chimney shaft to the digging site. A small fire was built below the chimney and as the warm air rose, gases and exhaled carbon dioxide from the men's breathing exited through the long wooden box and up the chimney while the air current drew fresh air into the tunnel.

The biggest problem was figuring the exact distance from the mine entrance to the enemy's works. "This was accomplished," Samuel P. Bates wrote quoting Pleasants, "by making five separate triangulations with a theodolite [a surveying instrument that measures horizontal and vertical angles] and taking their mean. The triangulations were made in our most advanced line of works, and within one hundred and thirty-three yards of the enemy's line of sharp-shooters."

The main gallery of the tunnel was completed on July 17 and was 510.8 feet in length. The enemy began to search for the mine on that date and operations halted until the next day. Two lateral galleries were dug under the Confederate works, the left gallery measured thirty-seven feet in length, the right measured thirty-eight feet long. All excavation ended at 6 P.M. on the 23rd. On the 27th men packed powder kegs in the galleries beginning at 4 P.M. and ended at 10 P.M. The charge consisted of 320 kegs of powder each holding about 25 pounds. That was the equivalent of four tons of powder. There were three lines of fuses spliced together for a length of ninety-eight feet.

Ninth Corps headquarters ordered Pleasants to detonate the mine on July 30 at 3:30 A.M. Pleasants wrote, "I lighted the fuse at a quarter past three A.M., and having waited until a quarter past four without any explosion having taken place, an officer and a sergeant (Lieutenant Jacob Douty, company K, and Sergeant Henry Rees, company F) of the Forty-eighth Pennsylvania Regiment, volunteered to go in and examine the cause of the delay. It was found that the fire had stopped where the fuses were spliced. They were re-lighted, and at sixteen minutes of five A.M. the powder exploded."[76] Both Douty and Rees survived the war.

General Meade, possibly realizing his mistake in doubting the efforts of Lt. Col. Pleasants and his men, wrote a commendation to the regiment on August 3, 1864. But he was under no illusions as to the success of the operation. After all, the whole point of the explosion was in the follow up by the infantry, not just to blow a large hole in the Confederate defensive line. Writing to his wife on July 31, 1864, he admitted the attack on July 30 was a failure.

> *At 5 A.M. yesterday the mine was most successfully exploded, throwing into the air, and subsequently burying, four guns and a South Carolina regiment. Our column immediately took possession of the crater and the adjacent part of the enemy's first line; but instead of immediately pushing on and crowning the hill in front, which was the key to the whole of the enemy's position, our men crouched in the crater and could not be got forward. Burnside and myself had a dispute, he not willing to admit his men would not advance; at the same time it was evident to all no progress was being made. In the meantime the enemy, seeing we did not come forward, rallied, and massing on the point held by our troops, drove them back, with confusion and the loss of a number of prisoners."*

On the day General Meade wrote his commendation to the Forty-eighth Pennsylvania, he wrote to his wife, "Our miserable failure will require an investigation, and authority has been asked of the President to appoint a court of inquiry."[77]

The Joint Committee on the Conduct of the War was just the congressional body to perform the investigation. Formed as a result of the battle of Ball's Bluff in the fall of 1861, this committee, chaired by the radical Republican senator Benjamin F. Wade of Ohio and created by the equally radical Republican senator Zachariah Chandler of Michigan, this committee held hearings from December 20, 1861, until the end of the conflict some four years later.[78]

Bruce Tap in his work *Over Lincoln's Shoulder* described the committee and its Republican majority this way: "[They] believed that the Union war effort would benefit by officers with staunch antislavery credentials." They discounted military science thinking military skill as little more than common sense. Battlefield success, they believed, would inevitably follow from correct political beliefs."[79]

Letter Number 39

In this letter Frank described the Battle of the Crater. Edward Porter Alexander wrote that he believed General Robert E. Lee only partially believed Alexander's report that the enemy were mining. Mahone was Major General William Mahone. Gibbes of course was Wade Hampton Gibbes who dueled with Emory Upton when they were cadets at West Point.

Petersburg, Virginia—Aug 2nd P.M. 1864

My dear Mother:
I sent you a dispatch a few days ago to tell you I was well and safe through the fight which though very desperate and at one time threatening to be very serious, turned out to be the greatest fizzle of the war. It was a very weak attempt on Grant's part and needs some other explanation to my mind besides the currently reported statement that the men on the line wouldn't fight— or rather charge our lines. Grant breached our lines by mining and when the smoke cleared away, had occupied the line with his troops. He then made two attempts to charge across to our reserve works but was easily driven back on each occasion. Instead of massing a corps and moving right ahead, he commenced digging and we had time to bring up two brigades of Mahones Division and got some mortars at work on them. At about 2 P.M. we charged and took the whole line and our men literally butchered them. The night before the attack I discovered that the enemy had negros in their entrenchments, the first I had ever seen, but the next day I saw many of them and some fought with bravery. We only captured about 150 of them. The Battery on the right of Pegram's (the one blown up) belongs to our corps and was one of

Gibbes— He fought his Battery with the greatest courage and judgment— about 10 o'clock he was wounded— knowing that there was other an officer present with the command to supply his place, I assumed command and as such went to the aid of his Battery— found a terrible state of affairs there— but finally assisted by Joe Haskell, I got one gun to work on the enemy from that direction. The day was awfully hot— and I suffered tremendously from heat.

Gibbes is shot through the upper right breast— the ball cutting the out artery and breaking his collar bone. He is doing well— is in good hands. The danger now is from secondary hemmorage, caused by the superation, which commenced last night. In a week his danger will be past if he lives that long. I am very hopeful. He is in good spirits and doesn't seem to entertain the slightest notion of dying. His wife will be here tonight. I am writing very hurriedly with Joe's mean pen, ink and paper. Haven't heard a word from you all in a week. Don't know any thing of Alex yet. Love to all.

Your affect. boy—
Frank Huger

Letter Number 40

Colston — Captain Frederick M. Colston from Maryland was ordnance officer in the battalion. At Gettysburg he was admonished by General Robert E. Lee for using his spurs on his balking horse.[80] News from Chicago referred to the Democratic Party's convention being held there where former Union general George B. McClellan was nominated their presidential candidate. Uncle Cle referred to Cleland Kinloch Huger (1818–1892) brother of Frank's father. Cleland served in the Rutledge Mounted Rifles at the outbreak of the war, then later served as chief ordnance officer in the Department of South Carolina, Georgia and Florida (http://www.sc.edu/library/socar/uscs/1994/chhuge94.html). Gen. Preston was Brigadier General John Smith Preston, Sr., Celly's father-in-law.

Clay House Thursday, Aug. 3rd, 1864

Dear Celly:

As Colston is going in this eve. I will send you a line merely to report ourselves as still quiet tho' we've been a little more active than usual during the last week. I understand that Joe Haskell also has leave and you will probably see him. I've never told him who made the cravat and it will be a pretty mess of fish if he goes thanking the supposed manufacturer of it. I'll go up to Petersburg tomorrow as I want to see Alexander for a little while. Its awfully dull here, nobody to see and nothing to do except catch the chill and fevers. I have 140 men on sick report today, besides a large number sent off to hospital. We seem to have gained a little success on the R. Road last Thursday, which if repeated often enough will wear Mr. Grant out. The news from Chicago will indicate what we must expect. For my part I look for peace next spring. Did uncle Cle get the bodies he went for. I suppose they have all gone home. Has Gen Preston gotten back? I hope he brings good accounts of the "sis"

I should on Pinck coming out and seeing me [the exact way Frank wrote it, nothing missing] but this is such a miserable country for the chills that I don't think it worth the risk. Tell Mother I will send Dick in about the first of next week with her things. He reports them all safe. I feel mighty like running the Blocade and paying you all a visit while nothing is going on here but unfortunately it can't be did. When is your next chance of sending letters to the Trans. Miss.? I'll have one ready. Love to Mother and Jones.

Your affect. bro.
Frank Huger

Letter Number 41

Dick was Frank's servant and seems to have been able to travel rather freely. Mrs. Anderson was identified earlier as the wife of Colonel Samuel Smith Anderson. Miss Sallie was Sallie Grattan, who had been engaged to Brigadier General Samuel Garland, Jr., of A. P. Hill's Corps. He had been killed at Fox's Gap at South Mountain before the Battle of Antietam. The General most probably was Richard H. Anderson in command of the First Corps in Longstreet's absence because of his wounding at the Wilderness.

Wednesday, 7th Sept, 1864
Near James River Co.

My dear Mother:

Dick arrived yesterday with his numerous traps for which I'm very much obliged, and you must be sure to thank Mrs. Anderson for the pillow which answers very well and is a great comfort. The weather has turned very cool and I hope the country will now get more healthy. The nights are splendid for sleeping. If Miss Sallie has come, you must remember me very kindly to her and tell her how much I regret that its impossible for me to get to Richmond or rather to get out of it as Gen. Lee's pass is required before a pass-port can be obtained. I reckon too that if she is only going to stay a few days that her time will be pretty thoroughly occupied by a young man who has the necessary documents and therefore I won't be missed. When is it that you and Pinck are coming out? I haven't a very inviting looking locality but I shall be very glad to see you. Good bye. Love to Celly and P. The General has just sent for me and I must ride.

Your affect. boy—
Frank Huger

Letter Number 42

Mrs. G. is Mrs. Galt, Dick's owner, from whom Frank leased Dick to be his servant.

Camp—Monday Sept. 12, 1864

My dear Mother:

I have just received your note which Jack Preston gave to some one at the Depot and write at once to say that as far as I know Thursday will be convenient day for you to come as far as I am concerned. I am now busy putting up some works to endeavor to make a new tower that the Yankees have built, untenable for them, and I may be able to destroy it. I expect to open tomorrow evening about 4 o'clock—you'll probably hear me as Richmond is in plain view from my position. On Wednesday I am on a Board that meets about three miles from here, but on Thursday I will have nothing to do. You had better come out on the 10 o'clock train on Thursday morning, and I will be at the depot at 11 with the ambulance. The evening train goes back at 5 o'clock. I don't know that I have any particular wants unless it is a bottle of vinegar and one other thing, if you have an old shirt that would answer for Dick—someone stole his while on the fence drying. I gave him Mrs. G. letter—rather affectionate tho it was. Dick disclaimed any intention of ever intending to say he didn't always have everything he wanted, but said he thought it was his old mistresses duty to give him something, which she had never done since he has been with me, now two years and a half. I'll send her a remittance today.

I left my Bible in my trunk. Please bring it out to me.

Give my kindest regards to General and Mrs. Preston and love to P. & Celly. If Thursday is at all favorable, I will be at the 11 o'clock train unless I hear to the contrary.

Your affect. boy
Frank Huger

Do send this letter to Ben the first Chance.

Letter Number 43

M. Grattan was Sallie Grattan. Celly's baby boy was named William Preston. The lost Petersburg vessels that turned up most likely were found in Halifax, North Carolina. The vessels must have been river craft to have made the trip.

Camp—Wednesday, Sept. 21, 1864

My dear Mother:

I have just received your note by M. Grattan and am mighty happy to hear the good news of darling Celly and the boy. Thank heaven she is doing well—do let me hear as often as you can.

I went to Petersburg on Sunday. Heard a rather good sermon from Mr. Platt. The Petersburg vessels reported lost are safe in Halifax.

I have been busy day and night since my return getting in some mortars, to operate on the canal. Hope to complete my business tonight.

Love to dear Celly. I'll come in to see her if I get a chance. I'll send Dick tomorrow evening. Send him to Fredericksburg, and keep him as long as you want him.

Your affect. boy—
Frank Huger

Letter Number 44

Major Jordan was Tyler Calhoun Jordan, commander of the Bedford, Virginia, battery in Frank Huger's battalion. Miss Mary was Mary Cantey Preston. She married John Thompson Darby, a surgeon in the Hampton Legion, on October 1, 1864.

Clay House—Friday night October 14, 1864 Lines near James R. Va.

My dear Celly:

As Maj. Jordans boy is going into town tomorrow morning, I'll make him the bearer of this communication of your old brothers congratulations upon your present good health and upon the advent of the little boy. I will certainly run and see him the first opportunity I can get—but we live in momentary expectation that Grant's plans will soon be developed and they may involve active operations on this line. Quien Sabe—I think they will. We have been quiet so long that in the doctrine of chances we should expect active work ere long, and besides common sense causes me to suspect that will endeavor soon to use the canal when I Hope we will kill ten thousand of them. I wouldn't be away if anything happened for the world and in the meantime the youngster will have a chance to grow—for you knew I never saw one under three months old, and if I should think him half as sweet as you do doubtless I'd eat him. Give him his uncle Frank's love—he's made me feel ten years older (between you and I, I pulled a half dozen grey hairs from my whiskers the last fortnight). So Miss Mary looked splendid as a bride Mother says, of course she did—, should liked to have seen her. Have you had a chance to send my fan, rather a primitive wedding gift—but curious in as much as it was made in the trenches at Petersburg, out of a solid piece of cedar. You must give my love to them all when you write, especially Liz [unclear, may be Indy]. She's my main stay of the family now. I got a letter from poor Tilghman's brother—Tench—he said my mother had informed me that he was in the Confederacy,—to the witch I didn't like to tell him the first letter you know, that "he was another"—, so I left him under the impression. He wants me to sell Lees mare. I have offered to become the purchaser, for by the recent order reducing the number of horses I had to sell one of mine; and I am compelled to have two.

In my trunk there is a pair of gauntlets that Joe Haskells sister made me last winter but the hand part is all worn off. Now I think it a good plan (don't you) for you to have some worsted on hand and when your friends come in and bother you by staying too long, just set them to work and you see there will be a double advantage—you won't be bothered by your friends, or familiars and I'll get a pair of gloves which would be just the cheese, especially riding at night this cold weather. I think it a good scheme.

The first day I have leisure I'll try and hunt you some birds. There are a good many in the neighborhood I hear. Love to all.

Frank Huger

When is Pinck coming out? This is good weather now for his visit.

Letter Number 45

Clay House Saturday Eve Dec 31st 1864

My dear Celly,

Guh this is a gloomy day for the winding up of another year of war. I hope it may soon brighten in more than one sense, and that next year there mayn't be a Yankee in a hundred miles of us. We have so much to be thankful for, that I'm sure we haven't much right to wish for more—but I can't help but wishing after that father and the boys were over here that we might all be together again. I hope you have had a pleasant time. Mine would have been a pleasant Xmas if only by contrast with the one of last year, but independently of that I have had a very pleasant time. On Saturday last I dined at Mrs. [unclear] where we had a superb dinner came back here about 2 o'clk Sunday—and found Dick cooking a fine turkey for dinner wh[ich] we washed down with a bottle of good grog, on Monday I dined with one of my captains, on the line who gave us a splendid feast—on Tuesday Alexander was here, and got very short commons. Wednesday about 12 o'clk I started off and went some into Dinwiddie to a frolic, rode 20 miles, and got there about 6 o'clk, danced all night and started back after breakfast next morning and got here that night at 9 o'clk after having a little more Xmas in Petersburg. I heard that Jennie Baran would be there in about ten days. The bad weather prevented the party from being fully attended but there were enough to have a pleasant time—and the [unclear] you last saw.

Tell Pinck please have my coat fixed at once. [Seems to have run out of paper].

F. H.

Letter Number 46

Following is a letter fragment in the Frank Huger file for the dates Aug. 2 to Dec. 31 1864. No date appears on the fragment but the subject matter seems to place it here.

The girls all looked very pretty—were not in full dress, but had on high bodies, and colored skirts—I'm sure of that for I heard an old lady say so. Since my return I have [unclear], and am now making preparations to open a school for my non-commissioned officers. Maj. Jordan being away keeps me busy—as I have no one to relieve me of the ordinary detail of business—but I hope he will be back soon. Then I'm going to run in and see you all. Do ask Pinck if he would take my grey sack [coat] to Kings, on Main Street, just above the Spottswood, on the opposite side, and have the collar cleaned and when it is done beg Mother to have these buttons on it replaced by these she told me she had taken off my old [Tweed?] coat.

Colston who is staying here now tells me he saw the Comodore taking care of himself the other night.—I got my new Yr. note from Miss Mary this morning—oh by the way, have you heard of Miss Sallie Hampton yet, and did Wade get away from the Yanks, when he was in Abington?

Tell Jones to send me back that "Eleanor's Victory" as it is about time I was returning it.—I'll send [Bracken, Barker] *for it on Tuesday. How's the boy. Kiss him for me—Love to little Seve, and tell her the bean soup we had yesterday couldn't be beat in Virginia, all pretty quiet except for mortars shelling Dutch Gap. We have only two rumors, one that Mr. Davis died last night, and the other that he has absconded with fifty thousand dollars in gold—you can't beat that in Richmond. Good bye*

Your affect. boy F. H.

1865

Letter Number 47

Eustis and Ben are Frank's two older brothers. The Peace Commissioners were a three-man team headed by Confederate vice president Alexander H. Stephens. They met with President Lincoln and Secretary of State William H. Seward in Hampton Roads in January 1865. Confederate general Edmund Kirby Smith (1824–1893) fought in the east until the summer of 1862 when he was sent west by President Jefferson Davis. Kirby Smith gave his name to the Trans-Mississippi; virtually cut off from the rest of the Confederacy with the fall of Vicksburg, this isolated region was also known as Kirby Smithdom. The boy is Celly's baby, William Preston. Sherman is of course Union general William T. Sherman while Hardee is Confederate general "Old Reliable" William J. Hardee. Uncle Pinck is Frank's father's brother Thomas Pinckney Huger. Of course we know that Frank too had a brother Thomas Pinckney Huger.

Lines near Howletts
February 5th, 1865

My dear father:

Mother sends me word that here will be a good opportunity of sending a letter in a few days so I will send in a line tonight in hopes that she may get it in time to send off with hers. About two weeks ago I wrote Eustis and I recollect sending a letter to Ben which I suppose he would get about the middle of January. I have just returned from Petersburg where I have been pretty much all the week on a Board of Officers—investigating some dirty transactions, and as the principal witness is in Texas, I moved I be sent out to bring him but the proposal was not received with the consideration I thought it merited, so we have concluded to do without him. What with being much occupied with my extended line, for I have 28 guns, and the numerous details incidental to officers, I have been very busy but I'm getting heartily tired of being in one place, and I often wish I could get General Kirby Smith's Dept., and if I was sure of getting anything to do I should like of all things to be there. What is the chance for a young fellow who ain't afraid of work? You will hear of course that Peace Commissioners have gone to Washington—they won't do half as much good as I will here, and will come back before long with fleas in their ears. The best way to make peace is to kill our enemies. Somehow I feel sanguine that this is our last winter campaign—and that the war will be terminated this summer. I hear good accounts of the boy. He is a fine little fellow, characterized by great dignity of deportment and a rapidly vanishing crop of hair.—which added to a very good temper, a splendid appetite, and a disposition to make as little noise as possible, makes him a great comfort. Little Celly plays 2nd violin—the little [unclear, may be Scoce] *monopolizing all the responsibility—baby talk is all the lingo used and as soon as I have mastered enough to be intelligible, I am going to get 10 days, and pay them a visit. Sherman appears to be rapidly advancing on Branchville, Hardee watching him. I hope for the best then but confess do not expect much. However, you will hear the result of the move by the time this reaches you. I feel mighty sorry for Uncle Pinck for I believe he has lost everything. Goodnight—love to the boys. We all want to see you much.*

F. H.

I have seen your letters of 20th and 31st Dec. The peace commissioners have gotten back. Lincoln says that we must preface any proposition for peace by laying down the implements of war and apologizing.

CHAPTER FOUR

Letters from the Trans-Mississippi

Letter Number 48

Before Benjamin Huger left for the Trans-Mississippi Department he made out his will on April 6, 1863. It was made out in Columbia, South Carolina, and witnessed by three. He left all his property to his wife, E. Celestine Huger, to be disposed of as she might wish. He appointed his wife executrix and his sons Benjamin Jr. and Thomas Pinckney executor.

This set of letters, some not complete, were written home by Ben senior, Ben junior and Eustis. Their war was different from Frank's. The following letter of March 23, 1863, was from Eustis to his sister. Eustis was in Little Rock, Arkansas.

> *"I was very glad My dear sister to get your letter on Saturday and was a little surprised to hear you were to be married so soon. I can only wish you every happiness and congratulate you on having such a good fellow for a husband."* Then Eustis wrote about the difficulty crossing the Mississippi River: *"There are so many Yankee Gun boats about, but I hope before long we will have the river clear of them.*
> *Your affect. Bro. Eus"*

Letter Number 49

Benjamin Huger wrote this very long letter without a salutation to his wife from Shreveport, Louisiana. It tells of his travels and conditions throughout Texas. Unfortunately there are parts that are very hard to read and decipher. Generals Drayton and Holmes are Thomas Drayton and Theophilus H. Holmes. Mrs. Smith was the wife of General Edmund Kirby Smith. Col. Stockton was P. Stockton, commander of the San Antonio arsenal.

Major Rhett, was Thomas G. Rhett, General Kirby Smith's chief of ordnance and artillery, Trans-Mississippi Department. Senator Wigfall was later on Brigadier General Louis T. Wigfall. A pistol marksman and duelist he took advantage of his reputation for dueling and supposed willingness to shoot people with whom he disagreed. Wigfall remained in the U.S. Senate after his state of Texas left the Union, acting as a Confederate spy. He bought arms for the Texas Confederates until expelled from the Senate in July 1861. Mr. Clemson was Thomas G. Clemson, the man in charge of the iron works.

Shreveport La. Oct. 23d 1863

Here we are back again at the place we started from more than two months since—. One month has been occupied traveling far distances, and a month in visiting different places—. I have written to you several times, but it is doubtful if you received my letters—We were so glad to find a letter here from Eustis last evening enclosing one from Pinck 30th Aug. and one from you of 9th Sept. He mentions the arrival of Genl. Drayton and Genl. Holmes Hd. Qrt. I presume you have carried out your intentions of going to Richd. [Richmond, Virginia] *about 1st Sept. & will address this there—We are both well now—tho as I have told you, Ben has had two or three chills but they have always been checked by quinine—We have rooms at the hotel here for the present & accept all invitations to dine & we breakfasted with Col Anderson really plush* [remaining words of the sentence are not clear except for hominy and some kind of cake]. *We will remain here till the end of the month, and then establish our office at Marshall—*

Leaving here in August we had some very hot weather but the nights soon getting cool, and we have had very favorable weather for our journey. From Houston we went by R.R.d [railroad] *for Galveston* [The entire sentence is unclear but he wrote they saw salt water and visited the fortifications. They took a carriage and four mules on the railroad to Columbus on the Colorado River and then took three days to go to San Antonio by the mule carriage.] *Spent 10 days there Col Stockton got there a day after me—left San A. on 8 Oct. to Austen, the Capital. Saw the Govt and state works—and came on all through prairie country & beautiful wads, thru Waco & Corsicana and struck the land on this side of the Trinity R passing thru Tyler to Marshall where we stopped a day & got here last evening 15 days from San A.—Mrs. Smith & her little girl are here now & as the weather is quite cool now it will probably be very healthful and she will remain the present and has offered me the use of her house at Marshall until she wants it.*

It is of course very hard scratching to get any comforts but we are very well off on the whole in Texas, and do not expect to starve. I hear the last accounts from Charleston are to 7 Oct. & the Enemy had made no further progress. God grant his plans may be defeated. I am very anxious to hear what has taken place; there is no use discussing events—all may be changed before you receive this. Maj Ezell, Q.M. Dept. told me he goes home (Macon, Ga.) on a visit, to return in two months. I send this by him & will beg him to endorse on it the probable time he will leave there that you may write by him on his return. If he does not leave tomorrow Ben & I will fill up a sheet & I write this to have something ready—

Oct. 24th Maj. Ezell has not yet left. I last evening recd. from San Antonio P's [Pinckney] letter of 21st August enclosing yours of 16th Aug.—as I tell you about I found later letters here—So you want to come over here!—Well if I cannot go back after a while, and have to remain here always it can be done, but I must get some money first & build you a cabin—These places are so crowded there is no room—all La & Ark pour their refugees into Texas and the Enemy have most of both those States. I hope however I will be able to return to you as the journey is most difficult & uncomfortable—and [word unclear] you can bring your own conveyance, impossible, on this side of the river.

I have not the control of one cent of public money & do not know when I can get any, until I do I will be unable to set up an office, or employ any clerks. I wanted to ask for Eustis as soon as I can get a place for him—If he was here now I would have to board him at the miserable hotel at $4 per day—In [town name unclear] Texas we paid $8.10 per day—the depreciation of our currency is a serious evil—

Oct 26th Maj. E tells me he expects to get off tomorrow—I laid this by till I heard from him—Genl. and Mrs. Smith have offered me the house they secured at Marshall (Senator Wigfall's)—It is a small house 4 rooms, but is comfortably furnished—and as Marshall is getting quite crowded empty houses cannot be allowed & they prefer my occupying it—I have a couple of office rooms there but no money to employ clerks. I can only pack away and keep the returns sent me. As Genl. Smith has his Chief of Ord. (Maj. Rhett) and the district Genls. Have theirs, I take no control, except for the Arsenal at San Antonio & operations of Nitre Mining Bureau—I write this to War Dept. by this opportunity—We will be quite comfortable & <u>quiet</u> at Marshall—So make yourself easy about us for the present. P's arrival [letter] of his visit to F. [Frank] is the first news we have had of the dear Boy. God grant he may get as safely thru all to come. Love for darling Celly. Her letter and the fine bottle of <u>brandy</u> [word unclear] to the Yankees and Mr. Clemson—We are much indebted to dear P for getting letters to us. Love for him—Remember us to all our friends God bless you. B. [Ben Jr.] may add a line—

As ever Yours BH

Ben spared his wife a description of the seamier side of San Antonio. A large population of unruly, transient wagon drivers (San Antonio was the northern terminus for overland trade with Mexico) regularly disturbed the peace. Few nights passed without a lynching, several murders and general rioting.[1]

Letter Number 50

McPherson is unidentified. The evacuation of Little Rock followed the capture of the place by Union general Frederick Steele in September 1863. This general advance of the Federals forced Confederate general Sterling Price to fall back from his fortified positions around Little Rock to the southern part of the state around Camden and Arkadelphia.

Bayard Taylor (1825–1878) was an American man of letters and poet. His translation of Goethe's *Faust* has become a classic. The book mentioned in the letter was based upon his five months spent among the gold diggings in California in 1849 when he was a special correspondent for the New York *Tribune*. His brother, Charles F. Taylor, was captain of Company H, 13th Pennsylvania Reserves, the Bucktails and was the regiment's colonel when he was killed at Gettysburg on July 2, 1863. Major Carr, who taught Ben Jr. to make corn husk cigars, was Charles Edward Carr, chief paymaster for the Trans-Mississippi Department.

The French reported to have been in Tennessee was Union general William French who commanded the Union Third Corps after Gettysburg. John Saunders was John Selden Saunders, lieutenant colonel and chief of artillery to General Pemberton. He was a prisoner of war at Vicksburg.

Shreveport La. Nov 4th 1863

My dear Pinck

I wrote a letter yesterday to Mother & gave it to McPherson, thinking that he would leave at once but he has been delayed until today; and I begin this to send off in three or four days by another opportunity — I have been expecting Eustis here for two or three days and last night he made his appearance and will add a P.S. to the letter McP. Is to take — Eus is looking pretty well, but is a little hard up in the matter of clothes having lost all but what he could carry in his pocket at the evacuation of Little Rock. He travels now on a basis of three shirts, and the rest of his wardrobe in proportion, and if one could only get three more shirts when the originals went to pieces, it would be by far the best arrangement, but we seem to be on our last legs here for everything except [unclear word] *& military supplies — I came across Bayard Taylor's travels in California in 1849 in* which he mentions the prices as a matter of astonishment; but in all cases where a comparison can be made, they are more than double here—Soap, which don't appear to be considered an article of prime necessity, formerly worth 10 [cents] is now worth $10. per lb. when it can be had at all, and I am told this morning that Virginia smoking tobacco has "riz" to $12. Per lb. consequently cigarettes, where one enjoys a good deal of puffing for very little smoke are growing popular. I took a two hours lesson from Maj. Carr and can now manufacture a corn husk cigar as well as any Mexican.

An Extra is out today with a letter from the correspondent of the Chicago Times dated Washington Oct. 17th in which he says that Genl. Lee has defeated the Yanks for 8 days, and driven them back to Washington and expressing much disgust at their defeat. I hope it may turn out true. We also hear that [General Ulysses S.] Grant is to command in Tenn. and [General William S.] Rosecrans is to relieve Meade in Va., but this is emphatically the land of rumors and we don't *know* anything until long after it has happened.

Nov. 6th—We are going over to Marshall [Texas] to [unclear word] and I will leave this here to go by Capt. Jones who will start in a very few days. I have given him a letter of introduction to you and you will find him a pleasant fellow—He can tell you more than I can write concerning ourselves. I received yesterday your letter of Sept. 19th which was ten days later than the last letter Eustis had. I hope by this time you are beginning to get some of ours, but you must remember that from Aug. 17th to Oct. 22nd we only sent two or three letters. Now that we are nearer to Headquarters we can write quite often *and I don't know that anyone has been captured going from here since July*—Mr. Clemson missed C. [capture?] coming this way & was probably not very discreet; but anyone who has made this trip and got here will understand the value of silence on the way home. Eustis and father will add a line to this. From your last letter I hardly think it probable that French was at the last battle in Tenn. but if the Chicago Times man is right he was probably in some fights in Va. What has become of John Saunders When we passed through Jackson I heard that he was and was not in Vicksburg, probably *not* I think.

Remember me most kindly to Miss Betty and write to Miss Fanny Kerr on the [word unclear] and get me some news from [word unclear]—Forden [word unclear] old Sergt & now Hospital Streward at Gen. Hospital N.Y. will do the underground business for you—Where is Capt. Arthur Sinclair. Love to Celly, and I would love to see her hand writing and not because it is so good either—I suppose that if the P's [Prestons] & Mother go to Richmond she will go too, but you make no special mention of her—Good bye—

Letter Number 51

Benjamin Huger wrote this part of the letter to his wife on November 7, 1863. He explained the handicaps he worked under. Col. Allston was Benjamin Allston, West Point class of 1853. F. was Frank.

Nov. 7 Sat. Ben forgot our last letters told us Celly & the two Mrss P's had arrived in Richd. [The rest of the sentence is unclear. Huger then wrote about having orders and transportation to Marshall, Texas. Some words are unclear, the letters very small and indistinct.] ... *but I get the comfort of a house* [in Marshall]*— and we will take it as quickly as we can. I can do little more than keep the records of the Ordnance Bureau— I should have been sent here a year sooner & furnished with means to create supplies. Now if I could create them, I am* [word or words unclear] *a Dollar & have not the funds to pay Clerks and office expenses —*

We have news from the other side to 22nd Oct—& the Enemy have made no progress any where so far — this morning we hear [word unclear] *has defeated a party of Yanks on the southern coast. If we can gain the advantage, tho that will not affect the war, it will help raise up the Opposition to Lincoln & a division of parties at the north is the only means of closing this war. Eustis is here with us, he returned to his post & I will apply for his transfer to the Ord. Dept. Major Carr and Col. Sam are well Col. Allston has not yet returned from Texas — I am going now to makes some calls before leaving & send this by Capt. Jones. You and dear* [unclear word] *must write to F. for me — I recd. a long letter from him on his return from the Penna. campaign — He could not have reached Chattanooga in time for the fight there, but hope he will help to finish the work and a decided success there will be invaluable to us. When mother writes to lieut E. tell her we cant send many letters, & count on your informing our friends concerning us. Love to all — God bless you*

         BH

Letter Number 52

The next letter is from Eustis and as it is undated probably followed Benjamin Huger's letter of November 7. The letter reveals that Eustis is both an optimist and a pragmatist.

My dear Mother

I don't know that I can tell you much more about ourselves. The country here is so large & the means of conveyance such that it consumes a great deal of time to do anything at all. I don't see that we could have got in any faster than we have—There is a good deal of want of system in some of the arrangements, which however we can remedy after a while, and when affairs get properly regulated so as to work steadily & smoothly along, I see no reason why we should not return east of the Mississippi This I should think would require some two or three months more and in the meanwhile, we will be quite comfortably fixed, and [near?] quite a large town with some pleasant society. I don't think it would pay for you to attempt the trip here, as the men who come only come carrying a pair of saddlebags—and to get to the Miss. you would have to buy a carriage & horses & drive across the state Miss. some 300 miles more—And it would be difficult to get clothes replaced here—if we were going to stay here for a long time, it might do to make the attempt, but as I don't see why we should not leave here by early spring at latest, it would hardly be worth the trouble. Our means too are limited here to pay, and everything is double the price it is with you— Flour $200 per barrel—Love to Celly & Pinck—and the rest if they are with you. Eustis

Letter Number 53

A letter fragment written by Ben Jr. to his mother. Ben is commenting on the Confederate postmaster general, John H. Reagan.

Marshall Texas, Dec. 19th 1863

"Just now I was introduced to a captain who offered to take letters to Richmond, but was just mounting his horse to start & I could not ask him to wait so I will send you a line by the Reagan's semi-weekly mail which I do not have much faith in."

Letter Number 54

General Huger wrote this letter to his wife the day before Christmas 1863. The letter may have been copied at some time after he wrote it because it is not in his normal handwriting. The writing is much smaller and the letters formed differently from General Huger's other letters. It describes the difficulties in sending and receiving mail and the efforts made to improve delivery. It also shows that the general had little to do out west.

General Wigfall was Brigadier General Louis T. Wigfall, identified earlier.

General Reynolds was Thomas C. Reynolds, who served as the Confederate governor of Missouri from 1862 to 1865. By 1862 the office was little more than a name.

General Huger had time to add to his letter and wrote an additional page on December 27. Because it helps to explain the relationship between General Huger and General E. Kirby Smith and his staff, the second half is repeated for the reader's convenience later on.

The reader may be wonder why General Huger reports to the chief of the Confederate Ordnance Bureau, Colonel Gorgas. Why did a general report to a colonel? According to Robert K. Krick bureau chiefs in Richmond, like Colonel Gorgas, had line officers, like General Huger, assigned to them to carry out the bureau's responsibilities.

Marshall Dec. 24th 1863

A young officer told me today, my dear wife, that he would go to Shreveport in the morning expecting to go across the River in a few days, so I will have a line for him, in case he should succeed in getting it on—Some of us have written weekly. The last we sent by mail, which the P.M. Genl promises will go—doubtful—As it is doubtful if any of them reached you, I must tell you we are here quite well & stay comfortable for these times—We have our office in the Court house square where Ben has Eustis & three other clerks examining the Returns & accounts. I am not troubled with much else to do, as the monies Col Gorgas wrote I would distribute have not as yet been placed at my disposal—So I have much leisure and occupy myself with Gen Wigfall's library. He has some very good works, and we have made some acquaintances among the ladies so we go out sometimes of an evening to visit them—We went last evening to see Gen. Reynolds of Missouri as he is Gov. of our part of the state, but Yankees have another there. So his residence here is safer than it would be in Misso [Missouri].—His wife joined him here some weeks since—He is a native of S.C. and his wife is also. She made her way across the river last Octo [October] and joined him—and there are a good many refugees from Arkansas here & in the neighborhood. This State is the asylum for all those whom the Yankees have driven from their homes. We have not heard a word of news for ten days passed, and are very much cut off from knowing what is going on elsewhere—Genl [Edmund Kirby] Smith is with the Army in Arkansas, no news from him as yet.

So tomorrow we will have our Christmas turkey, and make ourselves as con-

tented as possible— Our whole family were together at Xmas in Norfolk two years ago. When will that occur again? And darling Frank—I want so much to hear of him his last letter was 16th Oct— My last from you was 26th Oct. from Col Gorgas 9th Nov— Mr. Dunwoody will I hope deliver you our letters 7 Jany. Love for dear P & C, [Pinckney and Celestine his two youngest children] *remember us to W Preston— I send this as an extra, as I have little confidence in its reaching you, but* [unclear] *only with you we are all well—There is really little news to tell about us.*

God bless you all
Yours ever B H

Dec. 27th (Sunday) The gentleman who was to take this with him to his home to spend Xmas & said he would return here today and go on tomorrow. So I can tell you we three had our quail dinner [not turkey] on the 25th & went to a large party in the evening— with wine dancing & an [word unclear] and supper, we were invited to two or three houses to drink Eggnog— So we knew it was Xmas time once more. Not a word of news of any kind and here we are at the close of the year 63. Three years of war— if it does not come to a close in another year, the chances are it will endure for many years more.

I will probably go to Shreveport [Louisiana] *in a few days & see the officers there & report to Col. Gorgas & the War Dept. results here so far—The command of which is that orders must be given from the War Dept. placing me in position here, if I am to remain. I was sent out only to give my "advice & valuable experience." Maj. Rhett is Chf of Ordnance to Lt. Gen. Smith— Genl. S. is otherwise occupied & leaves Ord. business to Maj. R. who wants none of my "advice and experience"; & as he acts* <u>by orders</u> *of Genl. S. I have no control whatever of the large operations he is carrying on & he has no idea of letting me have any if he can help it— So as far as Ord. matters are concerned I might as well be anywhere else.*

Letter Number 55

General Huger mentions Mr. Stringfellow but does not describe him. Frank mentioned him in some of his letters as well. Beyond being a friend of the family, nothing else can be said of him.

Jany 6th, <u>1864</u>

My reliable messenger got drunk Christmas & got his head broke & could not go—An officer goes tomorrow, Shreveport, & I possibly may go too, & I hear a messenger is to be sent to Col [George W.] *Rains at Augusta so I send a package to him, to forward.*

Eustis has an enclosure ready, I suppose he has told you of the cold. My inkstand has been within 8 feet of a roaring fire & is frozen hard. I am writing with some other till I melt it — everything freezes I never felt such cold and it is 10 degrees colder here than "57 — I have no doubt it has been a severe winter everywhere. We all keep quite well — hope you do likewise. <u>Melted ink.</u>

I enclose a letter I have just rec: [received] *from Mr. Stringfellow whom I told you about in one of my letters. Send this to our Mr. S with my kind regards. Nothing from you since 26th Oct. No news. Crossing the Miss.* [Mississippi River] *now must be difficult as the weather and the Yankees have both to be overcome. Well this year is the Yankee Election — If their party don't quarrel among themselves they* <u>ought to</u>. *God grant they may. Love to all*

Your Husband B H

Letter Number 56

The following is a letter fragment lacking a date, but it was written by Ben Huger Jr. because it mentions father and Eustis. In all likelihood it was written from Trans-Mississippi. Mr. Stringfellow is mentioned again.

Crossed sheets are mentioned in this fragment. There are some letters in the file where lines are written across a page at right angles to lines of writing. They are unable to be read.

The bearded Oliver Middleton was Oliver Hering Middleton Sr., a planter from the Colleton District. His only son, Oliver Hering Middleton Jr., was killed in Virginia in May 1864 while serving with the Charleston Light Dragoons.

... another piece. Had I any idea that my yarn was to be so long I would have spared you the crossed sheet, but you are not annoyed with them often —

Eustis is sitting with his feet cocked up by the fire & is about as entertaining as could be expected of one who has had a good dinner & a long walk after it & Father has not come back & I expect he has had an apple toddy brewing after the euchre [card game] *— Remember to Mr. Stringfellow. I did not know until meeting his brother that he was in Petersburg. Mr. D. can probably tell him who his brother is going to marry, if he don't know already. Here it is after ten & Father has returned minus the grog but plus the card party — He is looking very well and has a white beard that would do to match Oliver Middleton's beard. — Give my* love to the sisters whom I would much like to see and after "Rackensac refugees won't it be a treat— Our friends of today would be a treat to meet with anywhere— but some are mightly the reverse— Love to Celly & Pinck & Jack who I hope keeps out of bullet tracks— I wish I had time to write to Frank, but with this" feed on my hands, have had no time until tonight— Goodbye— and I miss [unclear word, begins with D] in the morning. I will be as badly disappointed as ever Jim Bankhead was.

Letter Number 57

Letter from Benjamin Huger to his wife from Marshall, Texas, dated April 8, 1864. Col. Gorgas was Col. Josiah Gorgas, chief of the Confederate Ordnance Bureau. Twice in the letter he used the term "F & G." It appears to have meant pretty well off.

My dearest little Sevee,

"I got a note from Col. Gorgas ... saying he had not forgot us all on this side of the river, and would provide means for us. Up to this time I have had no means supplied me, so I have little responsibility, or trouble and only regret I cannot render the service, which I think I might under different circumstances.

I am afraid our communications are growing more difficult, but hope yet to receive some letters from you— I am more entirely separated from you now than in Europe, or Mexico, except the four months our communications were cut off; when a four months brought change, now it seems as if there was never to be a change for the better—This war must cease next year, or it will become chronic and last an indefinite time.

From dear Frank I have not heard except through your letters, since his of 1st Jan! I hope he was able to pay you a visit last month as he proposed.—and little Pinck and dearest Celly it seems a century since I left them instead of less than one year."

Ben continued the letter the next day. April 8 had been appointed for a day of prayer. He wrote the following account of the church on the base.

"We have a nice little Ch[urch] here but the bad boys have amused themselves throwing stones and breaking all the coloured glass windows."

Letter Number 58

In the next letter portion Ben Jr. wrote to his younger brother Pinck about the Red River Campaign under Union general Nathaniel P. Banks.

Marshall [Texas] May 1st 1864

My dear Pinck,
"Before this reaches you, you will have heard of the defeat of both columns of the Yankee Army that was to drive every Rebel South of the Sabine River. The last from [Nathaniel P.] Banks was that he had destroyed his stores and was making his way to Alexandria. Our Cavalry in his rear helping him on. He has met with a most disastrous defeat."
Ben Jr.

Letter Number 59

On June 24, 1864 Ben, writing to his wife from Marshall, Texas, told of the death of Confederate general Leonidas Polk. It was just as well that the cause of his death was not mentioned. Polk, killed at Pine Mountain on June 14, 1864, had his body badly mangled by a three-inch solid artillery shot.

"We heard today the death of Genl. [Leonidas] *Polk* — a contemporary of mine at W.P. [West Point]. *The cause of his death not mentioned* — but the position he held was enough to [unclear] *a man of his years* — and as it was about the position I was entitled to from my rank I doubt if I could have bourne the trials of it better than he did, and should be thankful my banishment spares me all such trials and responsibilities."

Letter Number 60

Marshall, [Texas] July 12, 1864

My own dear wife,
"News comes in to us daily, principally from Northern papers, and it does

appear to me that the inevitable revolution at the North, which is duly progressing, and will soon culminate, and burst with a fearful crash —. At our last accounts gold in N.Y. had jumped from 220 to 238. Yesterday news came it was up to 270 and that Mr. Chase, and most of the Treasury officers had resigned, as rats desert a sinking ship."

Letter Number 61

Marshall, [Texas] November 12, 1864

"I am so rejoiced my dear wife to get your letters informing us Celly's troubles were all safely over and she and Boy doing well, & that he was two weeks old." Ben approved of his grandson's name, William Preston.

CHAPTER FIVE

Postwar Letters

Finally on November 11, 1865, Frank received a final receipt of his parole granting him the right "to go to his home and there remain undisturbed." Frank Huger entered the railway service in 1865 and worked in the railroad industry until his death. He began as secretary of the Norfolk & Petersburg Railroad, holding that position until 1867. During part of that time until 1867 he also held the positions of secretary of the South Side Railroad and from January to May 1867 secretary of the Virginia & Tennessee Railroad. From May 1867 to June 1, 1880, Frank was master of transportation of the Virginia & Tennessee Railroad. Having found employment with the railroads Frank had an easier time transforming into civilian life than many others, including his old friend and superior Edward Porter Alexander.

General Edward Porter Alexander wrote the four letters that follow to Frank Huger. They survive in the Huger Family Papers at the Virginia Historical Society. They are included because they supply a vivid look at Huger's mentor and best friend during the trying months immediately after the war. Alexander's letters also reveal inferentially some interesting details about what he knows of Huger's undertakings during that bitter era. Furthermore, as one of my historian friends told me as I considered using these: "Anything written by Porter Alexander is well worth reading."

Letter Number 62

Washington, Georgia

Sept. 1st 1865

Dear Frank. U will immediately report to the undersigned where U R.; how U. R.; what U R doing; how you like it, & especially how I shall direct this letter in order that it may reach U. for I havnt the faintest idea & am going to send it on to Lewis Webb & ask him to advertise for U. I have altogether 2 much to say to put it on a single sheet even if I were disposed to risk so much writing on such a poor chance of its getting to U. The few facts which will give U a general idea of my situation &c are that I cant get the means to leave the country & therefore cant go to Brazil & be a soldier as my whole heart is set to do that therefore has to be at least postponed & I am seeking something to do here. A speculation & two employments present chances. [Next word is blurred, maybe Spec.] *is to buy the right for an ice manufacturing machine for California & go there with it. I have* [blurred, possibly the word is seen] *it—a small one—making very nearly a ton of ice a day at cost of $3.00. It is simple & sure. If I succeed in getting the right I want U to go into it with me so communicate with me. I will know result this month—(Sep.) I hope—That failing I want to get either superintendency of R.R. from Augusta to Atlanta wh. will soon be vacant or professorship in college somewhere may be at Columbia.* [South Carolina].

No special news to write but I long to see U till I can't rest, & wd [would] *retreat from Gettysburg again to be with U & the old Battalion one night more. The Haskells are all at home but Langdon gone to Ark. & have all been to see me but John who is married & therefore cannot come. My family are all well & would send love but have all gone to bed.*

I have no time for more having to write another letter tonight. Remember me to all friends in your vicinity—if U have any vicinity—
     Most sincerely yours
     E. P. Alexander

To
Col F Huger
Car YaRa? [Unclear as to the meaning].

Letter Number 63

Alexander referred to his wife as Mrs. Micawber. She is a character in Charles Dickens's *David Copperfield*.

            Washington Geo. Dec. 26th 1865

Dear Frank
 Your letter of Oct. 27th reached me a short while ago. The first[,] last & only tidings of you which have ever come to me beyond a few vague rumors & a recent letter from Gibbes saying that you were now working under Mahone. I have picked up a precarious subsistence this summer in various ways & at last have taken to the last business you (or myself either) wd. have ever dreamt of seeing me do anything but get in jail at—viz horse speculation, but I tried it a

month ago and did very well changing $2000 to $3000 at it in three weeks. I am now trying it again with a fair prospect, but it is about played out with this attempt. I am also going in with Gilmer in some sort of lumber business in Sav.[annah] hardly know what yet. Maybe a saw mill — maybe fire wood — maybe shingles, staves &c. I think there is a heap of money in some cotton & rice plantations to be leased near Sav. I was recently offered a three years lease on which I think there was $60,000 profit <u>sure</u> maybe more but it wanted $15,000 Capital & I could only raise one half. I have been quite in favor of getting you & the Haskells & Willie Mason & Gibbes to make a company of R.R. Contractors & Joe Haskell is very strong for it. It is a business wh. [which] can be expanded indefinitely if prosperous & requires not a heavy capital.

I have been offered some contracts on road from Augusta to Columbia, (direct) & wd take it even now if they wd offer a price wh. wd pay. They only offer 10 cts in gold per yard. Before the war it used to be 12 cts for earth wh. counted in both Excavation & Embankment, & 17 cts for what counted but once. Now labor & provisions are at double prices & 10 cts don't pay. I am in negotiations at present with New Orleans Express Co. wh. wishes to extend its field for a position in this state but fear they cant pay a living rate. If they don't, & nothing else turns up I will take the Prof. of Chem &c at V.M.I. or a Prof.ship at Columbia S.C. I hear very beguiling accounts from Mexico & if I didn't have a family would go there to see it, but I "cant desert Mrs. Micawber." I have written to Stevens about it & if he says well I may try & send "an intelligence officer" to select a position for me. I am very hurried <u>today</u> with business as I leave for Sav. tomorrow. Give my love to all inquiring friends — My wife sends her regards & is as anxious for me to get something wh. will include you as I am myself. Write me what prospects are under Mahone so that if I see anything better I can let you know. Remember me <u>specially</u> to J. D. Smith & send me your <u>photograph</u> & beg Smith to send me his —

Most sincerely yours
E.P. Alexander

To Lt. Col. F. Huger
Petersburg

Letter Number 64

Columbia Apr. 19th 1867

Dear Frank
    Don't think me a wretch for not writing to you since the Devonshire slates were tilted up (See Comstocks Geology) for the truth is that I have been so tangled

up in *Calculus for three months that I have hardly had a clear idea or a moment to smoke a jovial cigarette, & even now I have sneaked off from the inexorable* [mathematical symbol entered here that can't be reproduced is an integral for the X and Y axis] *for only long enough to write a scratch or so & then I must take to my assymptotes & run in my garden & plant some seed if I expect to have any vegetables this summer.*

I enjoyed seeing your father here as much, I'll bet, as you could yourself. He aint a bit older than I am & he can take life — smooth or rough — with sugar or straight in a way that does a fellow good for a year to look at for a day.

I have been hoping to hear of some betterment of your condition for some time & as I haven't yet heard shall now expect to hear it every day more confidently than ever for I know its bound to come & I only hope it will bring you in this direction. I havnt had time to work any at my book for two or three months & will hardly commence well at it again until July. I can get very little of the help I need from others, & sometimes feel almost in despair about it. I write to everybody I can hear of but get very few replies. Please keep a lookout for the addresses of all the Regimental field officers of the Corps you can hear of & send them to me. I particularly want the addresses of N.C. Ala. Miss & Flor. Regts — having not yet gotten one of the first & last states & only a very few of others.

Can you also send me the address of any of the Battn Officers who can give me a Battery History of Taylors Battery. I send you in another envelope some blanks which I wish you would give to Meyers. (I have forgotten his initials & so don't mail direct) & ask him please to fill them for his battery for all its fights in our Corps. By the way I'll send you two *& get you to forward one to whoever can tell me of Taylors Battery — or still better fill them yourself with all you can recollect of detail & incident of each battle for the whole Battalion — (My own memory aint enough to trust to.) & send me the address of Taylor's man. I want to get for an appendix a short Regtl or Battery History for each command.*

By the way also — do you know anybody *who has the published reports of* Williamsburg *&* Seven Pines. *I cant hear of them anywhere & I want them* bad *& right away. Some of the Petersburg people ought to have them for they are accessible to Richmond where they were published & they were not burnt out & they* must *have them.*

All of our crowd here send you lots of love & all say with me Cant *you ever get down this way on some railroad pretence —*

Hampton is about finishing his RR work & has not yet found any thing else to go at — Everything & everybody here blue & mostly *scared. Give my love to all my Petersburg friends & believe me*

Very Sincerely Yours
E P Alexander

Letter Number 65

Columbia Aug 16th 1867

Dear Frank

Please accept the usual excuses for my long silence & authorize me to plunge in medias res with what little I have to say in what very little time I have to say it in. As my new responsibility is a boy I welcome him with pleasure, & have sent his name to the conscript office for enrollment in Longstreets next Corps. I have also written to old Pete asking him if his unfortunate letter wasn't only a piece of strategy which our stupid people have misunderstood. I believe it. No answer yet. Am pegging away at my book but with low progress for lack of information — press of study. Still encouraged however to go on. Have just written a review of Swintons A. P. [Army of the Potomac by William Swinton] *for Presbyterian Review* published here, but rather doubt whether they will publish it. If they do I'll try & send you a copy. Am greatly obliged for notes of your father's & wd like to have a statement of what Brigs composed his & Hills divisions at Seven Pines. I have always known the falsity of many of the official reports & there [sic] notes are just the things to spot them. I have never yet gotten the official reports of the Battle of Seven Pines but D. H. Hill thinks he can get them for me.

Politics are hot and heavy in this state & it was pretty nearly cowed but I hope is reviving. Everything was in favor of voting for a convention until lately Perrys letters produced some change & Hills more wherever they have been read. The latter I gave to Hampton & they changed his views & we then tried to get him out in a letter & have succeeded tho. not in exactly the kind I hoped yet in one which will do good. I wrote the letter asking him to come out. (I suppose you will see both published together) but some moderate fellows struck out a sentence which had all the germ in it & changed the whole tone both of it & Hamptons. I am advising everybody here to buy a good breech loader & put it away to fight "for child and wife for home & life" & several other things perhaps "brimeby." [? Word unclear] If our garrisons were removed I believe we wd have a war of races in a month. I very highly & kindly appreciate your kind coal offer & while I wd not willingly exchange my present location & position, it is a state affair & may & I fear will go to pot at an early day in which case I wd be delighted to do so well as that looks. Please write me a little more fully about it, Where and what sort of hours & duty, — whether the "private energy & enterprise" could be without the jealousy of the company who generally desire to monopolise [sic] what their employees possess of that & very justly too.

Please give my love to each & all of your family for me when you see them — too many to enumerate by pen. Hampton & Jennie are flourishing. H is expecting to work another R. R. contract but has very little capital & is considerably down in the mouth. The R R Co will however help him I hope. I enclose photographs & love to the Camerons. Bena joins me in love. Very sincerely yrs.,

E. P. Alexander

Railroading

Frank's career in railroads is listed in "Who's Who in Railroading, North America, 1893." There is an unexplained gap in his work history between June 1, 1880, and April 1, 1882. On this later date he became Superintendent of Transportation for the Atlantic, Mississippi & Ohio and at the same time was Superintendent of the Western Division of the Norfolk & Western Railroad. He held both positions until July 1, 1888. On that date he became superintendent of transportation on the Norfolk & Western Railroad. As his obituary stated Frank held this later position at the time of his death in 1897.

The "Who's Who" account does not quite square with the history of the Norfolk and Western Railway as recorded in a book of that title by C. Nelson Harris. Mr. Harris wrote that the N&W began when Mr. Clarence Clark purchased the bankrupt Atlantic, Mississippi and Ohio Railroad at auction in Richmond in February 1881 for 8.5 million dollars. Frank Huger's Confederate comrade-in-arms, William Mahone, had been an officer in the AM&O. The Norfolk & Western merged with the Shenandoah Valley Railroad and hauled coal particularly from the Pocahontas mine in western Virginia.[1]

On March 14, 1884, a disastrous coal mine explosion and fire erupted in the Pocahontas coal mine in that small Virginia town on the border with West Virginia. One hundred fifty lives were lost. The explosion caused loose coal in the mine to catch fire. In order to extinguish the fire the mine was flooded and then sealed to smother the flames. Not until a month later were bodies recovered. The April 15, 1884, edition of the *New York*

Photograph of Frank Huger in later life (courtesy United States Military Academy).

Times reported, "Twenty-six bodies were boxed, and at 9 o'clock this morning [April 14] they were brought out at the entry and placed in a row for identification." The men were Negroes. They were identified by their clothes, boots and personal items found on the bodies. On behalf of the stricken families Frank wrote the following letter to the governor of Virginia.

Letter Number 66

Lynchburg, Va. March 14, 1884

Governor William E. Cameron,
Richmond, Va.:

Mr. Lathrop, superintendent of Southwestern improvement company, advises that so many families live out of the immediate vicinity, that it is difficult to determine at once what is necessary, but he thinks twenty-five hundred dollars will cover immediate necessities. The number of victims is now believed to be one hundred and fifty-four.

Frank Huger

The same "Who's Who in Railroading in North America, 1893" carried the following account of Frank's cousin, Frank K. Huger. He was superintendent of the East Tennessee, Virginia & Georgia railroad and Knoxville & Ohio railroad with offices in Knoxville, Tennessee. This Frank Huger was born December 5, 1845, at Clydesdale, Beaufort District, South Carolina. He entered railway service in September 1865, "since which time he has been consecutively, December 5, 1865 to 1874 (with the exception of 1872), on Northeastern (S.C.); 4 months baggage master, 1 year passenger conductor, 5 years cashier, 2 years superintendent; 1874 to 1878, agent South Carolina Rd, Augusta; 1878 to 1880 general freight agent Greenville & Columbia Rd; 1881, master transportation East Tennessee, Virginia & Georgia Rd; 1881 to date division superintendent."

The remaining letters Colonel Frank Huger wrote towards the end of his life. His thoughts and concerns returned to the Civil War.

Letter Number 67

This letter was found in the Frank Huger folder in the Huger Family Papers. The "Longstreet Book" in all probability was the old Confederate general's *From Manassas to Appomattox*. Longstreet's enemies must have been anticipating its publication from Longstreet's signing his book contract with the J. B. Lippincott Company on May 1, 1895. According to James I. Robertson, Jr., in his introduction to *From Manassas to Appomattox* in the reprint edition of the Civil War Series from the Indiana University Press, the first edition appeared in 1896. The date of the following letter is January 31, 1896. No grass was permitted to grow in the streets of Longstreet's critics. At the end of this letter someone wrote in a different hand from that of Frank Huger, "Gustavus W. Smith." However other letters in the file show that the man living at this New York City address was John A. T. Costello.

---

130 East 115th St
New York City
Jany 31st 1896

My Dear Colonel:
Again thanking you for the "Longstreet Book," I have to say: "His account of operations at Seven Pines is saturated with grossly inaccurate statements — malicious aspersions — and outrageous perversions.

Record Facts — clearly established by indisputable testimony — heretofore published — cannot be refuted by such means as are resorted to by General Longstreet."

If, in your judgement, [sic] *it should at any time, become essential, or even desirable, that the foregoing comments be made public, request you to attend to that matter for me, through the Press or otherwise.*
Very truly Your Friend Col. Frank Huger
Roanoke, Va.

Letter Number 68

The following letter was written to former Confederate cavalry leader Fitzhugh Lee, who in 1896 was U.S. consul-general to Cuba. Fitz was the nephew of General Robert E. Lee and the son of the general's older brother Sydney Smith Lee. Fitz fought through the entire Civil War from First Manassas to Appomattox. For the next twenty years after the war he was a farmer and then was elected governor of Virginia. As consul-general to Cuba he was in Havana at the start of the Spanish-American War and took part in it. He died at age seventy in 1905. Frank Huger described a scene from Gettysburg on the third day not long before Pickett's Charge.

Other Confederate officers he mentioned included Walter Herron Taylor, assistant adjutant general to General Lee at Gettysburg. Taylor rose to the rank of lieutenant colonel. Lieutenant Colonel Thomas Mann Randolph Talcott was engineering officer to Lee and Charles Scott Venable was aide-de-camp to General Lee.

Roanoke, Va., April 24, 1896.

Genl. Fitz Lee,
Lynchburg, Va.
My dear Fitz:

I was glad to get your note of the 20th. I wish, too, I could see you, and if I get a chance I will try and do so if you will kindly let me know when you expect to leave Lynchburg. If you get in any trouble in Cuba, or anywhere else, just send for me and I will bring the artillery to your relief at once and thus put an end to all your troubles. Your reference to that old Gettysburg matter makes me recall that on the morning of the 3rd day Genl. Lee seemed to have been advised that he should extend our right. He came to the vicinity of the peach [orchard] in the morning and sent a courier in to me, (I was then in command of Alexander's battalion), to say he would like me to see Genl. Alexander. I sent him word that Genl. Alexander had left me between 4:00 and 5:00 o'clock that morning and I had not seen him since. The courier then returned with the request that I would join Genl. Lee and party, which I did—on the Emmettsburg road back of the peach orchard. There were quite a number in the party besides Genl. Lee, and I recall Genl. Longstreet and Genl. A. P. Hill. I am not sure about Walter Taylor, but I think either he or Talcott were there, and a good many others; and, by the way, I think Charlie Veneble [sic] was there. We continued to ride towards our right, until when we got near the end of the orchard I advised Genl. Lee not to go into the "open," because the picket lines at that point were running disagreeably near to the road. Genl. Lee then said "Gentlemen we will dismount here and I will go a little on the right with Col. Huger." This he did, made a careful reconnaissance of the little Round Top and wooded mountain on the right, and remarked to me that the conditions of affairs he found on the right were different from what he had been led to expect, and, after a few minutes, returned to the group of officers. Longstreet was partially lying on the ground, and A.P. Hill was sitting on the top rail of a dilapidated fence, and the others were scattered about. Genl. Lee seemed in a very serious mood when we were coming back from our short walk to the right, and remarked very plainly about in the following words: "Gentlemen we will mount now and return to our post and carry out our original intention of attacking these people in the center." I of course, you know, was anxious for all the information I could get, and kept a close watch on Longstreet and A.P. Hill's face when Genl. Lee made this announcement, and I did not discover that either of them were anxious or spoiling for the prospective fight. They then mounted their horses, and I on foot accompanied them up the road until I got to the path that turned off to my battalion, when I bade Genl. Lee and the other Gentlemen good bye. The General very kindly extended his hand to me, and while shaking me by the hand remarked that he was going to attack these people in the center, and "I hope you won't let us get in any trouble while this is going on," to which I replied that we were in a good position, had a strong line of defense, and supported by Hood's and McLaw's Division they could not make any impression on us and that we would not get in any trouble in that vicinity; to which he replied by a kind gesture throwing off my hand, that "You are not going to have Hood's Division, as that will be used to assist in the attack." I do not pretend to quote the General's words, but I do say that he told me in the presence of several people that he was going to use Hood's Division for the purpose of making the attack which he contemplated that day, and this fact I mentioned to Jimmy Dearing whom I saw a few minutes after. I think that what Genl. Lee said to me was mentioned about an hour and a half before the attack took place. This is all I know about it, and I give it to you with pleasure, for it is exactly true, but you will please understand that I do not pretend, after this long lapse of time, to quote what Genl. Lee said literally.

By the way, I have been watching with a great deal of interest this Gettysburg controversy in all its phases, and have read Longstreet's book,—a tissue of nonsense, that he had better have died before ever having written. Genl. G. W. Smith, who saw Longstreet's book, commented on what he said of the Battle of Seven Pines in the following language:

"His account of the operations at Seven Pines is saturated with grossly inaccurate statements, malicious aspersions and outrageous perversions. Recorded facts, clearly established by indisputable testimony heretofore published, cannot be refuted by such means as are resorted to by Genl. Longstreet."

I wish you a safe and happy trip, and hope all will go well with you.

Yours very sincerely,
Frank Huger

Letter Number 69

Frank wrote the following letter J. Thompson Brown, who, as a lieutenant, brought back a number of items for Frank from Richmond. Frank was captured during the battle of Sailor's Creek on April 6, 1865.

Roanoke, Va., April 24, 1896

Capt. J. Thompson Brown,
Richmond, Va.
My dear Capt.:

I am in receipt of yours of the 23rd inst., and will try to carry out my promise to you in a few days. I write now simply to answer your inquiry in the last paragraph of your letter.

So much of the battalion as we took forward on the front road, (which consisted of 12 guns), did cross Sailors Creek at the bottom of that hill where Picketts Division was in line of battle on the left, and it was going up the ascent, on the west side of Sailors Creek that we were struck by the enemies cavalry. Then you know that Sailors Creek took a turn and went between our army and the enemy, and we crossed Sailors Creek after we were taken prisoners, but at a different point than the one we crossed with the guns herein referred to. I do not know whether the balance of the guns, which went on some other road, Crossed Sailors Creek or not, but I take it they did.

Yours very truly,
Frank Huger

Letter Number 70

Capture at the battle of Sailor's Creek brought Frank Huger's fighting to a close. In the following letter to the same J. Thompson Brown, Frank recounted the events that lead to his capture. Frank wrote that he gave a message for General George Pickett to a Confederate staff officer who assured Frank that he was indeed the man his uniform implied. The intelligence this officer carried was Frank's discovery that no enemy force was in front of Pickett's division. General Pickett believed to the contrary and had asked Frank to post his artillery to aid his division. Frank's orders prevented him from complying and therefore he wanted to send this intelligence back to Pickett. He sent another Confederate messenger to General Eppa Hunton who commanded Pickett's right brigade. "Neither of these messages were ever delivered," Frank wrote, "for the two supposed Confederate staff officers turned out to be Yankee spies, though dressed in full Confederate gray and wearing a star trimmed with black on each collar."

Horace Porter, an officer on General Grant's staff and whose years at West Point corresponded with those of Frank, wrote of such spies. On April 4, 1864, another active day according to Porter, brought the Union army to Wilson's Station, twenty-seven miles west of Petersburg. The next day, according to Porter:

There was a sudden commotion among the headquarters escort, and looking around I saw some of our men dashing up to a horseman in full rebel uniform, who had suddenly appeared in the road. I recognized him at once as one of Sheridan's scouts, who had before brought us important dispatches; said to him: "How do you do, Campbell?" ... Campbell then took from his mouth a wad of tobacco, broke it open, and pulled out a little ball of tin-foil. Rolled up in this was a sheet of tissue paper on which was written the famous dispatch so widely published at the time in which Sheridan described the situation at Jetersville, and added: "I wish you were here yourself."

Of the battle of Sailor's Creek Porter wrote only this:

Ord [General Edward O.C.] pushed out to Rice's Station, and [General Philip] Sheridan and [General Horatio G.] Wright had gone in against the enemy and fought the battle of Sailor's Creek, capturing six general officers and about seven thousand men and "smashing things" generally.[2]

Colonel J. Warren Keifer, commander of the second brigade, third division of General Horatio G. Wright's Sixth Corps, Army of the Potomac, identified the six captured generals in his account of the battle of Sailor's Creek. They were Joseph B. Kershaw, G.W.C. Lee, Seth M. Barton, Dudley M. DuBose, Eppa Hunton and Montgomery D. Corse.[3]

This letter is by far the longest letter of the group. For clarity I will insert my remarks in the text within brackets.

Roanoke, Va., May 11, 1896

Capt. J. Thompson Brown,
#1113 Main St., Richmond, Va.
My dear Capt.:

I duly received your favor under date of March 28, 1896, advising me you proposed to prepare an article on the Battle of Sailor's Creek, and asking me to send my personal recollections of that event, which I will try and do herewith — though the events occurred so long ago that you must make allowances for any discrepancies that may occur, and please do not hesitate to correct them if I should fall in any error, for I understand you simply want correct material for <u>you</u> to make the story as complete as you can. I have only, you must understand, to trust to my memory, which at best is treacherous, as I have not the leisure to hunt up authorities.

As I understand it, we were not engaged in the battle of Sailor's Creek proper, but that our battalion met its disaster on the morning of the 6th of April, 1865, several hours before the battle proper of Sailor's Creek, in which, therefore, we were not engaged.

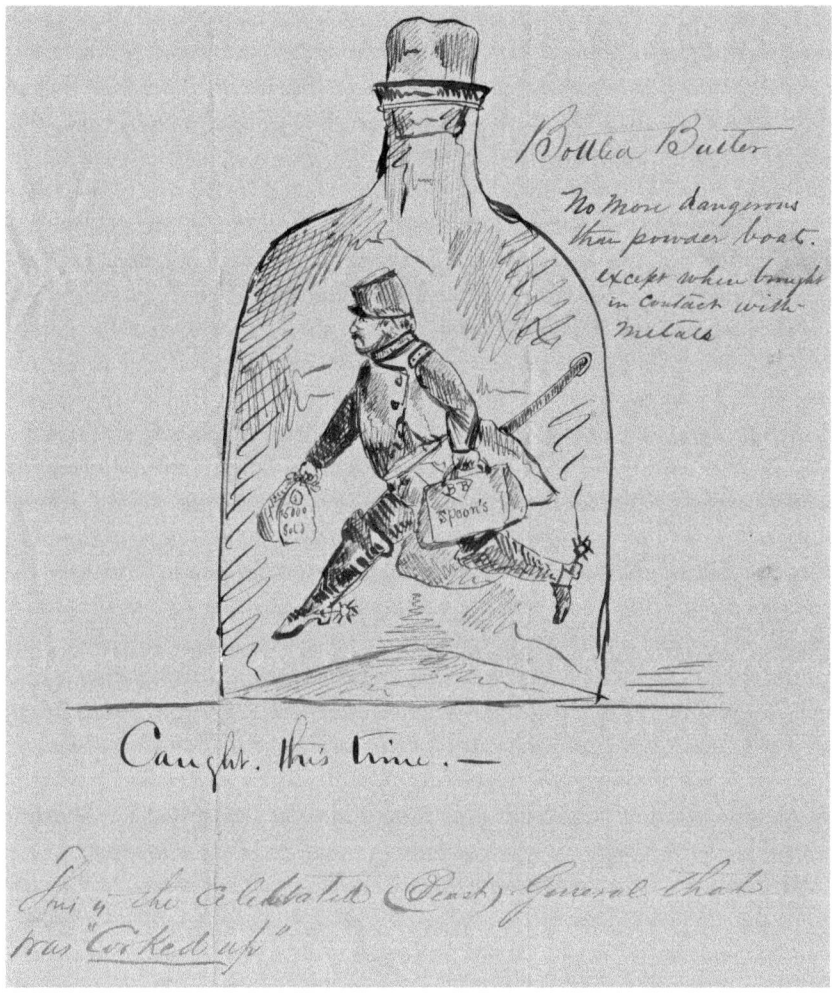

Caricature of Union General Benjamin Butler titled "Caught this time." The text on the illustration reads: "Bottled Butler No more dangerous than powder boats except when brought in contact with metals." This is a reference to Butler's reputation for stealing silverware. The caption on the bottom of the page reads: "This is the celebrated (Beast) General that was '*Corked* up'" (courtesy Virginia Historical Society).

At that time I was in command of the battalion formerly commanded by Col. E. P. Alexander, as I had been for about a year previously, consisting of six batteries as follows,—but you have all that, officers, men, the number of guns in each battery, character, &c., &c. When it was ascertained that Genl. Grant was moving his army from the vicinity of Malvern Hill to Petersburg, Genl. Lee ordered Pickett's Division and our battalion to proceed at once to Petersburg for the relief *of that place, (this date you can easily ascertain),—to cross the James River by the pontoon bridge near Drury's Bluff, which promptly did; and on the road to Petersburg we struck the enemy commanded by Genl. Benjamin Butler, and had to drive them off to east of the road and hold them there while a portion of our army used the road to Petersburg. On this account the force that was designed for the advanced relief of Petersburg found themselves on the Howlet* [sic] *House line between the James and Appomattox Rivers, where Genl. Butler was said to have been "bottled up" with his command, and there the battalion remained until the final abandonment of our lines on Sunday evening April 2, 1865, at which time the Division of Genl. William Mahone occupied the line with us in place of Pickett's Division, which had been sent to the right to the vicinity of Five Forks. On the retreat, when we reached Amelia Courthouse on the ?,* [Frank's spaces and question mark] *I met Genl. Alexander, Chief of Artillery of the First Corps, for the last time during the war, who gave me a slight insight into the situation, which I confess looked blue to me, as it had appeared for sometime, when I received directions from him to take as many of my guns as I could properly equip with horses in fair condition, so the artillery could move with celerity, and take the front road with them, and turn the balance of the battalion over to the care of Maj. T. C. Jordan with order to report the same to Genl. Lindsay Walker,* [3rd Corps chief of artillery] *who was moving on some other road with wagon trains, &c. In obedience to this order, we very soon had twelve (12) guns in motion to the front,—two guns from each battery; and that (?) night, (I think you must fix this, but it was the night of the 5th of April; so if we were at Amelia Courthouse on the 5th, that is all right, but if we were at Amelia Courthouse on the 4th it was the following night), I received orders to pass our army and report to the front. This was a most tedious and trying night's march, for our men were generally worn and tired out by continuous marching and fighting, with little food or rest, and had fallen asleep in their tracks and many of them in the road. Early on the morning of the 6th I met Genl. R. E. Lee, surrounded by a group of officers apparently his staff, at the forks of the road east of Sailor's Creek and about three-quarters of a mile or less, therefrom. (I think this distance is about correct, but you will know). He told me that the enemy had gotten in our front and that Genl.* [Charles W.] *Field, with his Division, was moving forward to attack; and that Genl. Mahone , with his Division, who had just left the high ground on the other side of the Creek, would support him, and that I should push on and join that force and report there to Genl. Field or Genl. Mahone. In reply to my question as to which road to take, he indicated the left-hand road, where two large gate-posts stood, (the gate, of course was gone, and the posts would have been gone, too, I expect, but for their large size), which we followed down an incline all the way to Sailor's Creek. We found Pickett's Division in line of battle without entrenchments just to the left of this road and about half-way down the slope, which was covered with thin undergrowth; I met Genl. Pickett with some staff on the right of the road. He informed me that the enemy were reported to be preparing to attack his front and requested me to get in line and help him out, but as we were under imperative orders to push on to the front I did not feel that I could loiter until he received further information; and I rode on down to Sailor's Creek, in which I watered "Jessie." I saw that Pickett's Division had not apparently crossed the Creek. The ascent on the other side for several hundred yards was through a deep cut, and the road sandy and deep, but about half way up to the plateau the road became better and the country heavily wooded. I rode, I think with only a single courier,— that young fellow whose name I am sorry I cannot recall, from [Captain Osmond B.] Taylor's battery. (Try and find out his name. He was a lumpy-faced quiet, intelligent boy, and as gallant as any man in the Army of Northern Virginia). On the plateau the road forked, one road going straight ahead and the other turning off to the left, and in the angle was a farmhouse with some outbuildings and surrounded by a dilapidated fence. Here some stragglers were met from Mahone's Division, who told me the Division had moved probably less than an hour before, and that [Brigadier General Edward A.] Perry had sent a few pickets down the road toward the enemy but they had no reserve. A large force of the enemy was seen on the high grounds, about a mile and a quarter, or a mile and a half, south of us moving in a westerly direction. I sent the courier back to meet the guns and hurry them forward, and then I saw a squadron of the enemies cavalry, about a quarter of a mile distant, emerge from a piece of woods and turn into the straight road above referred to, following Mahone's Division. I soon ascertained that there was no force of the enemy in front of Pickett's Division, and observing what I supposed to be a Confederate staff officer, and having received from him the assurance that he was, I sent him on a message to Genl. Pickett to give him the situation and urging him to extend his right up the hill to the junction of the two roads; and a few minutes after deeming this movement of the first importance, I called another staff officer and sent him on a similar errand to Genl. Eppa Hunton, who commanded Pickett's right brigade that day. Neither of these messages were ever delivered, for the two supposed Confederate staff officers turned out to be Yankee spies, though dressed in full Confederate gray and wearing a star trimmed with black on each collar. The enemy here commenced to shell the woods at the junction of the two roads very heavily, and my horse "Jessie" was hit by a bullet from a shrapnel, so I turned her loose and she ran back into our lines and was subsequently recovered. The enemy, who had concentrated a large body of cavalry in the low grounds near Sailor's Creek, ran over the sparse lines of Perry's pickets and came right on. I ran to the leading guns, two 12-pound howitzers of Capt. [William W.] Fickling's battery, and got them in line at close distance at once and loaded with canister, and the balance of the guns I intended to deploy in line on my right and left, and fired two loads of canister into the group of cavalry huddled together about 150 yards from us, when they charged us in a scattering way, many of them passing both flanks and sabering or shooting the gunners who were trying to move their guns into line. I think two pieces of [Captain George V.] Moody's battery came next to Fickling's guns, and I recall seeing Kelly, I think, (the lead driver of his front piece), shot down while trying to unlimber after being repeatedly called on to surrender. I do not think that any shots were fired from Moody's guns. [Major William W.] Parker's two 3-inch Rifles came next, but they must have been captured while in column of pieces, for they drove out on our right escorted by some Federal cavalry and in their full possession. (I reckon. [William M.] Evans can tell you all about this). Two shots were fired by the guns of Fickling, one from each gun, canister, and were reloaded, but only one gun was fired a second time, (the right-hand gun), as the friction primer failed at the left gun and before it could be replaced the enemy had rushed on us and sabered some and shot others of the detachment, and there were many more of the enemy than of our own men at the guns. You will please observe that there was no surrender, though previously the enemy had called on us to "cease firing and surrender"; but we were simply here "crowded out," and my orders to load could not be obeyed for the Yankees would not let us and did not have the courtesy to load themselves, which by the way, they should have done and turned the guns on the balance of our column in the cut and on the right rear of Pickett; but of course they were uncertain who was there, and where, and so they contented themselves by taking the guns off. I should remark here that when we were getting Capt. Ficklings's guns in line, (he being mounted and I on foot), I told that gallant officer to go to the rear and try and save all the guns if possible, for I realized that all that remained at the front would either be killed or taken. He remonstrated with me, and claimed that as the two guns were his he should be allowed to fight them, &c., but as time was very pressing I could only order him to proceed on the very important duty designated without being able to make him any further explanation of my reasons therefor except to assure him that I would look after his guns. As illustrating the mixed condition we were in I may mention here that I saw Capt. Fickling being led off the field a prisoner on foot a few minutes before I was taken.*

Right here, now, I will mention some personalities, which you must use very lightly, for where all did their best I have always thought that any parade of such matters was in bad taste and had better be left off.

When our guns were captured, or say 6 or 8 out of 12, I found myself practically alone, as far as I knew, but had my pistol, an army revolver, with six loads in it, and had to protect myself against only such men as rushed upon me to cut me down while I was trying to get to a small clump of young pines. While doing so I was I was fired at it seems to me by repeating rifles, and was charged by an officer followed by a soldier or orderly. I hit the former in the head with one shot, and he ceased to trouble me any more, and I only had time to cock and raise my pistol high enough to shoot the horse of the courier following him in the breast and jump out of the way, while the rider, who was encumbered with his overcoat, carbine, saber and canteen, and possibly some other accouterments, rolled by me down the hill. While looking out for the next chap, and a very few seconds thereafter, I was touched on the right side of my head by a pistol, and turning around I saw a Lieutenant of cavalry, I think of a Connecticut regiment, and then I saw for the first time that more of the enemies cavalry were in our rear than were in sight in my front, and I realized then that the jig was up, — rather accelerated by the officer who demanded my pistol, which I handed to him with one charge in the chamber. He saw the three small stars which I wore on my Collar and asked me if I was a general officer, to which I replied that I was not but was a field officer of artillery. He then inquired what command I belonged to, &c., to which I replied that I had, I believed, given him all the information I proposed to do. He then told me to step out towards the farmhouse at the junction of the roads and he would send a guard to take me to Genl. Meade's headquarters. I was immediately surrounded by several alleged cavalrymen, but who were really looters, who demanded my hat, — (the black felt that I had purchased from Dooley, the Richmond hatter, about a week before for about $300.00). Then some other thieves demanded my watch, which I refused to yield, but in the excitement I forgot about my hat, which was snatched from my head by a man on horseback who rode off with it. The efforts of the five or six remaining men seemed to be concentrating on my watch, and I was advised to give it up or I might lose my life, and this suggestion was enforced by a scoundrelly looking, (apparently Italian), devil touching me on the head with his carbine, which he carried across his lap as he sat on his horse. I firmly declined to give it up, when I was pushed backwards by one of the men who grabbed the watch chain, (which broke about the middle), and pulling out the watch he handed it to the man above mentioned on horseback, who rode off with it followed by several loud curses from me, during which another thief ran his hand into my sack pocket and took out a small bag of tobacco and my tooth brush. The latter I have often felt sorry I asked him for, as he could have no use for it, but he indignantly refused and broke it in pieces and stamped it in the mud.

All these things happened very rapidly, and I think it was about this time I met Evans, who very kindly gave me an artillery cap. The guard, who had just come up to conduct me to Genl. Meade's headquarters, was now with us, (and I think it was here, or about this time, that I met you, and some other members of *our old command, was it not?). We had only gone a very short distance when we saw apparently about a Division of United States cavalry in the low grounds on Sailor's Creek, massed, with a large number of officers in front and out of sight from the high grounds from which we had come. It proved to be Custer's Division, and he rode out and met me very cordially,* ([General George A.] *Custer was an old acquaintance of mine, having been at West Point while I was there, and was entered in the class two years after me but was graduated in 1861), saying to the guard that the whereabouts of Genl. Meade's headquarters was not known, and offered me a horse to ride, but this was declined with thanks. (Right about here I am mixed as to details and time, and if I have gotten, or do get anything wrong, you and Evans must adjust it). I think we went on and the guard put us in the "bull-pen" where there were a lot of Confederates. A short time after we were placed there a Lieutenant Arden, of the United States cavalry, brought an escort and took me off again in search of Meade's headquarters. As I would not give him assurance in reply to his request that if opportunity offered I would not attempt to escape, the Lieutenant had my mule led. While making slow progress on this account we were met by another Lieutenant of cavalry, on Custer's staff, who had my bridle returned and he dismissed the escort and took me to some wagons, there giving me something to eat, when he told me he was a Plebe at West Point when I was a first-classman, and was as kind and courteous as possible, as indeed was Lieutenant Arden. I have forgotten the name of this young officer, I am sorry to say, who thus relieved me from probably a long and useless ride, as Meade's headquarters were on the move and nobody knew where they were. I think it was just after this that I met Genl. Custer, who told me his Division, or some part of it, was going then to make an attack on a portion of our line, and suggested I go and see it done as he would like me to see them take our people in, which I did, and found the cavalry marching to the attack. They soon received a pretty severe fire, and in a little while came back in a hurry, much to Custer's chagrin I thought, which probably might have been increased by my remarking that I had frequently seen his men "try and take us in out of the wet just that fashion." He took it, though, good-naturedly and then proceeded to blame himself for letting me be exposed to our own fire, of which I tried to relieve him by saying that I had come there voluntarily, having nothing to do, &c.; but a little later the last and most destructive assault was made and our line was broken with a loss of many of our best officers and men, and the capture of a great many others,—among them Genl. Custus* [sic] *Lee,* [Joseph B.] *Kershaw,* [Eppa] *Hunton,* [Montgomery D.] *Corse, Commodore* [John R.] *Tucker, of the Navy, &c., &c. (You will please corroborate so much as I have stated and amplify this disaster). We were all, I believe, placed in an open field with a few fires burning, it being very cold, and of course it was raining, when early in the night a courier came to our temporary huddle and* brought several horses, with request from Genl. Custer, who was in our neighborhood, that I would come and spend the night with him, and bring over as many of the officers as the courier might have horses for. So about 6 or 8, or possibly a few more, of us went over to Custer's headquarters, which was in the midst of his cavalry in a hollow square formed by four field guns and caissons. There he gave us a very good field supper and made us very comfortable for the night,—I sharing Custer's blanket; and in the morning we were all sent off with the balance of the prisoners to Burkeville, while Custer's cavalry was off early, about 4:00 or 5:00 A.M., after the remnant of our army. It was the last time I ever saw him. The night I spent at Custer's headquarters he was the most courteous and kind to us and told the officer of the guard that we were all his guests and were not to be molested or annoyed in any manner, while of course, not mentioning anything to us about any parole, &c., assuming of course that his guests would do nothing not entirely agreeable to him. When we parted next morning I noticed that Genl. Custer was wearing a small pair of silver gilt spurs, and as I had on a pair of Mexican steel spurs, inlaid with gold, which my father, Capt. Ben. Huger, Chief of Ordnance to Genl. Scott's army, had procured in Mexico, I suggested to him to take my spurs and return them at some future time, for I was a prisoner and expected to do more walking than riding, which he at once accepted, casting aside his old spurs. Subsequently he wrote me from Washington that he was going to the West and had my spurs, to which he had become attached, and asked to be allowed to take them with him. Subsequently, after his unfortunate death, probably three or four months thereafter, a man walked into my office at Lynchburg one evening and gave me one of the spurs, which he told me had been recovered in the Black Hills, and that spur I have now. And, further, I will add right here that Custer issued an order to try to recover the watch of which I had been robbed, but did not succeed in finding it; but he very kindly sent me another watch, which is all he had succeeded in having delivered by his order, and begged me to accept it even if it should not prove to be mine, but I of course returned it.

Now you will recall that towards the close of the war it was rumored that from various causes there was an impression prevailing that some of our men were not as reliable as formerly. You must refute this idea, for in the main it was false. Speaking for our men, as well as for those whose conduct come under my observation, the insinuation was most unjust. My men never marched better, though the retreat was a very severe test in this direction, for we were going all the time, with nothing to eat, without shelter and embarrassed by blocked roads, and in some cases small bridges down. Then as to fighting, men never did better, nor could better have been done. Indeed the officers and men of the battalion always displayed the greatest intelligence and valor possible, they never shrank from any duty, and, as Genl. Alexander once wrote to me, "It was the work of supererogation to command such men." One only had to show them where they could get in, and in they went, and always maintained themselves just as well in the hundreds of fights they were in as they did at Fredericksburg, (both of them), or at Gettysburg. I can never say enough of their absolute bravery, coolness and courage, or their patience on the march, or fidelity at all times.

It is a great pity that the organization of the battalion could not have been in some manner kept up; but with four batteries from Virginia, one from South Carolina and one from Mississippi, this was impossible, for doubtless this would have led to a concerted action on the part of the command to place in some historical form its services during the war, but we have the satisfaction of knowing that we yield to no command anywhere in the Confederate service, either in the sense of duty better performed or as having been frequently called into action as we were.

You will, of course, refer to the death of Capt. O. B. Taylor, at Sailor's Creek. I never knew exactly how it happened, and only heard of it subsequently. He was a cool, gallant man. I recollect at Gettysburg the enemy were trying to crown a small hill on our left front with a battery of artillery, to which I called Taylor's attention, and told him not to let them do it, and they didn't. He commanded a battery of four 12-pound Napoleons, and kept his shrapnel so well scattered on that hill that not a shot was fired from it during the engagement of the 3rd day.

There were many others who suffered at the time of our capture, about whom probably you know more than I do, but if possible I think they should be done justice to in your proposed Memoir.

The final destruction of the Army of Northern Virginia was simply a repetition on a large scale of our disaster. That army was simply "crowded out" by a large excess of numbers, our force having been materially reduced by reason of hard fighting, poor rations, and they not supplied with regularity, and sickness, due to hard service.

I do not know that there is anything further that I can add to this reminiscence that will be interesting, and therefore I will now close it, with best wishes, and hope you will be able to get out your pamphlet in time to be available for the Re-union at Richmond about the 1st of July proximo.

Yours very truly,
Frank Huger

Letter Number 71

This letter helps to identify the recipient, J. Van McCreery. He had been a Confederate artilleryman along with his brother William J. McCreery, who was killed at Gettysburg. According to Jennings Wise in his work, *The Long Arm of Lee*, Miller's battery of Major Eshleman's battalion of the Washington Artillery fired the opening gun or Confederate signal gun. Eshleman's battalion was to the left of Alexander's, then under command of Frank Huger. The Confederate line of guns ran for about 1300 yards from the Peach Orchard south to Spangler's Woods. Frank Huger's battalion, of which Parker's Virginia Battery was a part, suffered the heaviest loss in personnel, about 28 percent.[4] Parker's battery initially deployed just west of the Emmitsburg Road opposite the Peach Orchard and then moved east of the Peach Orchard firing towards the Trostle barn after the repulse of Pickett's Charge. Parker's battery did not finally retire to a spot near Willoughby Run well west of the Emmitsburg Road until after dark about 8:30 P.M.[5] In this letter Frank gave important information about his family.

Roanoke, Va., May 12, 1896

My dear Van:

I was very glad indeed to receive your letter under date of the 8th of May, and glad to hear from you again; and I will now try and answer your questions to the best of my ability, though it has been so long since these events that I may fall in error from lapse of time.

The signal guns to open the artillery fire on the 3rd day at Gettysburg, (two guns), were fired by the Washington artillery,—I think the two right pieces, but I do not know what Company of that battalion occupied the right at that particular time. Capt. J. Thompson Brown, #1113 Main Street, Richmond, Va., or Maj. Evans, can give you the location of Parker's battery during the duel on the 3rd day and subsequently. Capt. Parker, with his battery, very gallantly held, late in the evening, what I now recall as our left of the peach orchard against the advance of the enemy. There was heavy picket firing there about dark, and I think Parker retired after you left. He was certainly the last of our guns to do so, and, as I have said, there was a heavy picket fire from the enemies line in this vicinity. To the best of my knowledge your guns were not posted to the right of the peach orchard, as Alexander's battalion joined the right of the Washington artillery, and Haskell was on my right with his battalion.

I am very glad to hear such good accounts of you and to know that you are all well. In 1879 I married Miss Julia Trible, and have had five children,— four girls and one boy. I lost my eldest girl when she was an infant. My eldest now is 14; the next is 12; the next 10, and the boy 6 years old. I very often recall my dear old friend, your brother, and have often and earnestly wished he could have been spared to us all and to his country in the trying times we have all gone through.

With the kindest regards and best wishes
Yours very sincerely,
Frank Huger

Mr. J. Van McCreery,
10 South First Street
Richmond, Va.

Letter Number 72

Roanoke, Va., June 5, 1896

Col. E. P. Alexander,
Agusta, Ga.
My dear Alex:

I heard from Capt. [J. Thompson] Brown, to whom I wrote to know if he could give the address of any survivors of [Captain Pichegru] Woolfolk's old battery who were at the battle of Gettysburg. He says he does not know of any, but he thinks if you will address Sergeant B. E. Poitiaux, who is now on the Police force in the city of Richmond, Va., and who was a Sergeant in Woolfolk's battery, he may be able to give you such information as you want.

Yours very sincerely,
Frank Huger

Letter Number 73

Roanoke, Va., June 5, 1896

Capt. J. Thompson Brown,
1113 Main St., Richmond, Va.,
My dear Capt.:

I am very much obliged to you for your letter of June 2, which I have read with a great deal of interest, but with some little surprise at the facility with which I forgot some things and get others mixed in the long lapse of time; and I am certainly very much obliged to you for setting me straight on points which you were kind enough to mention. Some of these days when I have a chance to look over your speech I have no doubt I will find a good many more that have gone clean out of my mind by this time.

When I am next in Richmond I hope I shall have the pleasure of seeing you I will certainly try to do so if time permits.

Very truly yours,
Frank Huger

CHAPTER SIX

Benjamin Huger

Born on November 22, 1805, Benjamin Huger came into an already distinguished family. His father, Francis Kinlock Huger, was aide-de-camp to General James Wilkinson in 1800 and adjutant general in the War of 1812. In the 1790s Francis was imprisoned in Austria for his attempt to free Lafayette from the prison at Olmütz. Francis' father, also Benjamin Huger, was killed at Charleston, South Carolina, during the British occupation in our fight for independence. Benjamin Huger's mother, wife of Francis Kinlock Huger, was Harriott Lucas Pinckney, daughter of Major General Thomas Pinckney.

Francis and Harriott Huger parented eight children. They were Anna Isabella Huger, born about 1803; Elizabeth Huger, 1804; Thomas Pinckney Huger, about 1804 or '05; Benjamin Huger, November 22, 1805; Francis Huger, 1811, Cleland Kinlock Huger, 1818; Mary Ester Huger, 1820 and Harriott Horry Huger, 1822. I have found no names of other children but the spaces between the births of the surviving children suggest that some may have died in childhood. It was a rare family at this time that experienced no childhood deaths.

Young Ben entered the U.S. Military Academy at West Point, New York, in 1821 at the age of sixteen. He graduated eighth of thirty-seven in the class of 1825. Upon graduation he received a second lieutenant's brevet but was quickly promoted to second lieutenant in the 3rd U.S. Artillery. He served as a topographical engineer until 1828 when he took a leave of absence to visit Europe, returning in 1830. While abroad he perfected his equestrian skills and studied the finer points of fencing along with artillery, engineering, chemistry and mathematics. Socially he met Lafayette, Sir Walter Scott and the Duke of Wellington. Upon his return he was on recruiting duty and then served at Fort Trumbull in New London, Connecticut. Following a year of ordnance duty Benjamin attained the rank of captain of ordnance in 1832, the year the Ordnance Department finally became separate from the artillery. From 1832 until 1839 and then again from 1841 to 1846 he commanded the arsenal at Fort Monroe. The break in the service came when he and three others traveled to Europe under orders of Secretary of War Joel

Poinsett to study European military establishments, particularly cannon foundries.[1]

In the late 1830s there were two schools of thought in the United States concerning gun metal for field artillery. Should cast iron replace bronze? Cast iron was much less expensive per pound than was bronze while bronze was more ductile. In April 1840 Secretary of War Joel R. Poinsett sent Major Rufus L. Baker, captains Alfred Mordecai and Benjamin Huger, and William Wade to Europe "to obtain such practical knowledge of the treatment of iron, that the Ordnance Department may dictate rules to the founders so as to ensure the selection of good metal, and the fabrication of good guns." Baker, Huger and Mordecai were army officers serving on the ordnance board. William Wade, a former army ordnance officer, was part owner of the Fort Pitt Foundry and interested in finding a way to make stronger iron castings. Sailing from New York on April 1, 1840, they did not return until November 21, 1840. During that time the team visited arsenals, foundries, mines, powder mills and other installations in Great Britain, France, Belgium, Germany, Norway, Sweden and Russia. The Swedes had rich iron mines and excellent foundries that allowed Sweden to use cast iron field artillery. The four Americans took excellent notes and made close and accurate observations. One result was that after 1842 there was an ordnance representative at every private foundry that cast guns for the army.[2]

Following are several letters from the Huger Family Papers relating to Benjamin Huger's trip abroad as a member of the team. The first two were written to Huger from a Thomas Moody.

Waltham Abbey, Essex
23th April 1840

"*Doubtless however you and your friends would like to see small arms, Gun Powder Manufactories and for other purposes I must ask permission of the Master General and Board of ordnance, from a circumstance which occurred about a year ago.*"

Moody wrote again from Waltham Abbey on April 28. This letter stated that Colonel Fox, secretary to the master general of the ordnance, was unwell and unable to meet with the team. The letter indicates that Huger was staying in London at the Royal Hotel, St. James Street. He was to meet with the director of the Polytechnic Institute.

One letter Benjamin Huger wrote home to his wife survives in the Huger Family Papers. It is addressed to Mrs. B. Huger, Pendleton, So. Carolina. Pendleton is in the northwestern part of the state, just southwest of Greenville. The Huger family owned considerable property in this part of the state. In 1845 and 1846 Benjamin Huger sought to sell one large tract and worked through his two brothers, Cleland and Thomas.

St. Petersburg July 30th 1840

My dear Wife,
    I wrote to you a week ago — soon after my arrival here — and tomorrow we go via Lubeck to Berlin, where I hope to find [unclear] — If I had moments leisure I should be over anxious, but I have been kept in such constant employment and excitement that time has flown, and it is with great regret that I am forced away from this grand place — having seen so very little. Last Saturday night we received an invitation from the Emperor [Nicholas I, 1825–1855] *to be at his grand Camp at Krasnoe silo³ — about 16 miles from here, on Sunday at 8 o'ck, — to be presented to him, & to see the maneuvers of the troops on Monday, Tuesday and Wednesday — so we got ready & left this very early Sunday morning got here in a couple of hours — were presented to the Emperor, at once — And witnessed all the maneuvers of the troops, got back here Wednesday evening and have been Employed since in seeing the Arsenal here. — There were 50.000 men in Camp. 36 thousand Infantry, 12, thousand Cavalry — and 2 thousand Artillery —. The Emperor Commanded in Person, — and a most magnificent sight it was, — I will describe it at leisure — I only write a line now, as a gentleman of my acquaintance leaves this tomorrow for St* [steam] *Boat direct to* [Le] *Havre & thence to London, and will deliver this to Messrs. C & S. to forward — it may perhaps reach you before my dispatch which I will forward from Hamburg.*
    We have been treated with marked attention here; and the visit has been a truly gratifying one —. I am as well as I can be — and if I could only catch a glimpse of you and the dear Boys — God bless them before I take my few hours nap I should be perfectly happy — Good night my own pet Love to all the good people with you.
                    Yours ever B.H.

Augt. 1 — Have got through July you see — we leave here at 1 PM today will visit the fortifications at Cornstad [Kronshtadt] *this evening & embark early 2 AM tomorrow morning for Lubeck — Good bye Yours*

From 1839 to 1846 Captain Huger served as a member of the U.S. Army Ordnance Board. This board provided technical service and had no administrative control over the Ordnance Department. Colonel Huger explained this distinction between the Ordnance Board and Ordnance Department in testimony before Congress on March 30, 1854. Questioned about his knowledge of the manner in which discipline was enforced under the civil superintendents, Huger replied: "As a member of the ordnance board, I knew something of the general management, but had no personal knowledge." When asked if the rules in force under the civil superintendents were approved by the ordinance board Colonel Huger replied: "It is the chief of the ordinance bureau who makes the regulations. The ordnance board has only to examine and approve of the changes in the model of the arms, machinery, &c. so as to avoid continual changes in the model, arms, or other articles in the use of the service."

Colonel Huger was asked next if the rules concerning discipline that were made by the superintendent were submitted to the ordnance board for approval. He replied: "They are not. The ordnance board have nothing to do with the administration of the armories."[4]

While on that board Huger designed an improved lever for opening and closing the breechblock on the Hall's rifle that was manufactured at the rifle works at Harpers Ferry Armory. An improvement to the well-made, well-designed Hall rifle was no small accomplishment. Huger's lever was called a fish tail and the wide design that resembled a fish tail or the flukes of a whale provided more surface for the thumb for easier operation.[5]

Benjamin Huger married his cousin Elizabeth Celestine Pinckney on February 7, 1831. They had five children; Benjamin, Eustis, Francis or Frank, Thomas Pinckney and Celestine Pinckney. Benjamin junior and Eustis served on their father's staff while Thomas, or Pinck, it seems, did not serve in the Confederate forces because of poor health. There is some evidence that he may have served briefly in some capacity.

During the Mexican War, Benjamin Huger was chief of ordnance under Major General Winfield Scott and received three brevet promotions to major, lieutenant colonel and colonel, the last promotion on September 13, 1847, for conduct at Chapultepec. He participated in the siege of Vera Cruz, having charge of the siege train. He fought at Cerro Gordo, Molino del Rey and took part in the capture of Mexico City. His service in Mexico made him an original member of the Aztec Club, organized in Mexico City in 1847. Following the end of the Mexican War he returned to command the Fort Monroe arsenal in Virginia. In 1851 Huger assumed command of the Harpers Ferry Armory, also in Virginia at the time. At Harpers Ferry Benjamin Huger made his most important contribution to ordnance development.

Huger had some questions concerning his brevet rank upon taking command at Harpers Ferry. While serving there he became involved in the controversy over civilian superintendents for the national armories. See Appendices I and II. In 1852 the State of South Carolina presented Benjamin Huger with a sword in recognition of his "long course of service in the Army of the United States, and more particularly, as displayed at the siege of Vera Cruz." South Carolina governor John L. Manning signed the resolution.

From 1854 until 1860 Huger was in charge of the Pikesville, Maryland, Arsenal just outside of Baltimore and then was appointed to the command of the Charleston, South Carolina, Arsenal in 1860. It was while serving in Charleston that he resigned his commission on April 22, 1861; at the time he held the permanent rank of major and the brevet rank of colonel. His son Benjamin Huger, Jr., received an appointment as first lieutenant of infantry in the Army of the Confederate States on May 20, 1861. On June 17, 1861, Benjamin Huger Sr. received his appointment as brigadier general in the Provisional Army in the service of the Confederate States. Confederate secretary of war L. Pope Walker signed both appointments. On October 7, 1861, the new secretary of war, Judah P. Benjamin, raised General Benjamin Huger to the rank of major general.

Huger's first command in the Confederate service was of the district of Norfolk, Virginia. Believing his forces too weak to resist attack Huger set fire to the navy yard, blew up the CSS *Virginia* and evacuated the city in May 1862, retiring before the hesitant force under Union general John Wool marched from Huger's old post, Fort Monroe. See Appendix II for Huger's report on these operations.

Major General Benjamin Huger commanded a division on the peninsula in 1862 and took part in the battles of Seven Pines, Gaines' Mill, Glendale and Malvern Hill. His movement at Seven Pines was interfered with to some extent by the march of General James Longstreet. Under a cloud, Huger lost his field command on July 12, 1862. His new post was that of inspector of artillery and ordnance. In 1863, about the time of the fall of Vicksburg he was sent to the Trans-Mississippi. There he saw to the establishment of the arsenal at Tyler, Texas.

Too late for General Huger's benefit, his conduct at Seven Pines received a defense from the astute E. P. Alexander: "No complaint is made of any disobedience, slowness, or non-performance, by any officer, except Huger, and the facts in his case distinctly relieve *him* from any blame whatever. Indeed, it is almost tragic the way in which he became the scapegoat of this occasion, the true history of which is even yet [1907] not generally understood. Gen. [Gustavus W.] Smith, however, in 1891, published all the facts for the first time with documentary proof."[6]

According to Frank E. Vandiver Huger's appointment to the position of chief of the Bureau of Ordnance, Trans-Mississippi Department, was in part to get him out of the way. His former subordinate at Harpers Ferry, James Henry Burton, now superintendent of all Confederate Armories, was irked at Huger's inspection of Burton's operations in Macon, Georgia. Vandiver wrote about this episode as follows: "Possibly reflecting lingering resentment over past trouble in Mexico, Gorgas told Burton: 'Gen. Huger's orders are intended to cover all Ordn Establishments. He will do no harm, if he can do no good.'"[7] Still Burton must have believed he had an obligation to report to Huger. For example Huger was well enough informed on the progress of the Macon Arsenal to state it would permanently employ eighteen hundred workers. On January 7, 1863, Burton wrote to Huger about the difficulty of getting skilled workmen. "The demand for this class of labour so greatly exceeds the supply that it is in vain to expect to meet it, and to a great extent this class of mechanic dictates the wages they receive." A few days earlier, on January 2, John W. Mallet, head of the Confederate States Central Laboratory wrote to Huger and reported progress made thus far on the laboratory.[8]

General Edmund Kirby Smith may have considered Huger to have been a fifth wheel. Smith already had Major Thomas G. Rhett as chief of ordnance and artillery in his Trans-Mississippi Department. General Smith may have seen Huger, coming as chief of the Bureau of Ordnance, as redundant.

The following letters summarize Major General Benjamin Huger's service in the Trans-Mississippi. His letters, as well as those of his two sons, Benjamin Jr. and Eustis, express the same sentiments.

Alexandria, La. July 6, 1863

Col. J. Gorgas, Chief of Ordnance:

Colonel: I have arrived this place, and as General E.[dmund] K.[irby] Smith has his headquarters at Shreveport, I have sent him copies of my orders, both to that place and to Monroe, as it is not known where he is at present. I shall await his orders. I remain, very respectfully, your obedient servant.

Benj. Huger Major-General, &c[9]

Ordnance Bureau, Trans-Mississippi Department,
Marshall, Tex., January 15, 1864.

Maj. J. P. Johnson,
Assistant Inspector-General;

Major: As requested by you, I have the honor to submit the following report:

In the early part of last year I was ordered to proceed to this department, to give such advice and assistance as my enlarged experience enabled me to do, and for this purpose I would report to Lieutenant-General Smith, &c.

On my arrival at General Smith's headquarters, Vicksburg and Port Hudson has fallen, and we were in a great measure isolated from the rest of the Confederacy. General Smith issued a general order, announcing me as the chief of the bureau of ordnance for this department, and directing all the returns and reports, heretofore made to Richmond, to be made to me. The officers of the Niter and Mining Corps also to report to me.

I made a tour of inspection through the country, visiting the different establishments for manufacturing ordnance supplies, and on my return, with the approval of General Smith, I established the office of the bureau at this place, where the returns from the different arsenals and the troops are sent.

These returns are recorded and examined in my office, corrections required when necessary, and then filed, to be transmitted to Richmond for settlement at the Treasury, when opportunity may offer. As the department placed no funds under my control, and the officers procuring supplies wanted money, not advice, I could render no assistance.

The only arsenal under my control is the Texas Arsenal, San Antonio, commanded by Col. P. Stockton. All other establishments and all contracts for supplies are under the control of the acting chiefs of ordnance and artillery. I know nothing of their proceedings until they render their accounts to this office, when I have only to see that the expenditures have been properly and legally made. The intention of the War Department seems to be to distribute the funds through me (which would give me control of the expenditures), as the Chief of Ordnance at Richmond has sent me authority to draw to the amount of a million and a half for ordnance; but as he has omitted to state who to draw upon; I could only refer his letters to the commanding general, and up to this date I have been unable to get the first dollar for the expenses of the department. Under these circumstances, I must refer you for all information as to procuring the ordnance supplies to Maj. T. G. Rhett, chief of ordnance and artillery, on the staff of Lieutenant-General Smith.

The Niter and Mining Corps are employed as follows:

1st. Mr. Thomas G. Clemson, in charge of iron works, has the furnace in Marion County in blast; is making pig iron and castings. He is about erecting another furnace in Davis County, in the same neighborhood, and proposes to put up a third in Anderson County, near the Trinity River.

2d. Maj. Isaac Read and Lieutenants Sprigg and Harrison, in charge of niter works and other mining operations. As the niter caves in Northern Arkansas and the lead mines in Sevier County have all been abandoned from the approach of the enemy, Major Read has gone with all the forces at his disposal to work the very productive niter caves in Western Texas. These caves have already yielded a good deal of niter, and Major Read is confident we can get from them all that we require. There is now a year's supply on hand, provided the powder mill to be established here was at work, which is not likely to be for some time. Sulphur and copperas [a greenish crystalline, hydrated ferrous sulfate used in the manufacture of fertilizers, ink and water purification] *are also being obtained by this department.*

3d. For preparing lead, niter, &c., by purchase, Capt. R. H. Temple has been stationed at San Antonio, and has procured these articles to the extent of his ability.

The supply of such articles is sufficient, except iron, of which we want an unlimited quantity, and I have directed every exertion to be made to proceed with this manufacture.

All of which is respectfully submitted by your obedient servant,
Benj. Huger
Maj. Gen. and Chief of Bureau of Ordnance, Trans-Miss. Dept.[10]

Major Thomas G. Rhett's position may be better appreciated from some of his correspondence to Major J. P. Johnson, assistant adjutant and inspector general. From this correspondence it would appear that Major Rhett had things pretty well in hand. In a letter to Johnson from Shreveport on October 22, 1863, Rhett wrote as follows:

Major: I respectfully report for your information as follows: Establishments for ordnance work were in full operation at Little Rock, Arkadelphia, and Camden, and a shop for repairs of arms at Fort Smith; but, by reason of movements recently ordered, and the approach of the Federal forces, all these workshops and establishments have been removed to places of safety: the machinery, tools, stores, and men from Little Rock Arsenal to Tyler, Tex.; the machinery, tools, stores, and men from Arkadelphia to Marshall, Tex.; and the machinery, tools, stores and men from Camden to Shreveport, La.

I am establishing at Tyler a laboratory for fabricating battery and small-arms ammunition, carpenters' and blacksmiths' shop and shop for repairs of arms. I am also in treaty for the purchase of a manufactory of small-arms located at that point, and which is now carrying out a contract with the State of Texas for making guns.

At Marshall, Tex., I am having buildings erected for the manufacture of small-arms, smiths' and carpenters' shop powder-mill and magazine, and am concentrating at that point large supplies of heavy material, such as saltpeter, sulphur, lead, and iron, and I intend it to be a depot for supplies arriving from Mexico.

At Shreveport, La., are established, and now in operation, a foundry, harness, carpenter, and smiths' shops, and laboratory for fabricating battery and small-arms ammunition. The foundry is now going good work, and is turning out 9 and 11 inch shot and shell, 30-pounder Parrott shot and shell, Brooke shot for 32-pounder gun (rifled), 3 inch rifle shell and shot. 3.8-inch rifle shell and shot, 2.25 inch rifle shell and shot. 6 and 12 pounder projectiles, Navy fuses, heavy castings for powder-mill &c.

The laboratory turns out from 7,000 to 10,000 rounds per day; other shops doing equally well, notwithstanding an unusual amount of sick among mechanics employed and detailed. I have here gathered some good machinery, and intend increasing it from time to time; also erecting buildings for arsenal, magazine, shops, &c. (in addition to those already in position), and putting up a large reverberatory furnace. This department has now at this point 100,000 pounds of flat bar railroad iron, 70,000 pounds road and flat bar iron, 100 kegs nails, and — tons of pig-iron.

There are ordnance workshops at Houston, Tex., and an arsenal of construction at San Antonio. There is a powder-mill at this last-named point belonging to a contractor, of no great value, as far as I am able to learn.

I have contracted for supplies of stores in quantity, for which payment is to be made in cotton. Contractors have now en route to and close upon Marshall 30,000 pounds of lead, 50,000 pounds of English powder, trace-chains, wood screws, canvas, axes, flannel, paper, files, cones, &c. Fair quantities of these important articles are now coming forward, but a fatality has attended the introduction of arms, accouterments, cartridge paper, and acids into this department. A great many arms have been captured and lost while in transit from Richmond and other points east of the Mississippi, some 7,000 or 8,000 stand have been taken into Vicksburg for safety and there lost. Not long ago a vessel with 12,000 stand was captured off the coast of Mexico while trying to run in, and still more recently another, having on board 10,000 guns, 5,000,000 percussion caps, and 2,000,000 rounds of small-arms ammunition, run in just off the mouth of the Rio Grande, and had succeeded in getting ashore only 4,600 guns of her whole cargo, when she was seized and taken off by a French cruiser. I have no information going to show whether these arms were the property of contractors or already belonged to the Government and sent around from Bermuda.

This department should have at least 30,000 more guns, about a third of them for cavalry. Accouterments are also wanted in quantity, material and workmen having been so scarce as to prevent a supply being provided by manufacture.

Funds are badly needed. A million dollars sent to the depository at Alexandria, La., intended for use of this department, was turned over to quartermaster's department, District of West Louisiana, by the depositary. This action will check my operations materially.

I state, in conclusion, without hesitancy, that did we have the 30,000 additional arms and accouterments and a supply of percussion caps, that I could provide for all other wants of my department.

I am, major, very respectfully, your obedient servant,
Thos. G. Rhett,
Major and Chief of Ordnance and Artillery, Trans-Miss Dept.

About three months later he wrote:

Office of Chief of Ordnance and Artillery
Trans-Mississippi Department
Shreveport, La., January 19, 1864

Maj. J. P. Johnson,
Assistant Adjutant and Inspector General:

Major: I am unable, from the absence of most of my officers from their posts (several being on a board of examiners at Camden, and others absent, to appear before said board), to furnish you with as full a report as I could wish, and therefore confine myself for the present to those points which seemed most important, viz, ammunition, powder, lead, and caps. From reports furnished my office, there about 150,000 pounds of powder in this department, 140,000 pounds niter, and about 30,000 pounds of sulphur. These supplies are being increased by shipments from Mexico, and I will in this way be enabled to supply the needs of my department, if the enemy do not cut us off from Rio Grande. Caps can only be obtained in small quantities, and are bought up whenever they can be found. Lead is supplied from Mexico, and there are several hundred thousand pounds on the way, besides sufficient for present consumption in depot at Marshall, Tex. I am putting up at Marshall, Tex., powder-mills and cap-machines, which, when finished, will supply all that can be used; and the other works, such as gunsmiths' and machine shops, foundries, &c., are being put up at Marshall and Tyler, Tex., and also at this point. A laboratory, in charge of a skillful chemist, is in course of construction. These works are under competent officers, who are pressing them forward *rapidly, and I have no doubt of my ability to supply all wants of ordnance stores in a short time, provided money be promptly furnished me when called for.*

The armies in the field are pretty well supplied with small-arms and artillery ammunition. The removal of the works from Camden, Arkadelphia, and Little Rock, and putting up the necessary buildings and foundries, has caused me to be very backward in my ability to meet the calls made upon me for ordnance supplies; but in a few months I hope to be able not only to meet all such calls, but to have a large surplus of manufactured stores on hand for any emergency that may arise.

A more complete and correct report, if needed, can be made as soon as my officers return, and send you at any point you may desire.

I am, sir, very respectfully, your obedient servant,
  Thos. G. Rhett,
  Major and Chief of Ordnance and Artillery, Trans-Miss Dept.[11]

Some explanation about Lieutenant General Edmund Kirby Smith and his Department of Trans-Mississippi may be in order. The Trans-Mississippi was made a separate department in May 1862. The Trans-Mississippi region included Texas, Arkansas, Missouri, Indian Territory, that part of Louisiana west of the Mississippi River and the Arizona Territory. Although a large area geographically Confederate president Jefferson Davis devoted his main attention to Virginia and Tennessee, thus relegating the region to secondary importance. On January 14, 1863, Lt. Gen. E. K. Smith received the appointment to command the Southwestern Army. Soon thereafter on February 9 Smith took command of all Confederate forces west of the Mississippi River, making Alexandria, Louisiana, his headquarters. After the fall of Vicksburg and Port Hudson, the region was virtually isolated from the rest of the Confederacy.[12]

With the loss of Arkansas in late 1863, the Confederacy was denied access to raw materials as well as suffering the loss of arsenals there. To replace these important manufacturing centers, the Trans-Mississippi Department established an arsenal at Tyler, Texas with related facilities at nearby Marshall, Texas. Although it would be hard to tell from General Huger's letters home, historian Frank Vandiver wrote:

> For some months [Col. Josiah] Gorgas himself had been particularly concerned about supplying arms and ammunition to Texas. San Antonio Arsenal had been nursed along, and other plants in that city [population approximately 8200] were contributing greatly toward maintaining a modest store of munitions for "Kirby Smithdom." But a large establishment of fabrication, backed by adequate and convenient iron resources, had to be provided before

any real progress toward filling the critical shortages in the West could be made. The answer, probably fostered by the wisdom of Huger, was the erection of a large armory at Tyler, Texas. Under the able guidance and command of Lieutenant Colonel G. H. Hill, this installation soon became indispensable to the western commanders and overshadowed other ordnance plants in the Trans-Mississippi."[13]

On December 27, 1863, General Huger wrote his wife a letter describing his position under General E. Kirby Smith.

> *"I will probably go to Shreveport* [Louisiana] *in a few days & see the officers there & report to Col. Gorgas & the War Dept. results here so far—The command of which is that orders must be given from the War Dept. placing me in position here, if I am to remain. I was sent out only to give my 'advice & valuable experience.' Maj. Rhett is Chf of Ordnance to Lt. Gen. Smith—Genl. S. is otherwise occupied & leaves Ord. business to Maj, R. who wants none of my 'advice and experience'; & as he acts <u>by orders</u> of Genl. S. I have no control whatever of the large operations he is carrying on & he has no idea of letting me have any if he can help it—So as far as Ord. matters are concerned I might as well be anywhere else."*

Indeed General E. Kirby Smith's biographer, Joseph H. Parks, did not include Benjamin Huger in the index to his biography. Scant recognition of General Huger's contribution in Trans-Mississippi is given on pages 379–80 in Robert L. Kerby's book, *Kirby Smith's Confederacy: The Trans-Mississippi South, 1863–1865.*

Confederate major general John Bankhead Magruder, like Huger, did not perform well during the Seven Days battles on the Virginia peninsula. Magruder's performance at Malvern Hill was especially poor. Magruder too left Virginia for a post in the Trans-Mississippi. Huger wrote the following entry in a letter home dated Marshall, Texas, November 27, 1863.

"John Magruder for reasons of his own ... pigion [sic] holes the proceedings of the B<u>d</u> & does not send them on to Hd [Head] Qr [Quarters] — I will work him in the end, his impudence is astounding." [Huger Family Papers].

Confederate general E. Kirby Smith surrendered his army of the Trans-Mississippi on June 2, 1865. Throughout the month of May the army had been dissolving. So rapidly had the soldiers gone their separate ways that of the approximately 60,000 troops in the Trans-Mississippi Department, only 17,515 remained to be paroled.[14]

After the war Huger lived on a farm in Fauquier County, Virginia. He returned to Charleston not long before his death in 1877 although his remains lie in the Green Mount Cemetery, Baltimore, Maryland.

The following obituary and brief biography of Benjamin Huger was written by his friend and colleague, ordnance officer Colonel Alfred Mordecai.

Benjamin Huger
No 399 — class of 1825
Died at Charleston So.Ca. Dec 7th 1877 — Aged 72

Benjamin Huger was born in Charleston So.Ca. November 22nd 1805. He belonged to a French Huguenot family who settled in South Carolina after the revolution of the Edict of Nantes, and many of whose members served with distinction, in military and civil employments, in the state and general governments —

His father, Col. Francis K. Huger, who was adjutant General in 1813, was when a very young man, engaged in the chivalrous enterprise of rescuing Gen. La Fayette from confinement in the Austrian prison of Olmurz [sic].

Young Huger entered the Military academy in 1821, and soon endeared himself to his comrades there by the amiable disposition, high tone of character and fine spirit which marked his course through life — On leaving the Academy he was appointed to the Artillery branch of the service; a few years afterwards he went on furlough to Europe, and spent some time there for improvement in professional and general knowledge.

In 1832, when the Ordnance Department was reorganized as a separate branch of the Army, Huger, then a second lieutenant, was selected by a Board of officers for appointment as a Captain in the New Corps — In this capacity he was placed in command of the Arsenal of Construction at Fort Monroe, where his efficient and valuable services justified his selection by the Board for extraordinary promotion; whilst his brother officers and many visitors to that frequented post were always received with courteous and liberal hospitality by him and his amiable and excellent wife, a member of the distinguished family of the Pinckney's of South Carolina.

As commander of the Fort Monroe Arsenal for many years and as a member of the Ordnance Board and of other Boards of like character, Capt Huger bore an important part in the reorganization and improvement of the system of Artillery and of the general armament and equipment of the troops, and in furtherance of these objects he was selected by Mr. Poinsett, Secy. Of War, as a member of a commission appointed in 1840 to visit the foundries and Military establishments of Europe.

When Gen. Scott was appointed to the command of an Army for the invasion of Mexico, in 1847, he selected Capt. Huger as the chief ordnance officer of that army, and placed him in command of the siege train and batteries of heavy artillery, in addition to his other duties of providing for the armament and equipment of the troops.

Gen. Scott's reports of the campaign bear the strongest testimony to the ability and efficiency with which the operations of these batteries in the siege of Vera Cruz and in the battles in the Valley of Mexico were conducted. In his report of the operations immediately preceding the occupation of the City of Mexico Gen. Scott makes special mention of the decisive effects of the heavy batteries XXX [Mordecai wrote these three crosses, they are not strike outs] *superintended by Capt. Huger chief of ordnance with this army — an officer distinguished by every kind of merit.* For "gallant and meritorious conduct" on these several occasions, Capt. Huger received the successive brevets of Major, Lieut. Colonel and Colonel in the United States Army and a sword of honor was presented to him by his native State.

After the Mexican War he was employed on Ordnance duties at Fort Monroe and other arsenals as superintendant of the Armory at Harpers Ferry and as Inspector of Ordnance at the Foundries — In the performance of the last mentioned duty he was stationed at the Pikesville Arsenal near Baltimore, at the outbreak of the late Civil War. He then Apl. 22nd 1861 resigned his commission in the Army of the United States and was for a short time in command of the Maryland Guards of Baltimore, where his judicious conduct restrained the rash proceedings of the imprudent.

He soon entered the Confederate service, with the rank of brigadier general and was assigned to the command of the Department of Norfolk Va. was promoted to the rank of Major General, and with his Division took part in the battles of the peninsula and in the operations around Richmond. He was on special service in the South Western Department where the war was ended.

After the war Gen. Huger lived for a short time in Baltimore, where he had the misfortune to lose the loved and faithful companion of his married life, and also his oldest son — He then retired to a farm which he purchased in Fauquier County Va where he spent nearly all the rest of his life; solaced by the affectionate care of children and grand children, and beloved and respected by his neighbors, as he had always been by his companions in arms. A change in his family arrangements made it necessary for him to leave this pleasant retreat in the autumn of 1877 and to turn his steps further South — His heart had been seriously impaired for about two years and was gradually declining; but he was fortunately able to reach his native city, where he died on the 7th of December 1877. Surrounded by members of his family and other friends.

In accordance with his own wish, his remains were taken by his sons to Baltimore, and laid by the side of those of his beloved wife and son, in Greenmount Cemetery.

This tribute to the memory of a gallant soldier, a kind friend and a good man, expresses very inadequately the love and esteem entertained for him by one who can look back on the recollection of a friendship of more than fifty years, uninterrupted by a harsh word or thought. The general estimation of his excellent qualities is well expressed in the words of an obituary notice in a Charleston Journal, on the day after his death.

"Having lived more than the three score years and ten usually allotted to man, he has gone down to the grave beloved by all for the kindness of his manner and the benevolence of his heart and honored by those who knew him best for the strict integrity and unblemished purity of his character."

Alfred Mordecai
Of the class of 1823.

APPENDIX I

Technical Developments at Harpers Ferry

The official small arms of the United States in 1855 were the altered model 1822 rifle-musket, .69-caliber; the altered model 1842 rifle-musket, .69-caliber; the altered model 1841 rifle, .58-caliber; the new model 1855 rifle-musket, .58-caliber; the new model 1855 rifle, .58-caliber and the new model 1855 pistol-carbine, .58-caliber.[1] U.S. Ordnance Department chief Colonel Henry Knox Craig referred to the .58-caliber arms as "the latest improved arms." The term altered meant that the model was altered from flintlock and smoothbore to a rifled, percussion lock arm. The year 1855 was selected for replacing all smoothbore arms with rifled arms for all branches of the service.[2]

The Ordnance Department conducted extensive tests between 1849 and 1855 to arrive at the arms Colonel Craig called "the latest improved arms." Adopting a rifled arm required ordnance men to decide upon the particular rifling and design of an elongated or cylindro-conical bullet. Brevet Colonel Benjamin Huger was a key player in these tests. The importance of his contributions to small arms development must be considered to do justice to his overall military reputation.

The difference between a rifled as compared with a smoothbore arm is the inscription of spiral grooves cut into the interior surface of the bore of the barrel. There are, however, a number of considerations to be addressed before the best rifling and bullet combination can be made. Colonel Huger supervised the work and the tests that would help those choices to be made. For example, how many spiral grooves should be cut? Should there be an even or odd number? Should the grooves and the lands be of the same width? How deeply should the grooves be cut? What is the best rotation or twist for the rifling to impart a stabilizing rotation to the bullet? Should the depth of the rifling grooves be uniform throughout the barrel or of decreasing depth as the rifling proceeds to the muzzle?

There was also the question of gaining. Advocates of gain twist rifling saw an advantage in a very slight rotation of the rifling from the breech to midpoint in the length of the barrel, then increasing the rate of twist from midpoint to the muzzle. The theory was that starting out with very little rotation of the rifling, lead would not strip off from the bullet. Then, when under the velocity produced by the powder gas, the bullet would gain rotational spin as it passed through the increased rifling twist of the last portion of the barrel.

Writing from Pikesville Arsenal on the outskirts of Baltimore, Maryland, on March 18, 1854, where he had just been transferred following his superintendence at Harpers Ferry, Huger summarized his work on the rifle and bullet design. His report began:

> *The Colonel of Ordnance* [Colonel Henry K. Craig] *having authorized experiments to be made at the Arsenal* [Harpers Ferry] *with rifles, firing elongated bullets, on the "tige" and Minié principles, seven rifles of musket caliber* [.69] *were made.*
> *The length of the barrel for all was 33 inches.*[3]

The two principles, tige and Minié, were the methods used to expand an undersized bullet that could easily be run down the rifled barrel and then expanded to seize the rifling. Both were of French army design and Colonel Huger, years before, had done his post graduate work in that country following his graduation from West Point in 1825. The tige principle used a tap or a mild blow of the ramrod to expand the soft lead bullet into the rifling. How hard a blow the bullet received was determined by the individual soldier, and although drilled to exercise a somewhat uniform blow, a certain amount of excess deformity of the ball was unavoidable with this method. On the other hand the Minié principle, named for French army officer Captain Claude-Etienne Minié, (1804–1879) used the force of the powder gas to expand the bullet into the rifling grooves. About 1847 Minié designed an elongated bullet into the hollow base of which resided a small iron disc. The force of the gas from the burning powder charge forced the iron disc deeper into the hollow forcing the sides of the bullet into the rifling grooves.[4]

While all seven of Colonel Huger's experimental rifled barrels were the same length and caliber, they varied somewhat in weight; four were the same (Huger did not give the weight for these four but they probably weighed about three pounds), two weighed about a pound more and one made of cast steel weighed several ounces more than the first four. Huger addressed the subject of rifling.

> *With expanding bullets, there should be an odd number of grooves in the bore of the barrel, in which case,* a groove *will be opposite a* land; *for when the ball is forced, each land tends to push the opposite part of the ball into a groove, conse-*

quently the ball is less deformed than where the number of grooves is even, where a land *would be opposite a* land, *and a* groove *opposite a* groove.⁵

Huger found that five grooves were sufficient. The Hall rifle had seven lands and grooves. Later tests confirmed that three lands and grooves of equal width were sufficient to provide the proper rotary twist to stabilize the bullet. The experiments also showed that a twist rate of one full turn in six feet was the optimum rate. A faster twist, one full turn in less than six feet, increased what was known as *derivation*—a French term—used to describe the tendency for the ball to travel in the direction of the rifling twist. In other words if the rifling was cut so that it turned from right to left the ball will fly to the left of point of aim and vice versa. As a result Huger discovered that in arms with a twist of one turn in four or five feet the sights had to be corrected to compensate for the derivation.

Huger's experiments found that gain twist provided no advantages. It was more difficult to cut such rifling and the bullet became deformed when it hit the point where the increased twist began. Today gain twist is coming back in favor in modern sporting arms (target rifles) because with the latest generation of machine tools a smoother transition between the varying twist rates can be made; there is no speed bump at midpoint, so to speak. In Huger's day the juncture at midpoint in the barrel where the twist increased was like a pothole in the road.

The tige principle proved to be inferior to the Minié. In order for the bullet to be expanded by a blow from the ramrod it had to rest on something solid. So to provide a kind of anvil for the bullet, an iron pin was inserted into the face of the breech plug, the powder charge surrounded the pin but did not cover or bury it. Then the ball could not yield under the ramrod blow, resting as it did on the iron pin or tige. But the pin made cleaning the arm more difficult.

The Minié principle was sound as a principle, but the original method of its implementation left room for improvement. Huger's supervision fostered improvement in bullet design. The problem of Captain Minié's design was that the iron expander disc often times was driven by the force of the powder gas too far into the bullet, causing it to break. To remedy this shortcoming Huger turned to his acting master armorer at Harpers Ferry, the young Virginian mechanic and machinist James Henry Burton. Burton began his employment at Harpers Ferry in 1843 and had been instrumental in the adoption of machine tools, particularly trip hammers, to the armory production of small arms. Under Colonel Huger's direction Burton began to design an expanding base bullet to replace that designed by Captain Minié. Before he finally settled on a workable design, a bullet officially named the Harpers

Ferry bullet, Burton designed and tested three basic designs. There were also several modifications to each of these three major designs.

During Burton's trials he wrote the following letter to Colonel Huger explaining the results of his tests. Major John Symington commanded the Harpers Ferry armory prior to Benjamin Huger and Burton had worked under his supervision. Major Symington would have the misfortune to command the Allegheny Arsenal just outside of Pittsburgh, Pennsylvania, when it suffered an explosion and fire on September 17, 1862, killing and maiming a large number of women and girls who worked there.

U.S. Armory H. Ferry
Jan. 27th 1854

Dear Sir,

According to promise I send you a hasty account of facts developed at the last trial of the hollow elongated bullet for the Rifle. In the first place, I fear that the bullet, of which you have a sample with you,—will have to be set down as a failure, whether fired with or without the expanding conical piece in the base of it. The practical result, so far as the number of hits in the target is concerned,—is no better than our former trial with the Minié bullet. So far as could be discerned (firing over water) the bullets frequently <u>burst</u>, as several pieces of something fell in the water—wide of the mark when the arm was fired. I observed also that the barrel became again very foul after six or eight discharges,—so much so that it had to be wiped out before the bullets could be pushed home: a result very different from that occurring in the use of the Rifle of Musket caliber, [0.69] in which <u>musket</u> powder is used. And here I think I have made a discovery that will prove of much advantage in the use of the Rifle hereafter, whether with or without the improved ammunition.

My opinion is now pretty firmly fixed,—after what has been developed in practice,—as regards this fact: viz: that the rifle powder now used in the service is <u>too fine in the grain</u>, and consequently <u>too quick</u> and <u>instantaneous in its ignition</u> for the size of the bullet the rifle carries, causing the bullet to "strip," or fail to follow the grooves of the barrel in many instances where it would not occur with powder of a <u>coarser</u> grain and <u>slower combustion.</u> Again, I believe it is an established fact that fine powder will foul and cake in a barrel to a much greater extent than coarse and these causes, perhaps, operate to a certain extent in producing the failure of the last or hollow bullet. At any rate, the failure was so entire, that I abandoned the further trial of this bullet. After making the best of my disappointment at the result (for disappointed I <u>was</u> most <u>egregiously</u>) I deter-

mined to test an idea I have had for some time in reference to the Rifle especially and of which I have spoken to you several times since the subject has been under consideration, viz: that _paper_ is _not the material_ for patching the rifle bullet; and so long as it is attempted to be used, so long will _failure_ result Profiting by my experience thus far I made up some cartridges as follows: first— the _simple_ elongated bullet like the one you have with you, but _solid,_ with _nothing_ attached to it except a simple linen patch, cut circular, and in diam. 1.3 inch. This was placed over the muzzle of a spare barrel and the bullet placed concentric with it and then pressed down with the hand into the barrel to the depth of the third groove from the base of the bullet. This drew the patch very nicely over the base of the bullet, and it was then secured to it by a simple threat wound twice around it and tied: the thread laying in the third groove of the bullet, which suits the purpose exactly. The bullets were then dipped into melted tallow (as the base of the _cartridge_ has heretofore been treated) and the cartridges made up in other respects as heretofore. I like this about the ammunition thus made up:— there is _no grease outside._ I made a hasty trial with these cartridges, and the result is _good._ The arm is loaded with fully as much _facility_ as with the former cartridges and I think the ball enters the muzzle of the barrel with decidedly _more_ ease than the former ones did with the _paper_ patch, there being no projecting corners caused by the folds. It was in this trial that the fact was developed that the use of _musket powder_ in the _Rifle_ will give better results than the use of the present Rifle powder. I fired _20 rounds_ with musket powder without wiping out, and the last bullet went home with almost as much ease as the first: and when the breech was taken out of the barrel for cleaning it, there was not near as much foulness observed as had been previously after firing only five or six rounds with Rifle powder.

 I should have remarked before that the "modus operandi" of loading with the above described ammunition, was simply to pour in the powder— _break off_ the bullet from the cartridge and remove _all_ the _paper_ from it, push the bullet home, (which is done without exertion) and settle it down upon the charge by a _simple, gentle_ blow with the ramrod. This seems to expand the bullet sufficiently to fill the grooves of the barrel: at least I infer as much, as the shots fired thus were _all good._ I observed, however, that the rifle, when fired with musket powder _twice hung fire_ in the twenty rounds fired. It may be that it is too coarse for the rifle: and my opinion is that it should be of a size of grain about _midway_ between the musket & Rifle powders. At all events, it seems to me a subject that would bear further investigation, involving as it does such important results as have been mentioned. I would observe here that much trouble was experienced a few years since, in the proof of rifle barrels, by them being bulged: caused, I am inclined to think, by the "brisante" [brisance] _(to quote from Major Symington)_ quality of the powder. It seemed to possess too much of a _bursting_ property.

In conclusion I must apologize for the disconnected manner in which these remarks have been thrown together and hope you will succeed in understanding my meaning notwithstanding its ambiguity; and would also express the opinion that we have hit upon the <u>simplest</u> and <u>best</u> description of ammunition for use in the Rifle. Perhaps I should also offer an apology for the great length of this epistle and would do so were it not that I know the interest you take in such matters generally, and this in particular. I shall proceed to make up enough ammunition to compare with the practice with the regular service ammunition which by the way has not yet arrived, as the express Co. refused to take it and it had to be sent through the Q. M. at Balt[imore]. I design making a similar experiment as just described with the Rifle of Musket calibers as soon as possible.

I am yours truly
Jas. H. Burton
Col. Benj. Huger
U.S.A.

In his report of March 18, 1854, from Pikesville Arsenal, Colonel Huger explained the drawbacks to the first two of Burton's bullet designs. The first idea Burton had for the Minié replacement featured an elongated bullet with a sharp cone-shaped recess in its base. Inserted into the cavity was a cone cast onto a circular base the same diameter as the bullet. This cone was cast from a lead and tin alloy harder than the bullet. This alloy cone was larger than the recess in the bullet so the circular base onto which the cone was cast did not come up flush with the base of the bullet but stood away by about one tenth of an inch. Like the original Minié bullet, gas pressure from the powder charge drove the circular based cone into the bullet and expanded its sides into the rifling grooves. The circular base prevented the cone from being driven too deeply into the bullet and damaging it as the iron disc had frequently done to the Minié ball.

Colonel Huger reported this bullet performed well at 200 yards. The problem was that the inserted hard alloy cone fell out after a short distance in flight and, as Huger wrote, "[m]ight do injury in firing <u>over</u> our own men."

Burton's next major design was based upon the tige principle. He designed a bullet that comprised two cast lead parts. The main body of the bullet was cast with a vertical cavity in its center and a flat across its top. The second piece was cast with a pointed or spitzer top and a long cylindrical body, not unlike a long stemmed mushroom. This second part was made to be inserted into the cavity of the first part. These two castings were assembled in the arsenal and the soldier loaded the bullet with both parts already combined. It its initial state the mushroom cap did not rest on the bullet but was apart from it by about one-tenth of an inch. Upon running the bullet down the barrel and onto the powder charge, the soldier then gave the bullet a rap with the ramrod to drive the two lead components more tightly together as well as expanding the lower part into the rifling. This bullet performed to satisfaction out to 200 yards but its flaw was in the fact that the blow to expand the bullet compressed the powder charge beneath it and made it cake. This caused no problem during the trials, Huger reported, because the arm was fired immediately upon loading. In actual service, however, the arm may remain loaded for some time before being fired and this caking may lead to a misfire. That Colonel Huger could foresee this possibility was in all probability a result of his personal combat experience in the Mexican War.

As tests and experiments continued James Burton discovered that the force of the powder gas was sufficient to expand a hollow based bullet, especially if the edges around the cavity were thin. Therefore the final Harpers Ferry bullet designed by Burton under these tests was a hollow base bullet. The cavity was in the form of a truncated cone. Later, in experiments conducted by Lieutenant James G. Benton, the cavity shape was modified to that of a cone.

Huger's experiments showed that the coarser granules of musket powder performed better than the finer rifle powder. Musket powder resulted in less fouling than rifle powder. These tests that Colonel Huger supervised paved the way for the adoption of the .58-caliber for the service arms. The choice of .69-caliber went back all the way to the American War of Independence when France provided the colonies with its shoulder arm, the Charleville. Huger's tests were made for the most part with .69-caliber barrels and to a much lesser extent with three rifle barrels of .54-caliber. Going from the round ball to the elongated bullet increased the weight of the slug considerably. Sixty-nine caliber musket balls in the editor's collection weigh on average about 450 grains. There are 7,000 grains in a pound so the .69-caliber musket ball weighed about one ounce. This is why the Charleville was also referred to as sixteen gauge. Gauge was based upon a ball size the number of which would equal a pound. So sixteen gauge is the size of a bore that will accept a ball one-sixteenth of a pound. Twelve gauge would admit a ball twelve of which would equal a pound.

When elongated bullets were cast for the .69-caliber arms the weight ranged from 650 grains to 810 grains depending upon the design of the bullet. These new bullets weighed about two ounces or twice that of the round ball. The powder charge was sixty-eight grains of musket powder. Colonel Huger had this to say:

"There are objections to using the elongated bullet in any form with the musket caliber—0.69 inch viz:

1st. The great weight of the ball, which, for the 'tige' weighs 1 oz. This makes the weight of the ammunition to be carried by the soldier quite burdensome, and the transportation of sufficient supplies over our extended frontiers would be very expensive.

2d. With this weight of ball, the charge of powder must be limited by the recoil the men can bear."[6]

Appendix II

Supplemental Letters

From Huger Family Papers, Virginia Historical Society, Box 1 of 8, 2006.0187

April 9th/50

My dear Huger
    Since writing to you yesterday about fuse metal I have seen mentioned other proportions of composition to type metal besides 16 lead to 1 antimony — I [unclear, think perhaps] that may be too soft, & yesterday I tried 12 lead & 1 antimony, which I think will answer very well — I directed the antimony to be got as pure as possible —...
                      Yours A. Mordecai
    If you find 12 to 1 too soft, add more antimony.

Editor's note: Huger and Mordecai were looking for a hard lead alloy for fuse metal. Type metal referred to was printers' type, which was a hard lead alloy to stand the pressure of the printing press. Competition shooters who choose to shoot lead bullets at relatively high velocities mix antimony with lead in various proportions to achieve a hard lead alloy for casting bullets.

Appointment to Command of Harpers Ferry Armory

Benjamin Huger

Fort Monroe Arsenal
July 26th 1851

Col H. K. Craig
Ordnance Dept.
Sir,
    I have received your instructions of the 24th inst.' and shall immediately

make all preparations to turn over the Command of this Arsenal to Major Ramsay when he arrives.

As regards my assignment to the command of the Harpers Ferry Armory, as that [Huger crossed out "that" and replaced it with "it"] *is one of the largest establishments in charge of the Ordnance Dept. and has always been assigned to a field officer I do not wish to take it in preference to the seniors, Majors Bell and Harding and Br. Major Mordecai, all of whom are entitled to that Command before myself.*

[Unclear, blurred] *honneur the public interest requires that I should be selected for that post, I request you will lay my claim before the Secretary of War to be assigned to duty by brevet according to command.*

I am Col Your ob. Servt.
Benj. Huger Br. Col.

Ordnance office
July 29th 1851

B. Col. B. Huger
Ft. Monroe Arsenal

Sir,

Your letter of the 26th inst. was received yesterday. Col Craig is now temporarily absent from the Ordnance office having left here yesterday afternoon. Before leaving he instructed me to inform that your service at Harpers Ferry Armory could not be dispensed with and that your assignment to duty according to brevet rank must be left for future consideration.

I am Respectfully
Your ob. Servt. Wm. Maynadier
Capt. Of Ord.
In charge of Ord. Dept.

Fort Monroe Arsenal
July 31st 1851

Colonel H. K. Craig
Ordnance Dept.

Sir,

In reply to your letter of the 29th inst. I beg leave to state that I did not intend to ask to be relieved from the assignment to Harper's Ferry Armory; but if, as stated in your letter of the 29th inst. "that my service at Harper's Ferry Armory cannot be dispensed with" I claim "that as it is one of the largest estab-

lishments in charge of the Ordnance Dept. and has always been commanded by a field officer, my being selected for this command does put me on duty as a field officer. The regulations require before an officer can exercise brevet rank in this case that he should be specially assigned in orders, I therefore request you to write at your earliest convenience explain the case to the Secretary of War, and ask his authority to give the necessary order."

      I am Sir Your ob. Servt. Benj. Huger
      B. Col.

            Ordnance office
            Washington July 31st 1851

Bvt. Col. B. Huger
Fort Monroe Arsenal
Sir,

 As requested in your letter of the 26th July 1851 your claim to be assigned to duty by brevet according to the command at Harper's Ferry Armory has been submitted to the Secretary of War — He stated that his decision in the Case of a similar application from Bvt. Lt. Col. Ripley was applicable to yours. That decision was on a letter from Bvt. Lt. Col. Ripley dated US Armory Springfield Feby 14 1851 applying to be recognized as entitled to the pay of his brevet rank, under the law and according to the usages of the Army and the previous decisions of the War Dept. in like cases. It was dated War Department April 29 1851, and was in these words; The persons employed at Springfield Armory are civilians only, and though the station is an important one, the portion of it that may be military does not constitute a command according to the Rank of Lieut Colonel."

      I am very Respectfully ect.
      Wm. Maynadier
      Capt. Of Ordnance

Activities at Harpers Ferry Armory, Military/Civilian Superintendents

 The following excerpts are from the Establishment of the Harpers Ferry Armory, extracts from 33rd Congress, 1st session, House of Representatives, Miscellaneous Document No. 76, May 18, 1854. They can be found on-line at http://wvculture.org/history/businessand industry/harpersferryarmory05.html. The text contained Colonel Benjamin Huger's answers to questions asked by the congressional committee, whose members were Mr. Stanton, Kentucky; Mr.

Dawson, Pennsylvania; Mr. Dickinson, Massachusetts; Mr. Faulkner, Virginia; Mr. Vansant, Maryland; Mr. Sapp, Ohio; and Mr. Keitt, South Carolina.

While Colonel Huger's answers to the questions asked him are included here to list some of his achievements while in command at Harpers Ferry Armory, the testimony overall and the purpose of the committee was to determine if military supervision of the national armories was superior to the civilian superintendents who had been in charge prior to the administration of President William H. Harrison. The mission of the committee was stated as follows:

> *"Resolved, That a special committee of seven members be appointed by the Speaker, to inquire and report to this House whether the appointment of military officers to superintend the manufacture of firearms at the national armories, ... is compatible with the public interest, and consistent with the nature and character of our civil government;..."*

This testimony was given to the committee by Colonel Huger on Thursday, March 30, 1854.

Q. Can you say in what respect changes have been made conducive to the order and economy of the establishment?

A. The order requiring the men to furnish their own oil and files has produced that effect. Formerly, the government furnished the oil. Now, the men are charged with it. The consumption now, in comparison with what it was under the old plan, is small. It is the same way with the files. I cannot state exactly what the reduction amounted to, but I suppose some of the papers on file in the department will show it. The men became more careful in the use of the oil and files when they were aware they were charged to them. Notwithstanding this charge, owing to the exercise of care and more facilities, the workmen's pay amounts to more now than it did then. [The idea of charging the workmen for sperm oil and files originated at Springfield Armory in 1850.][1]

Q. Were the rules printed and accessible to the workmen, and were any rules enforced which were merely verbal?

A. Major Symington [John Symington commanded at Harpers Ferry immediately before Colonel Huger] had them written and posted up. I had them printed. Verbal orders, which may be construed into rules, were also made from time to time.

Q. What is the character of the buildings at Harper's Ferry, and are they constructed with an eye to economy and convenience?

A. They are well constructed, and are excellent shops. Only one shop built under the civil system remains, and that has been thoroughly repaired.

The buildings under the civil system were very ordinary. Those now erected were built after the plan of the French arsenals, with plenty of light, the only expensive item about them being cast-iron window-frames.

Q. What changes have been made in any of the buildings since you took charge of them?

A. A machine-shop at the rifle-works has been built, and the machinery for the tilt-hammer shop at the musket factory has been erected. The bell-shop and boring-mill have been repaired. The rolling-mill has been nearly finished. Some new roofs have been put on the shops, and a blacksmith shop has been thoroughly rebuilt in the interior.

Q. Why was it that this blacksmith shop had to be rebuilt in the interior?

A. A tall shaft was made, as an experiment, to answer as a draught for all the forges. This plan, which succeeded very well in other places, failed there — owing, no doubt, to the fact of the place being surrounded by mountains. I remedied the failure there by paving the floor all over, putting in new forges complete, with a sheet-iron stack to every two forges, and by building a ventilator above the whole roof. These improvements to remedy this defect cost several thousand dollars. It was somewhere between six and eight thousand dollars.

Q. Under the military superintendence, have the improvements in the facilities of manufacturing arms kept pace with the improvements in private armories, and armories in other countries which you have visited?

A. They have. The improvements have been great, and have been assimilated, as far as we could, to the advance in machinery in the country generally. Whilst I was in charge, I visited manufactories at the north, and more than once sent a principal workman to do so, and to procure machinery. As far as the machinery is concerned, the establishment is far ahead of any I have seen in Europe.

I visited the royal manufactories at Enfield, England, the only government establishment in that country; the large contract factories at Birmingham, England, two of the French armories at Mulzig and Chatteiraut, and the government manufactory at Potsdam, in Prussia. All of these establishments are under military superintendence, except the contract factories at Birmingham. These factories make for the government, by contract, the parts of an arm. The government has a small shop at Birmingham where, under the supervision of a royal inspector, the parts made by contract are inspected and verified, and some of the minute work of an arm finished.

Q. Do the national armories of this country keep pace with the best private manufactories?

A. I cannot say positively. The attempt has been to keep up to the best machinery, &c. Some of those establishments have the very best.

Q. Is not the machinery at Harper's Ferry more highly finished than that in private factories, and for that reason more expensive?

A. Of this I have no exact knowledge. I have purchased machinery of those establishments, which I have always understood to be the same as that used by them.

Q. Can you state whether arms are manufactured at our national armories as cheaply as they are furnished by contractor; and how do the two description of arms compare with each other?

A. Some years since, the private factories were permitted to furnish arms to the government at the same price per arm as it cost the government to make them in its own armories. Of late years the price has been so reduced in the national armories, that the private factories have not furnished any, because they could not do it so cheap. I think it was since the Mexican war that they stopped. The government has continued to procure rifles from those factories, which compare favorably with the rifles manufactured at the national armories, but for which they have to be paid more.

The following testimony Colonel Huger gave the next day, March 31, 1854. It had to do with costs, production numbers and workmen's conditions.

Q. What expenditures, in your judgment, rightly enter into the cost of arms at the armory?

A. In my judgment, all materials used in its construction, all the ordinary repairs of the building and machinery to keep them in good order, and the wages of labor used in their construction; that is, all the appropriations made by Congress for the manufacture of arms, and such portion of the appropriations for repairs and improvements as is actually applied to the repairs of the shops and machinery.

Q. What expenditures are directed by the ordnance regulations to be charged to the manufacture of arms?

A. I could not state in detail, as there other items independent of those contained in the regulations, which are charged to the manufacture of arms: for instance, when I went to Harper's Ferry I ordered the grounds to be lit; the question arose as to whether the item of light should be charged to the cost of the arm. The department decided that it should be charged to the cost of the arm. The expense warming the shops is also charged. In addition to this, the wages of foreman, expenses of office hire, of clerks, are charged to its cost; all of which expense amounts to the same, whether there is one gun made, or one hundred. We also debit the buildings and machinery, every year, with a depreciation, on account of their use.

Q. In your opinion, is the property, machinery, &c., at the armories, in such a condition as to make necessary a continuance of the usual special appropriations, made every year, to the extent they have been for the past few years?

A. I think not. So far as Harper's Ferry is concerned, appropriations for machinery will be wanted, but none for buildings, as they are all in the best condition. At Springfield there will be some wanted, as the shops are very narrow, and unfit for their purposes.

Q. With the present machinery and improvements, can you give an idea of the extreme capacity of the armories?

A. About 40,000 stand a year.

Q. State what is the usual number of arms made each year at the armories?

A. There have been made at Springfield 20,000 arms, and at Harper's Ferry 16,000 or 17,000 arms in a year; but without having papers before me, I think I can say the average at Springfield has been 16,000, and at Harper's Ferry 12,000 arms per year. The appropriation would only justify the manufacture at Harper's Ferry of 750 muskets and 250 rifles per month. These arms have been distributed mostly to the States; the army receives but a small portion of them; some are kept in store. There now about half a million of arms on hand, to the best of my knowledge.

Q. Had you any difficulty in procuring a suitable supply of skilful [sic] and competent workmen for Harper's Ferry armory?

A. There were a great many workmen (but they were not very competent) constantly applying for situations. Competent men from abroad would not come there, because they did not like the place.

Q. Please state whether the workmen employed are cheerful and contented, and give ready obedience to the regulations and discipline of the establishment?

A. There has been a great deal of discontent evinced since the discussion of the proposed change in the system of superintendency; but it has been shown principally by those who have responsible duties to perform, and who, anticipating a change, are afraid that they might offend men under them; not by open insubordination, because no man is permitted to remain in the armory who practices that.

Q. How frequent are the discharges of workmen, and generally for what causes?

A. The discharges were very few during the time I was superintendent, for any other cause than exhaustion of appropriations. I had painful duty to discharge one-third of the men at one time on account of the appropriation having been reduced.

Q. Is the usual military education such as to give an officer practical knowledge of the qualities of the various materials which enter into the construction of an arm?

A. Not the military education at West Point; but the officer having charge of an armory, will soon acquire a knowledge to a sufficient extent. At West Point they learn the sciences, and receive a better theoretical education than a man outside of it could possibly acquire; but it is not necessary for the commandant of an armory to be acquainted with the particular branches of work there executed; he has officers under him that understand them. Even if he did, his military duties would consume too much of his time to enable him to look over all the various branches.

Q. What, in your judgment, should be the qualifications of a master-armorer, in view of his duties as prescribed by the ordnance regulations?

A. As his duties are to attend to all mechanical operations, and also to the inspection of the materials and finished work, as well as to distribute out all work, he should be a practical mechanic, capable of superintending all the operations; sufficiently informed If the working of machinery and its principles to be able to recommend the most suitable and best for the purposes required.

Q. What advantage, if any, does a military officer have, that a civilian would not have, in making improvements in arms, machinery, &c., and in the development of the inventive capacity of the workmen at the armories?

A. The advantage he has is, that his place is not dependent on the pleasure of those under him. The officers sent to those places have great experience, and understand the organization of men better than a civilian would. They have a practice in the use of arms, and on that account may know more about arms than a civilian would.

This is the end of the questions for Colonel Huger by this committee. His testimony gives a snapshot of his projects and accomplishments at Harpers Ferry Armory.

Benjamin Huger's Report on Operations at Norfolk

Copy

Headquarters Dept. Norfolk
Norfolk Va. Febr. 16th 1862

General S[amuel] Cooper
Adjt. & Insp. Genl.
Sir

I submit for the consideration of the Secretary of War a proposed arrangement of the Brigades of this division, rendered necessary by the movement of the enemy.

I had sent the 6th Va. Regt. Col. [Thomas Jefferson] *Corprew to the Currituck bridge, with orders to hold that point and prevent the enemy from passing through the South branch of the Chesapeake and Albemarle Canal.*

General [Henry A.] *Wise on his retreat from Nag's head came to Currituck Bridge, assumed command, removed the battery of three 32 pdrs. erected there and began abandoning the place before any enemy appeared. Soon after two or three row boats came up, fired a few rounds, which fell short, and our troops left. The enemy have not advanced since, and our Cavalry pickets are still there.*

I had no report from General Wise for two days, but heard he was falling back on Norfolk. I sent yesterday to establish batteries near Great Bridge, on the north branch of the Albemarle and Chesapeake Canal to block that passage and visited that place to day. I found General Wise there, with the five Companies of the 6th Va. Regt. Five pieces of artillery under Col [Charles Frederick] *Henningsen, and about four companies of his* [General Henry A. Wise] *Legion under Col* [John Harvie] *Richardson.*

I enquired of General Wise why he abandoned his position at Currituck bridge <u>without orders,</u> but could get no satisfactory answer. He said he intended to occupy a position on N. W. River, but on reaching there in a snow storm found no quarters for his men he fell back to Great Bridge, twelve miles south of Norfolk where he now is.

I must be allowed to consider General Wise supernumerary with his army and relieve him from duty. His Legion has no doubt fine material, but I consider it entirely disorganized and I shall feel stronger if it is removed.

I am Sir, Very respectfully
(signed) Benjm. Huger
Maj. Genl Commdg.[2]

Benjamin Huger Asks for a Court of Enquiry

Charleston, South Carolina
November 1862

Honr. G. W. Randolph,
Sec'y of War
Sir,

As I hear Genl. J. E. Johnston has reported for duty I hope before he is assigned to any distant command the "exigencies of the service" may permit you to grant me the Court of Enquiry promised. As Genl Johnston's published report of the battle of "Seven Pines," ignored the presence of the Division I then commanded at that battle, it is but justice to the whole of the Division, as well as

myself, that the Court of Enquiry [word faded and unclear] by the President should be assembled as soon as possible.
>Very Respectfully Your Obt. Servt.
>Benj Huger Major General[3]

Benjamin Huger Appointed Inspector of Ordnance and Artillery

>Adjutant and Inspector General's Office,
>Richmond, August 26, 1862.

GENERAL ORDERS,
No. 62

Major General Huger having been appointed Inspector of Ordnance and Artillery for the C. S. Army, is authorized to inspect and examine into all the establishments of the Ordnance Department, and the Works of all Contractors for this Department, including all foundries, and mines of iron, lead, copper and nitre working under permanent contract, and the condition and armament of all forts and batteries, and to give such orders and instructions as will tend to increase their efficiency. All Commanding Officers and others in charge of such works, are required to give him all facilities and assistance in their power in the performance of his duties. Such orders and instructions as he may consider necessary, and as do not conflict with the Orders of this Department, will be considered the Orders of the War Department, and will be transmitted, at once, through the office of the Chief of Ordnance. Reports of inspections will be remitted to the War Department, through the same channels. The rules and mode of inspection will be, in other respects, in conformity with section II of the Regulations of the Ordinance Department and are required to furnish transportation to himself and his aids and assistants, on his order. Where there are no lines of transportation, he will procure it, and keep an account of the actual expenses; which account will be paid by the Quartermaster's Department, on his certificate and order.[4]

Orders to the Trans-Mississippi Department

>Head Quarters Dept. Trans-Miss.
>SHREVEPORT, LA. JULY 27TH, 1863

General Orders
No. 32.

Major General B. Huger is announced as Chief of the Bureau of Ordnance for the Department of the Trans Mississippi. All returns and reports, required by the Regulations to be made to the Chief of the Bureau at Richmond, will in future be made to Maj. Genl. Huger.

The Chief of the Nitre & Mining Bureau and Iron Interests West of the Mississippi, will also report to Major Genl. Huger.

By command of
Lieut. Gen'l E. Kirby Smith,
S. S. ANDERSON,
Ass't. Adj't. Gen'l.[5]

Parole of Honor Papers

Following the surrender of General E. Kirby Smith's Trans-Mississippi Department Major General Benjamin Huger and his two sons, Benjamin Jr. and Eustis, signed the following papers. They were numbered 57, 406 and 717 respectively. The general signed on June 12, 1865, and gave his residence as Richmond, Virginia; Ben Jr. signed one day later than his father and gave his residence simply as Virginia. They both signed at Shreveport, Louisiana. Eustis signed on August 7, 1865, at the arsenal at Marshall, Texas, giving his residence as Elizabeth City Co., Virginia. He served as first aide de camp on ordnance duty to his father at the time of his signing his parole papers.

The oath on the printed paper read: "I, the undersigned, Prisoner of War, belonging to the Army of the Trans-Mississippi Department, having been surrendered by General E. Kirby Smith, C. S. A. Commanding said Department, to Major General E. R. S. Canby, U. S. A., Commanding Army and Division of West Mississippi, do hereby give my solemn PAROLE OF HONOR, that I will not hereafter serve in the Armies of the Confederate States, or in any military capacity whatever, against the United States of America, or render aid to the enemies of the latter, until properly exchanged in such manner as shall be mutually approved by the respective authorities."

Signing the Parole of Honor, approved by two Union officers, granted to the signer the following: "The above named officer will not be disturbed by the United States Authorities, as long as he observes his parole, and the laws in force where he resides." Imprinted on the bottom of the form was the name of the provost marshal general, Brigadier General George L. Andrews.[6]

APPENDIX III

Ordnance Chief Colonel Henry Knox Craig on Civilian Superintendents of the National Armories

ORDNANCE OFFICE
Washington, Feb. 8th, 1853

The subject of a change in the system of management of the National Armories is now before the Legislature of the country. Misrepresentations in regard to it have been extensively circulated. These misrepresentations, if suffered to pass unnoticed, may mislead many to the advocacy and support of a measure fraught with serious mischief to the public service in one of its important branches. As the person charged with the immediate administration of that branch, and responsible for its proper management — it is my duty to see that it receives no injury which it may be in my power, honestly, and truthfully to prevent. I therefore present the following statement, and ask the members of the National Legislature to give it a careful examination, and to pause and enquire, before taking a step, which my long experience, acquired in a life devoted to this particular business, and my best judgment and reflection tell me, will very seriously injure the public interest.

In April, 1841, the Civil Superintendents of the two National Armories were removed from office by direction of the President of the United States, and Officers of the Ordnance Corps were detailed to direct the concerns of each of the Armories, agreeably to the 9th Section of the Act of February 8th, 1815, which places the public armories under the direction of the Ordnance Department.[1]

In the following August, a Board of Citizens was appointed by the War Department, to examine into the condition and management of one of the Armories. That board made a full examination; and their report is published in Document No. 297, House Reps., 27th Congress 2d Session. I respectfully ask your attention to it, particularly to their views in regard to the system of Superintendence on page 5 of the Document.

By the 2d section of the act of the 23d of August, 1842, the offices of Civil Superintendents of the Armories were abolished, and their duties were devolved on officers of the Ordnance Corps to be detailed by the President, and this system of superintendence has continued since. When the officers of the Ordnance Corps took charge of the Armories, they found many abuses existing, the correction of which, and the complete reformation of the manner of conducting operations, were imperatively demanded by the public interest. This reformation was violently opposed by those who had been profiting by the abuses. They availed themselves of the plea of military despotism, and oppression of citizens by officers of the Army, and succeeded in arraigning the Superintendent of Springfield Armory before a Court of Enquiry on various charges. The proceedings of that court, which show a full, impartial and patient investigation of all the allegations against the Superintendent, involving also the comparative merits of the military and civil systems of superintendence, are published, in full, in Senate Document No. 344, 29th Congress, 1st session. I respectfully refer you to this document for information on the subject, and particularly to the testimony of Mr. Pomeroy , page 150 to 152; and to the opinion of the Court, as derived from testimony under oath, pages 199 to 205. The diminution in the cost of arms, and the improvement in their quality, found, by this enquiry, to have taken place, since the superintendence of the armories by Ordnance officers, have steadily continued; and the operations of the last fiscal year will show a far greater return for the amount expended, than was ever exhibited in the best days of the civil superintendence. At the same time, the workmen receive as good, if not better wages, than are paid at private establishments for the same services and skill, and they actually receive more than they did under the old system. Of these assertions there can be no doubt, for they are demonstrated by facts and figures.

The saving of labor on a musket, at Springfield Armory, since 1841, is $3.84, making a total on 23,000 manufactured in 1851 of more than $88,000. The average pay received by each workman in the year 1840-'41, the last of civil superintendence, was $37,87 per month; in the year 1850-'51 it was $38,84. An examination of the arms, made under the two systems, will shew immediately and conclusively, a great superiority in quality for those last made. The Springfield Armory, taken altogether, will compare favorably, in all respects, with the best conducted manufactories in our country; and it is now fully equal, if not superior, to any manufactory of arms of any other nation.

Although the Harper's Ferry Armory is still behind that at Springfield, the improvements there, since the change of the system of superintendence, have been many and important, and are steadily advancing. It had run down, under the old system, more than the other, and requires more time to bring it up; but at both establishments a like system of administration is producing a like effect. No one acquainted with this Armory prior to 1841, and the mode of conducting operations there at that time, who will visit and examine it now, can fail to be struck with its improved condition and better management. At both Armories, abuses, disorder and confusion have given way to regularity, order, efficiency, and economy; the mode of manufacturing and the quality of the manufactures have been improved; arms are made at less cost; the workmen are better paid; their moral character is of a higher grade, and the great majority of them are satisfied and contented. These are the fruits of the system now existing.

That some of the workmen, employed at the Armories, should have been discharged, is not to be wondered at. They had acquired, under the loose management of the old system, habits altogether unsuited to the stricter one of the new. A change of measures was absolutely necessary to a faithful, efficient and economical government of the establishments, and it was impossible to effect it without a change of men. The removals and discharges have been as few as possible, consistently with the public interest, and have, in no instance, been made without cause, and, good cause. Political influence or personal feeling, I have good reason to believe, and do consciouniously believe, have had nothing to do with them.

If the present system of superintendence should be abolished, this Department will still do its best for the proper management of the Armories, but I have not the least doubt that it will prove highly injurious, almost ruinous, to the efficiency of these establishments and to the interests of the country connected with them.

One argument has been advanced in favor of the proposed change, which seems plausible, and on that account may be worthy of such brief notice, as may be requisite to expose its fallacy. It is, that the superintendence of the National Armories is not a proper duty for *Officers of the Army*, who should be at the head of troops in the field; in command, only, of trained and disciplined soldiers. This is very true of a certain portion of the Officers of the Army. But the laws of our land include, in our Army, other officers, besides those to lead and command the troops; and define their duties too, which, if less brilliant and striking in their nature are not the less essential to the efficiency of the Military service. Among these officers, are those, whose duty and business it is to erect fortifications, to survey roads, to provide food, clothing and shelter for the troops, to transport all Military supplies, and to contrive, construct and supply all arms and munitions of War. These duties require education and experience for their proper performance; and the officers who perform them, first selected for their peculiar fitness for such occupations, have since added to that fitness the advantages acquired by experience.

To the Ordnance Corps of the Army is entrusted *by law* the construction and preparation of all arms and ammunition. Under the direction of the Ordnance Department the National Armories are placed *by law*. To remove its officers, therefore, from the immediate charge of these establishments, and to place them under civilians, who will doubtless be men of high political influence, either personally or through their friends, and whom *a department of the army* cannot, from the nature of things, control, will be to do the great injustice to that Department of requiring from it by law, that which the passage of the law, now before you, will deprive it of the means of accomplishing.

H. K. CRAIG,
Colonel Ordnance.

APPENDIX IV

Men at West Point When Frank Huger Attended

Alexander, Edward Porter—(1835–1910) Born in Georgia. West Point class of 1857. Chief of artillery in General James Longstreet's First Corps, Army of Northern Virginia. Rose to the rank of brigadier general in the Army of Northern Virginia and held the post of chief of artillery in that army. Commanded the Confederate artillery barrage at Gettysburg prior to Pickett's Charge.

Ames, Adelbert—(1835–1933) Born in Maine. West Point class of 1861. Became a Union general. Colonel of the 20th Maine. Fought throughout the Civil War, wounded at First Manassas. Served as brigadier general in the Spanish-American War.

Anderson, Robert—(1805–1871) West Point class of 1825. Commanded at Fort Sumter.

Babcock, Orville E.—(1835–1884) Born in Vermont. West Point class of 1861. Served throughout the Civil War, became aide-de-camp to General Ulysses Grant.

Bayard, George D.—(1835–1862) Born in New York. West Point class of 1856. Commanded First Pennsylvania Cavalry, killed at Fredericksburg, Virginia.

Cushing, Alonzo H.—(1841–1863) Born in New York. West Point class of 1861. Killed at Gettysburg, July 3, 1863, fighting his Battery B, 4th U.S. Artillery, during Pickett's Charge.

Custer, George A.—(1839–1876) Born in Ohio. West Point class of 1861. Cavalry officer during the Civil War, made brigadier general before the Battle of Gettysburg. Captured Frank Huger at Sailor's Creek in 1865. Killed at the Battle of Little Big Horn.

Dearing, James—(1840–1865) Born in Virginia. West Point class of 1862, resigned in 1861. Confederate officer, he may have been the last officer to die, April 22, 1865.

DuPont, Henry A.—(1838–1926) Born in Delaware. West Point class of 1861. Served in the Union Army throughout the Civil War with the Army of the Potomac. Remained in the army until 1875. Active in Delaware politics.

Field, Charles W.—(1828–1892) Born in Kentucky. West Point class of 1849. Confederate general.

Gibbes, Wade H.—(1837–1903) Born in South Carolina. West Point class of 1860. Served in the Confederate service, wounded at the Crater. Brother-in-law to E. P. Alexander. Fought a sword duel with Emory Upton as a cadet.

Gibbon, John—(1827–1896) West Point class of 1846. Union general, commanded a division in the Second Corps, Army of the Potomac. Served in the west during the Indian wars.

Gilmore, Quincy A.—(1825–1888) Born in Ohio. Union general and engineer.

Hardee, William J.—(1815–1873) West Point class of 1838. Confederate general. Author of *Rifle and Light Infantry Tactics*.

Hartsuff, George L.—(1830–1874) West Point class of 1852. Union officer.

Heintzelman, Samuel P.—(1805–1880) West Point class of 1826. Commanded the Union 3rd and 4th Corps early in the war.

Henry, Mathis W.—(1838–1877) Born in Kentucky. West Point class of 1860. Served in the Confederate service throughout the war. On Jeb Stuart's staff, horse artillery and commanded an artillery battalion in John B. Hood's division.

Howard, Oliver O.—(1830–1909) West Point class of 1854. Union officer, commanded the Eleventh Corps, head of the Freedman's Bureau.

Lee, Fitzhugh—(1835–1905) Born in Virginia. West Point class of 1856. This famous cavalry officer was nephew to General Robert E. Lee. Wounded in 1859 on the western plains, Lee instructed cavalry at West Point from 1860 until the outbreak of the Civil War. Served throughout the war under Jeb Stuart. Elected governor of Virginia and served in the Spanish-American War.

Lomax, Lunsford L.—(1835–1913) Born in Rhode Island. West Point class of 1856. Confederate cavalry general.

Lovejoy, George Steptoe—(1839–1862) Attended West Point.

Mahan, Dennis H.—(1802–1871) West Point class of 1824. Lifelong instructor at West Point.

Marmaduke, John S.—(1833–1887) Born in Missouri. West Point class of 1857. Confederate general.

Meade, Richard Kidder, Jr.—(1835–1862) Born in Virginia. West Point class of 1860. Left the Federal service for the Confederacy after the bombardment of Fort Sumter. Killed at Petersburg.

Merritt, Wesley—(1836–1910) Born in New York. West Point class of 1860. Union cavalry officer, conspicuous at Brandy Station. Service on the western plains, service in Spanish-American War. Attained rank of major general.

O'Rorke, Patrick H.—(1836–1863) West Point class of 1861. Killed at Gettysburg, colonel of 140th New York.

Pegram, John—(1832–1865) Born in Virginia. West Point class of 1854. Confederate general, killed at the end of the war.

Pelham, John—(1838–1863) Born in Alabama. Attended West Point. Captain Pelham's Battery of Horse Artillery. Killed in action at Felly's Ford, Virginia, March 17, 1863.

Porter, Horace—(1837–1921) Born in Pennsylvania. West Point class of 1860. Served throughout the Civil War as ordnance officer, then on General Ulysses Grant's staff.

Ramseur, Stephen D.—(1837–1864) West Point class of 1860. Confederate general, killed at Cedar Creek.

Reno, Marcus A.—(1834–1889) West Point class of 1855. Civil War service in which he received brevets for meritorious service. With Custer at Little Big Horn.

Reynolds, John F.—(1820–1863) West Point class of 1841. Commanded Union First Corps. Killed at Gettysburg, July 1, 1863.

Rosser, Thomas L.—(1836–1910) Born in Virginia. West Point class of 1861, resigned before graduating. Classmate and friend of George A. Custer. Confederate cavalry officer, served under Jeb Stuart.

Schaff, Morris—(1840–1929) West Point class of 1862. Union ordnance officer. Wrote the book *The Battle of the Wilderness.*

Schofield, John M.—(1831–1906) West Point class of 1853. Instructor at West Point, Union general.

Stoughton, Edwin H.—(1838–1868) Born in Vermont. West Point class of 1859. Union general.

Upton, Emory—(1839–1881) Born in New York. West Point class of 1861. An abolitionist, Upton fought a duel with swords with classmate Wade Hampton Gibbes. Union officer during the Civil War, military intellectual who wrote on military policy for the United States and infantry tactics.

Warren, Gouverneur K.—(1830–1882) West Point class of 1850. Union general, engineer, commander of Federal Fifth Corps in Overland Campaign.

Webb, Alexander S.—(1835–1911) West Point class of 1855. Taught mathematics at West Point 1857–1861. Division commander in the Federal Second Corps.

Weir, Robert W.—(1803–1889) Held position of drawing instructor at West Point for forty-two years.

Whistler, James McNeill—(1834–1903) attended West Point, American artist.

Wilcox, Cadmus M.—(1825–1890) West Point class of 1846. Confederate general. Author of *Rifles and Rifle Practice* and *History of the Mexican War.*

Young, Pierce M. B.—(1836–1896) Born in South Carolina. West Point class of 1861, resigned before graduation. Confederate general.

Appendix V

Report of the 1840 Board of Ordnance

Writing his annual report for 1839 to Secretary of War Joel R. Poinsett, Lieutenant Colonel George Talcott, chief of ordnance, provided some background leading to the secretary's appointing a four-man board to go to Europe the following year. The following excerpt is from the *Report from the Ordnance Department, Report of the Secretary of War,* November 29, 1839, page 87.

"With reference to the operations of this department during the present year, I respectfully state, that the board of ordnance officers has been assiduously engaged in reducing to a system the mode of fabricating all kinds of ordnance stores, in fixing their patterns, forms and dimensions, and preparing drawings of the same. Comparative trials have been made of different field guns of brass and iron, with a view to decide their proper weight and dimensions, as well as the material most suitable for field artillery. Brass guns have been manufactured which afford evidence of skill in that branch of the arts. The trials with iron are still in process, and will be prosecuted as long as the season will permit.

"In connection with this subject, I am bound to advert to the advantages to be derived from establishing a national foundry, at which by suitable trials and experiments some process could be adopted, whereby a greater uniformity in the quality of castings might be attained. If a larger number of cannon can be fabricated perfectly similar in their qualities, the heavy proof, to which all are now subjected, might be applied to but a small proportion, and the residue be tested with full services charges only. This course would prevent the greater number of guns from being injured in proving, as no doubt has been sometimes the case."

One year later [December 5, 1840], writing his annual report to Secretary of War Poinsett, ordnance chief Talcott wrote:

"Having repeatedly recommended, without effect, the establishment of a national foundry; having reason to fear the most serious consequences to the service from the want of proper regulations to govern contracts with private establishments; with your consent, I sent to Europe the board of officers who had been for some time employed in fixing the patterns, forms, and dimensions of the artillery, in order that they might acquire such information as would enable the department permanently to regulate this important branch of the service. I am happy to state that, wherever they have been, the national establishments have been thrown open to them, and, with praiseworthy liberality, every facility afforded to their researches. They have returned home, after having attained all the data which were expected from their investigations; and the knowledge they have acquired will be applied to the practical improvement of our ordnance. A concise report of their of their proceedings while in Europe is herewith transmitted, in connexion [sic] with that of the officers in charge of the Ordnance Department."[1]

The four member board consisted of Major Rufus L. Baker, captains Alfred Mordecai and Benjamin Huger and foundry man William Wade. They sailed from New York on April 1, 1840, and arrived in London on April 17. From time to time the board split into two, two-man teams and visited different sites. While in Great Britain they traveled to the foundry at Woolwich, the naval establishment at Chatham, the small arms manufactory at Enfield, Waltham Abbey powder works, the cannon foundry at Gospel Oak, the Alfreton Iron works, and iron works at Low Moor and Carron.

Leaving Great Britain they proceeded to Sweden again to visit foundries, iron works and iron ore mines. Leaving Sweden on July 15, 1840, they proceeded to Russia via Finland, arriving at St. Petersburg on July 22. Their report substantiates Huger's letter home from St. Petersburg dated July 30, 1840. Russia had the most extensive and best arranged foundry for casting bronze guns the board had visited. Leaving Russia from St. Petersburg the board traveled to Berlin via Hamburg and reached the Prussian capital on August 10. From Berlin they visited the cities of Liege and Antwerp and then moved on to France. Their travels in France took them to Douai where they observed cannons cast in clay as opposed to the sand casting made by the Russians. From there they went to the cannon foundry in Strasbourg, one of the oldest, then on to Mutzig. Although the machinery at Mutzig was described as "rude" the factory was converting flintlock arms to percussion, an operation being considered at home by Colonel Talcott. Here the board split once again with two men going to Metz to observe experiments being conducted on ballistic pendulums. The French were testing the relation between the length of bore to initial velocities. The members met in Paris and visited other sites in France before returning to London. Back in Great Britain they made side trips to Wales before leaving to return home on November 1, 1840. They arrived in New York on November 21.

It was not all note-taking. The board made a number of purchases, primarily of castings. They bought cannons enough for two field batteries from each of the three Swedish foundries. The board bought additional cannons of iron and bronze from the foundries in Liege. They purchased a number of swords and sabres in Berlin, books and models they considered important in Paris and numerous samples of gun powder and of pit-burnt charcoal.

The small arms manufactory at Enfield was not Great Britain's main source of small arms at this time. Most British arms were made by private makers in Birmingham. There private makers fabricated the parts which were then refined and fitted together at government works. Not until the Crimean War demanded a large supply of small arms and the realization that they could be made with interchangeable parts by machine tools did Enfield become Great Britain's major armory. In its endeavor to increase arms production at Enfield the British government turned to American machine tools and American mechanical know-how to set up and supervise the Royal Small Arms Factory at Enfield, England.

While the construction of suitable artillery was the major focus of the board in Europe, small arms manufacturing was also a topic of interest. The conversion from flintlock to percussion lock was going on widespread throughout as witnessed at Mutzig. Indeed Colonel Talcott had shown his interest in the percussion lock. After writing his reluctance to accept many of the designs in arms attempting "to increase the rapidity of firing, such as facilitating the loading by opening the breech, or by multiplying the chambers," he admitted of approving of one recent development in firearms.

"There is, however," he wrote, "one improvement, which has been fairly tested in the field by the armies of Europe, and which presents so many decided and ascertained advantages, that I am constrained to recommend, its adoption into our service — I mean the substitution of percussion for flint locks. The alteration may be made on the muskets now in the arsenals, and measures ought to be adopted to construct all new arms, whether rifles or muskets, with percussion locks."[2]

Chapter Notes

Chapter One

1. Boatner, *Encyclopedia*, 532–33; Commager, *Spirit*, 1078.
2. Woodward, *Mary Chesnut*, 280.
3. Rhoades, *Scapegoat*, 23; Tate, *Eyelids*, 36.
4. Remini, *Andrew Jackson*, 175.
5. Freeman, *R. E. Lee*, vol. 1, 46–47.
6. Curti, *The Learned Blacksmith*, 90.
7. Hilen, *Longfellow*, vol. 6, 123; Donald, *Charles Sumner*, 114, 117.
8. National Archives and Records Administration, M331, Compiled Service Records of Confederate General and Staff Officers and Nonregimental Enlisted Men. Cited hereafter as NARA.
9. Weinert, *The Confederate Regular Army*, 122.
10. Elliot, *Winfield Scott*, 649.
11. Remini, *Andrew Jackson*, 299.
12. Freehling, *Prelude*, 340–43.
13. Woodward, *Mary Chesnut*, 42.
14. Racine, *Gentlemen Merchants*, 438–39.
15. Scharf, *Confederate States Navy*, 287n.
16. Woodward, *Mary Chesnut*, 222.
17. Porter, *Naval History*, 178, 183; Hearn, *Admiral Porter*, 54.
18. Woodward, *Mary Chesnut*, 385. Meta Huger was Margaret Deas Huger, wife of John Middleton Huger.
19. Cleaves, *Meade*, 357–58; Meade, *Life and Letters*, vol. 1, 266.
20. Meade, *Life and Letters*, vol. 2, 278.
21. Racine, *Gentlemen Merchants*, 856 n4.
22. Ibid., 804–05.
23. Freehling, *Prelude*, 105, 119, 202, 216.
24. Coit, *John C. Calhoun*, 53, 257; Freehling, *Prelude*, 217.

Chapter Two

1. Donald, *Charles Sumner*, 309.
2. Stampp, *America in 1857*, 128–29; Huston, *The Panic of 1857*, 16; Curti, *The Learned Blacksmith*, 131–32.
3. Crary, *Dear Belle*, 22n, 23, 58.
4. Ibid., 22.
5. *Report of the Secretary of War, 1840*, 25.
6. Connell, *Son of the Morning Star*, 28–30.
7. Price, *West Point*, 52.

8. Ibid., 9; Anderson, *Whistler*, 25–31.
9. Schaff, *Old West Point*, 37–38; Crary, *Dear Belle*, 29–38.
10. Schaff, *Old West Point*, 53.
11. NARA.
12. Ibid.

Chapter Three

1. Glatthaar, *General Lee's Army*, 119–21.
2. Simpson, *A Good Southerner*, 267–68.
3. Musicant, *Divided Waters*, 80; Freeman, *R.E. Lee*, vol. 2, 13.
4. Trotter, *Ironclads*, 65.
5. O.R. 51, part 2, 102, 105–06; Freeman, *R.E. Lee*, vol. 1, 507–08.
6. Freeman, *R.E. Lee*, vol. 2, 13.
7. Ibid., vol. 1, 119.
8. Krick, R.K., *Lee's Colonels*, 387.
9. Harsh, *Taken at the Flood*, 1.
10. Holmes, O. W., "My Hunt after 'The Captain,'" *Atlantic Monthly*, December 1862, 749.
11. Johnson, *Artillery Hell*, 18, 24, 48, 88.
12. Freeman, *Lee's Lieutenants*, vol. 1, 611.
13. Ibid., 260.
14. Huger Family papers, November 4, 1863; Woodward, *Mary Chesnut*, 116; Freemon, *Gangrene*, 33.
15. NARA.
16. O'Reilly, *Fredericksburg*, 503; Gallagher, *Fredericksburg*, 26.
17. Gallagher, *Fighting*, 169–70.
18. Krick, Robert E. L., *Staff Officers*, 175.
19. Dew, *Apostles*, 60–61, 63, 68–73; Woodward, *Mary Chesnut*, 44, 621.
20. Gallagher, *Fighting*, 163.
21. Woodward, *Mary Chesnut*, 9, 430–31, 442–43, 535; Wise, *Long Arm*, vol. 1, 419, vol. 2, 984.
22. Vandiver, *Ploughshares*, 191.
23. Freeman, *Lee's Lieutenants*, 20, 231, 278.
24. Gallagher, *Chancellorsville*, ix.
25. Krick, Robert K., *Smoothbore Volley*, 1.
26. Krick, Robert E. L., *Staff Officers*, 153.
27. Coddington, *The Gettysburg Campaign*, xi.
28. *Home Remedies*, 63.
29. Woodward, *Mary Chesnut*, 541, 544, 547, 550.
30. Gallagher, *Fighting*, 162; Krick, Robert K., *Parker's*, 180.
31. Coddington, *Gettysburg*, 537.
32. Gallagher, *Fighting*, 273.
33. Woodward, *Mary Chesnut*, 51 n 5.
34. Freeman, *R. E. Lee*, vol. 3, 163–66.
35. Wert, *General James Longstreet*, 303; Cozzens, *The Terrible Sound*, 59.
36. Longstreet, *From Manassas*, 436–37.
37. Krick, Robert E. L., *Staff Officers*, 329; Roland, *A. S. Johnston*, 285.
38. Tate, *Eyelids*, 273; Norman, *Spiller and Burr*, 40.
39. Krick, Robert K., *Parker's*, 397–400; Pfanz, *Ewell*, 279; O. R., Series 1, vol. 36, part 1, 1085.

40. Johnson, *Battles and Leaders*, vol. 3, 638.
41. NARA.
42. Roland, *A. S. Johnston*, 325.
43. Krick, Robert E. L., *Staff Officers*, 307; Longstreet, *Manassas*, 497–98.
44. Krick, Robert E. L., *Staff Officers*, 334.
45. Longstreet, *Manassas*, 343–44.
46. Gallagher, *Fighting*, 612 n 72.
47. *Confederate Field Manual*, last page, no number.
48. Gallagher, *Fighting*, 323.
49. Woodward, *Mary Chesnut*, 537.
50. Gallagher, *Fighting*, 337.
51. Woodward, *Mary Chesnut*, entries for January and February 1864, 659.
52. Woodward, *Mary Chesnut*, 591.
53. Krick, Robert K., *Parker's*, 252–53.
54. Castel, *Decision in the West*, 44.
55. Woodward, *Mary Chesnut*, 536.
56. Gallagher, *Fighting*, 595 n 19.
57. Woodward, *Mary Chesnut*, 595.
58. Gallagher, *The Wilderness*, ix.
59. Steere, *The Wilderness Campaign*, 1.
60. Matter, *If it Takes All Summer*, 342, 349.
61. Humphreys, *The Virginia Campaign—1864*, 1–9.
62. Rhea, *North Anna*, 153.
63. Ibid., 131.
64. Gallagher, *Fighting*, 338.
65. Ibid., 597 n 65.
66. Freeman, *Lee's Lieutenants* vol. 2, 169.
67. Woodward, *Mary Chesnut*, 665–66.
68. Krick, Robert E. L., *Staff Officers*, 62.
69. Gallagher, *Fighting*, 441, 445, 446.
70. Simpson, *A Good Southerner*, 83.
71. Greene, *The Petersburg Campaign*, i.
72. Krick, Robert E. L., *Staff Officers*, 238; Greene, *Petersburg Campaign*, 482 n 5.
73. Gallagher, *Fighting*, 468.
74. Woodward, *Mary Chesnut*, 623.
75. O. R., Series 1, vol. 40, part 3, 810.
76. Bates, *History*, vol. 1, 1199–1202; Marvel, *Burnside*, 390–91.
77. Meade, *Life and Letters*, vol. 2, 217–18.
78. U.S. Congress, *Army of the Potomac*, vol. 1, introduction.
79. Tap, *Over Lincoln's Shoulder*, 2.
80. Gallagher, *Fighting*, 265–66.
81. Kerby, *Kirby Smith's Confederacy*, 178–79.

Chapter Four

1. Harris, *Norfolk & Western*, 7–10.

Chapter Five

1. Johnson, Robert U., ed. *Battles and Leaders*, vol. 4, 719–20.
2. Ibid., 721–22.

3. Wise, Jennings C., *Long Arm of Lee*, vol. 2, 664, 677, 693–94.
4. Krick, Robert K., *Parker's*, 179, 188–89.

Chapter Six

1. Birkhimer, *Artillery*, 265. Major Rufus L. Baker, Captain Alfred Mordecai and former ordnance captain and foundry-man William Wade along with Huger made up the team.
2. Schneller, *A Quest for Glory*, 65–66.
3. Krasnoye Selo, literally Red Village, was outside St. Petersburg and was the czar's summer residence.
4. U.S. House of Representatives, *Harpers Ferry Armory*, Huger's testimony.
5. Huntington, *Hall's Breechloaders*, 86, 225.
6. Alexander, E. Porter, *Military Memoirs*, 93.
7. Vandiver, *Ploughshares*, 157.
8. Iobst, *Civil War Macon*, 165, 197, 244.
9. O. R., Series 1, vol. 22, part 2, 907.
10. Parks, *Kirby Smith*, 351–52.
11. O. R., Series 1, vol. 22, part 2, 1139–1142.
12. Current, *The Confederacy*, 613–14.
13. Vandiver, *Ploughshares*, 191–92.
14. Parks, *General Kirby Smith*, 474–78 n 43.

Appendix I

1. *Small Arms, 1856*, 87; Wilcox, *Rifles and Rifle Practice*, 200.
2. Fuller, *The Rifled Musket*, 2, 4.
3. *Small Arms, 1856*, 11.
4. Tate, *Eyelids*, 42–55.
5. *Small Arms, 1856*, 11–12.
6. Ibid., 14.

Appendix II

1. Tate, *Eyelids*, 33.
2. NARA, 331.
3. Ibid.
4. Ibid.
5. Ibid.
6. Ibid.

Appendix III

1. Senate Document No. 345, 2nd Session, 27th Congress.

Appendix V

1. Report of the Secretary of War, 1840, 21.
2. Ibid.

Bibliography

Primary Sources

Huger Family Papers. Virginia Historical Society. Mostly papers from box 5 of 8 marked 2006.0187.

Mordecai, Captain Alfred. *Report of Experiments on Gunpowder made at Washington Arsenal in 1843 and 1844.* Washington: Gideon, 1845.

National Archives and Records Administration, Compiled Service Records of Confederate General and Staff Officers, and Nonregimental Enlisted Men, M331. Surname Range Hu-Hul. Referred to in notes as NARA M331.

"Report of the Secretary of War, December 5, 1840" in Message from the President of the United States to the Two Houses of Congress at the Commencement of the Second Session of the Twenty-Sixth Congress." Washington: Blair and Rives, Printers, 1840. Printed by order of the Senate of the United States, December 9, 1840.

Senate Document No. 345, 2nd Session 27th Congress.

U.S. Government. *Reports of Experiments with Small Arms for the Military Service, by Officers of the Ordnance Department, U. S. Army.* Washington: 1856. Reprint, Arendtsville, PA: Dean S. Thomas, 1984.

U.S. House of Representatives, "Establishment of Harpers Ferry Armory, extracts from.33rd Congress, 1st session, Miscellaneous Document No. 76." May 18, 1854.

Secondary Sources

Abana Books. *Home Remedies from Amish Country.* 5th ed. Millersburg, OH: Abana Books, 2005.

Albaugh, William A. III. *Tyler, Texas: The Story of the Confederate States Ordnance Works at Tyler, Texas 1861–1865.* Wilmington, NC: Broadfoot, 1993.

Alberts, Don E. *Brandy Station to Manila Bay: A Biography of General Wesley Merritt.* Austin, TX: Presidial Press, 1980.

Alexander, Edward P. *Military Memoirs of a Confederate.* New York: Scribners, 1907.

Anderson, Ronald, and Anne Koval. *James McNeill Whistler: Beyond the Myth.* New York: Carroll & Graf, 1994.

Barry, Captain William F., Major William H. French, and Major Henry J. Hunt. *Instructions for Field Artillery, 1861.* Reprint, New York: Greenwood Press, 1968.

Bates, Samuel P. *History of Pennsylvania Volunteers, 1861–5; Prepared in Compliance with Acts of the Legislature, Four Volumes.* Harrisburg, PA: Singerly, 1869.

Bauer, K. Jack. *The Mexican War, 1846–1848.* Lincoln: University of Nebraska Press, 1974.

Benton, Captain James G. *A Course of Instruction in Ordnance and Gunnery; Compiled for the Use of the Cadets of the United States Military Academy.* New York: Van Nostrand, 1862. Reprint, Gettysburg, PA: Thomas, n.d.

Birkhimer, William E. *Historical Sketch of the Organization, Administration, Matériel, and Tactics of the Artillery, United States Army.* Reprint. New York: Greenwood Press, 1968.
Boatner, Mark M. III. *Encyclopedia of the American Revolution.* 3rd ed. Mechanicsburg, PA: Stackpole Books, 1994.
Castel, Albert. *Decision in the West.* Lawrence: University Press of Kansas, 1992.
Cleaves, Freeman. *Meade of Gettysburg.* Dayton: Morningside Bookshop, 1980.
Coddington, Edwin B. *The Gettysburg Campaign: A Study in Command.* Reprint. Dayton: Morningside Bookshop, 1979.
Coit, Margaret L. *John C. Calhoun: American Portrait.* Columbia: University of South Carolina Press, 1991.
Commager, Henry Steele, and Richard B. Morris, eds. *The Spirit of Seventy-Six.* New York: Da Capo Press, 1995.
The Confederate Field Manual, 1984 reprint of *The Field Manual for the Use of the Officers on Ordnance Duty.* Richmond: Ritchie and Dunnavant, 1862. Reprint, Gettysburg, PA: Thomas, n.d.
Connell, Evan S. *Son of the Morning Star.* San Francisco: North Point Press, 1984.
Cozzens, Peter. *The Terrible Sound: The Battle of Chickamauga.* Urbana: The University of Illinois Press, 1992.
Crary, Catherine S., ed. *Dear Belle: Letters from a Cadet & Officer to His Sweetheart, 1858–1865.* Middletown, CT: Wesleyan University Press, 1965.
Current, Richard N., ed. *Encyclopedia of the Confederacy.* New York: Simon & Schuster, 1993.
Curti, Merle. *The Learned Blacksmith.* New York: Wilson-Erickson, 1937.
Dew, Charles B. *Apostles of Disunion: Southern Secession Commissioners and the Causes of the Civil War* Charlottesville: University of Virginia Press, 2001.
Donald, David H. *Charles Sumner and the Coming of the Civil War.* New York: Fawcett Columbine, 1960.
Elliott, Charles W. *Winfield Scott: The Soldier and the Man.* Cranbury, NJ: The Scholar's Bookshelf, 2006.
Freehling, William W. *Prelude to Civil War.* New York: Harper Torchbooks, 1965.
Freeman, Douglas S. *R. E. Lee: A Biography.* 4 vols. New York: Charles Scribner's Sons, 1934.
_____. *Lee's Lieutenants: A Study in Command.* 3 vols. New York: Charles Scribner's Sons, 1944.
Freemon, Frank R. *Gangrene and Glory: Medical Care during the American Civil War.* Madison, NJ: Fairleigh Dickinson University Press, 1998.
Fuller, Claud E. *The Rifled Musket.* New York: Bonanza Books, 1958.
Gallagher, Gary W., ed. *Fighting for the Confederacy: The Personal Recollections of General Edward Porter Alexander.* Chapel Hill: University of North Carolina Press, 1989.
_____. *Chancellorsville: The Battle and Its Aftermath.* Chapel Hill: University of North Carolina Press, 1996.
_____. *The Fredericksburg Campaign: Decision on the Rappahannock.* Chapel Hill: University of North Carolina Press, 1995.
_____. *The Wilderness Campaign.* Chapel Hill: University of North Carolina Press, 1997.
Gibbon, Brigadier General John. *The Artillerist's Manual, Compiled from Various Sources and Adapted to the Service of the United States.* New York: Van Nostrand, 1859. Reprint. Dayton, OH: Morningside, 1991.
Glatthaar, Joseph T. *General Lee's Army from Victory to Collapse.* New York: The Free Press, 2008.
Greene, A. Wilson. *Breaking the Backbone of the Rebellion: The Final Battles of the Petersburg Campaign.* Mason City, IA: Savas, 2000.
_____. *Whatever You Resolve To Be.* Baltimore: Butternut and Blue, 1992.

Harris, C. Nelson. *Images of Rail Norfolk and Western Railway Stations and Depots.* Charleston, SC: Arcadia Publishing, 2009.
Harsh, Joseph L. *Taken at the Flood: Robert E. Lee and Confederate Strategy in the Maryland Campaign of 1862.* Kent, OH: Kent State University Press, 1999.
Hearn, Chester G. *Admiral David Dixon Porter.* Annapolis, MD: Naval Institute Press, 1996.
Heitman, Francis B. *Historical Register and Dictionary of the United States Army, from its Organization, September 29, 1789, to March 2, 1903.* Washington: Government Printing Office, 1903. Reprint, Lake Monticello, VA: Olde Soldiers Books, 1988.
Hilen, Andrew, ed. *The Letters of Henry Wadsworth Longfellow,* Vol. 6. *1875–1882.* Cambridge, MA: Belknap Press, 1982.
Humphreys, Andrew A. *The Virginia Campaign: 1864.* Reprint, New York: The Blue & the Gray Press, n.d.
Huntington, R. T. *Hall's Breechloader.* York, PA: Shumway, 1972.
Iobst, Richard W. *Civil War Macon.* Macon, GA: Mercer University Press, 1999.
Johnson, Curt, and Richard C. Anderson, Jr. *Artillery Hell: The Employment of Artillery at Antietam.* College Station: Texas A&M University Press, 1995.
Johnson, Robert U., and Clarence C. Buel, eds. *Battles and Leaders of the Civil War.* New York: Thomas Yoseloff, 1956.
Kerby, Robert L. *Kirby Smith's Confederacy: The Trans-Mississippi South, 1863–1865.* New York: Columbia University Press, 1972.
Krick, Robert E. L. *Staff Officers in Gray: A Biographical Register of the Staff Officers in the Army of Northern Virginia.* Chapel Hill: University of North Carolina Press, 2003.
Krick, Robert K. *Lee's Colonels: A Biographical Register of the Field Officers of the Army of Northern Virginia.* Wilmington, NC: Broadfoot, 2009.
_____. *Parker's Virginia Battery, C. S. A.* Wilmington, NC: Broadfoot, 1989.
_____. *The Smoothbore Volley that Doomed the Confederacy.* Baton Rouge: Louisiana State University Press, 2002.
Longstreet, James. *From Manassas to Appomattox: Memoirs of the Civil War in America.* Bloomington: Indiana University Press and Kraus Reprint, Millwood, NY, 1976.
Marvel, William. *Burnside.* Chapel Hill: University of North Carolina Press, 1991.
Matter, William D. *If it Takes All Summer: The Battle of Spotsylvania.* Chapel Hill: University of North Carolina Press, 1988.
Mays, Thomas D., ed. *Let Us Meet in Heaven: The Civil War Letters of James Michael Barr, 5th South Carolina Cavalry.* Abilene, TX: McWhiney Foundation Press, 2001.
McCaffrey, James M. *"Surrounded by Dangers of All Kinds": The Mexican War Letters of Lieutenant Theodore Laidley.* Denton: University of North Texas Press, 1997.
Meade, George, ed. *The Life and Letters of George Gordon Meade.* 2 vols. New York: Charles Scribner's Sons, 1913.
Musicant, Ivan. *Divided Waters: The Naval History of the Civil War.* Edison, NJ: Castle Books, 2000.
Niven, John. *John C. Calhoun and the Price of Union: A Biography.* Baton Rouge: Louisiana State University Press, 1988.
Norman, Matthew W. *Colonel Burton's Spiller and Burr Revolver: An Untimely Venture in Confederate Small-Arms Manufacturing.* Macon, GA: Mercer University Press, 1996.
O'Reilly, Francis A. *The Fredericksburg Campaign.* Baton Rouge: Louisiana State University Press, 2003.
Parks, Joseph H. *General Kirby Smith, C.S.A.* Baton Rouge: Louisiana State University Press, 1954.
Pfanz, Donald C. *Richard S. Ewell: A Soldier's Life.* Chapel Hill: University of North Carolina Press, 1998.
Porter, David D. *Naval History of the Civil War.* Secaucus, NJ: Castle Books, 1984.

Price, B. Byron, David Reel, John Pultz, Roger Echo-Hawk, and Joan C. Troccoli, eds. *West Point Points West*. Denver: Institute of Western American Art, Denver Art Museum, 2002.

Racine, Philip N., ed. *Gentlemen Merchants: A Charleston Family's Odyssey, 1828–1870*. Knoxville: University of Tennessee Press, 2008.

Remini, Robert V. *Andrew Jackson and the Bank War*. New York: W. W. Norton, 1967.

_____. *The Life of Andrew Jackson*. New York: Harper & Row, 1984.

Rhea, Gordon C. *To the North Anna River: Grant and Lee May 13–25, 1864*. Baton Rouge: Lousiana State University Press, 2000.

Rhoades, Jeffery L. *Scapegoat General: Benjamin Huger*. Hamden, CT: Archon Books, 1895.

Roland, Charles P. *Albert Sidney Johnston: Soldier of Three Republics*. Lexington: University Press of Kentucky, 2001.

Schaff, Morris. *The Spirit of Old West Point*. Boston: Houghton, Mifflin, 1907.

Scharf, J. Thomas. *History of the Confederate States Navy*. Avenel, NJ: Gramercy Books, 1996.

Schneller, Robert J. Jr. *A Quest for Glory: A Biography of Rear Admiral John A. Dahlgren*. Annapolis: Naval Institute Press, 1996.

Simpson, Craig M. *A Good Southerner: The Life of Henry A. Wise of Virginia*. Chapel Hill: University of North Carolina Press, 1985.

Steere, Edward. *The Wilderness Campaign*. Harrisburg, PA: Stackpole Books, 1960.

Tap, Bruce. *Over Lincoln's Shoulder: The Committee on the Conduct of the War*. Lawrence: University Press of Kansas, 1998.

Tate, Thomas K. *From Under Iron Eyelids: The Biography of James Henry Burton, Armorer to Three Nations*. Bloomington, IN: AuthorHouse, 2005.

Trotter, William R. *Ironclads and Columbiads: The Civil War in North Carolina: The Coast*. Winston-Salem, NC: Blair, 1989.

U.S. Congress. *Joint Committee on the Conduct of the War*. Millwood, NY: Kraus Reprint, 1977.

Vandiver, Frank E. *Ploughshares into Swords: Josiah Gorgas and Confederate Ordnance*. College Station: Texas A&M University, 1980.

The War of the Rebellion: A Compilation of the Official Records of the Union and Confederate Armies. Washington: Government Printing Office, 1890.

Weinert, Richard P. Jr. *The Confederate Regular Army*. Shippensburg, PA: White Mane Publishing, 1991.

Wert, Jeffry D. *General James Longstreet: The Confederacy's Most Controversial Soldier*. New York: Simon & Schuster, 1993.

Wilcox, Cadmus M. *History of the Mexican War*. Washington: Church News Publishing, 1892.

_____. *Rifles and Rifle Practice an Elementary Treatise upon the Theory of Rifle Firing, Explaining the Causes of Inaccuracy of Fire, and the Manner of Correcting It, with Descriptions of the Infantry Rifles of Europe and the United States, Their Balls and Cartridges*. New York: Van Nostrand, 1859.

Wise, Jennings C. *The Long Arm of Lee*. 2 vols. Lincoln: University of Nebraska Press, 1988.

Woodward, C. Vann, ed. *Mary Chesnut's Civil War*. New Haven, CT: Yale University Press, 1981.

Index

Numbers in **_bold italics_** indicate pages with photographs.

Abert, John James 12
Aiken, David W. 72
Alexander, Edward Porter 29, 34–36, 49, 51, 55, 58, 63, 75, 78–79, 81–82, 103, 139–40, 145–46; artillery battalion 52, 69; book 130–31; civilian pursuits 127; Crater 105; Gettysburg 135; leave 82, 101; letters 127–32, 148; Seven Pines 153; wounds 64, 93, 97, 100
Alexander, George D. 83
Alexandria Boarding School 11; see also Brimstone Castle
Allegheny Arsenal 168
Allston, Benjamin 119
Amelia Court House 140
The American Anti-Slavery Society 17
American machine tools 194
Anderson, George B. 38
Anderson, Richard Heron 44, 49, 57, 102
Anderson, Robert 8, 17, 99
Anderson, Samuel S. 93
Andrews, George L. 183
Antietam, battle of 42–44
Army of Northern Virginia 47, 57, 70–71, 88, 98, 100, 146
Army of the James 92
Army of the Potomac 47, 88
Atlantic, Mississippi and Ohio Railroad 132
Aztec Club 93

Bacon, Thomas G. 72
Baker, Rufus L. 10, 150, 193
Ballistic pendulums 193
Ball's Bluff, battle of 105
Baltimore, Md. 22, 53, 61–62, 160
Banks, Nathaniel P. 125
Banks Ford 49
Baran, Jennie 111
Barksdale, William 63
Barry, William F. 54
Barton, Seth M. 138
Baylor, John Capron 51, 61, 66, 77
Beauregard, Pierre G.T. 72, 93, 95

Benét, Stephen Vincent 11
Benjamin, Judah P. 153
Benning, Henry L. 89
Benton, James G. 171
Bermuda Neck 95
Berryville, Va. 43
board of officers 193
Braddon, Mary E. 87
Bragg, Braxton 67, 69, 73–74, 79–81
Branch L. O'Brien 54
Brazil 128
Breckenridge, John C. 92
brevet rank 174–75
Brimstone Castle 12, 24
Brooks, Preston 23
Brown, J. Thompson (colonel) 71
Brown, J. Thompson (lieutenant) 71, 73, 75–76, 136–38, 147, 148
Brown, John 24, 27
Brown, Joseph E. 100
Buck, Miss 75, 86; see also Preston, Sally Buchanan
Buckner, Simon Bolivar 81
Bunker Hill, Va. 45, 66
Burnside, Ambrose E. 47, 52, 67, 74, 103
Burritt, Elihu 13, 24
Burton, James H. 154, 167–68; letter from 168–70
Butler, Andrew P. 23
Butler, Benjamin 76, 83, 92–93, 95, 140; caricature 139
Byrne's gargle 13

cadets, West Point class of 1860 22–23
Calhoun, John C. 15, 21
Cameron, William E. 133
Canby, E.R.S. 183
cannon casting 193
Carr, Charles E. 93, 117
Cass, Lewis 15
S.S. *Central America* 23
Cerro Gordo, battle of 152
Chancellorsville, battle of 57–59
Chandler, Zachariah 105

203

204 Index

Chapultepec, battle of 152
Charles Town, Va. (now West Virginia) 43
Charleston, S.C. 17, 20, 67
Charleston Arsenal 153
Charleville musket 171
Chattanooga, Tenn. 67–68, 70, 74, 76, 78–79, 119
Chesapeake Canal 181
Chestnut, Mary 7, 17, 52, 81, 87
Chicago, Ill. 107
Chickamauga, battle of 69, 79
Chimborazo Hospital 53
Christmas 110–11, 121–23
Clark, Clarence 132
Clemson, Thomas G. 115, 155
Cobham Station, Va. 94
Cold Harbor, Va. 95
Cold Stream Guards 76
Colston, Frederick M. 106, 111
Columbia, S.C. 47–48, 52
Cooper, Samuel 15, 40, 180
Corprew, Thomas J. 181
Corse, Montgomery D. 138
Costello, John A.T. 134
Court of Enquiry 181–82, 185
Craig, Henry K. 165–66, 173–74, 184–87
The Crater 102–4
Crimean War 194
Culpepper Court House, Va. 43, 48
Currituck bridge 181
Custer, George A. 26, 29, 36, 91, 144–45
Cutshaw, Wilfred E. 90
Czar Nicholas I of Russia 151

Dallas, George M. 15
Daniel, Junius 90
Darby, John Thompson 109
Davis, Jefferson 15, 56, 60, 67, 71, 80, 100, 112; administration 69, 159; as secretary of war 23
Department of Tennessee 100
Dialectic Society 29
Douty, Jacob 104
Drake, Edwin 24
Drayton, Thomas 114–15
Drayton, William 21
Duane, James 103
Du Bose, Dudley M. 138
Dunkin, Mary (aunt) 101
Du Pont Samuel F. 54

Early, Jubal 93, 99
East Tennessee, Virginia & Georgia Railroad 133
Edict of Nantes 161
Eleanor's Victory 87, 112
Ely's Ford 94

Eshleman, Benjamin F. 147
Eustis, Abram 8, 10–11
Evans, William M. 142
Ewell, Richard S. 61, 89

Falling Waters, Md. 66
Faquier County, Va. 160
Fickling, William W. 63, 141–42
Field, Charles W. 81, 87, 140
field guns, system of 10
flintlock to percussion conversion 193–94
Floyd, John B. 27, 32, 81
Forden (friend of Frank Huger) 45, 53, 58–59, 118
foreign arms factories 177
Fort Monroe, Va. 8, 149, 152–53, 162, 174
Fort Pitt Foundry 150
Fort Sanders, Tenn. 78
Fort Sumter, S.C. 8, 99
Fredericksburg, Va. 50, 58, 61
Fredericksburg, battle of 47–49
Freemantle, Arthur J.L. 76
French, John W. 30
French, William H. 54, 117
French ballistic tests 193
French Instruction for Field Artillery 9
Front Royal, Va. 43, 61
fuse metal 173

gain twist 165–66
Garland, Samuel, Jr. 107
Garnett, Mary 52
Garnett, Richard B. 63
garrisonians 24
Germana Ford 94
Gettysburg, battle of 54, 60, 62–64, 66, 117, 135
Gibbes, Wade Hampton 87, 105–6, 128–29
Gibbon, John 26, 28
Gilmer, Jeremy F. 68, 129
Gilmore, Quincy A. 65
Gordonsville, Va. 43, 45
Gorgas, Josiah 121–22, 124
Gourdin, Robert N. 17, 20
Gracie, Archibald, Jr. 78
Grant, Ulysses S. 66, 73, 81, 87–89, 95–98, 109, 139; Crater 105; rumor 100
Grattan, James F. 89
Grattan, Sallie 109
Great Bridge 181
Green Mount Cemetery 160
Greenville & Columbia Railroad 133
Gregg, John 92, 95
Grimes, Cary F. 44
Guiney's Station, Va. 51–52, 55, 57
gun carriages 9
Gwynn, Walter 41

Index

Hagerstown, Md. 66
Hall rifle 152, 167
Hallowell, Benjamin 11–12
Hampton, Mary Cantey 64
Hampton, Preston 91
Hampton, Sallie 111
Hampton, Wade 64
Hampton, Wade, III 63, 91, 97, 111
Hampton, Wade, IV 64
Hancock, Winfield S. 93
Hardee, William J. 26, 112–13
Harleston, Edward 47
Harpers Ferry, Va. (now West Virginia) 12, 24, 43, 79, 166
Harpers Ferry Armory 23, 152, 162, 167–68, 174–75, 186; condition 176–78, 186; cost of arms 178–79; superintendents 175–80
Harpers Ferry bullet 167–68
Harrisburg, Pa. 62
Harrison, William H. 176
Hartsuff, George S. 36
Haskell, John Cheves 60, 85, 98, 129
Haskell, Joseph Cheves 51, 60, 79, 85, 87, 98, 100, 106, 110, 128–29
Henderson, "Aunt" 47
Henderson, Mary 47
Henningsen, Charles F. 41
Heth, Henry 54, 92, 95
Heyward, Barnwell 63
Hill, Ambrose Powell 54, 58, 61, 135–36
Hill, Benjamin H. 100
Hill, Daniel Harvey 59, 71, 81
Hill, G.H. 160
Hoke, Robert F. 93, 96
Holmes, Oliver Wendell, Jr. 42–43
Holmes, Oliver Wendell, Sr. 42–43
Holmes, Theophilus H. 114–15
Hood, John Bell 52, 67, 69–70, 136
Hooker, Joseph 52, 62
Hopkins, Mark 24
Howard, Oliver O. 26
Howlett House 93, 95, 112
Huger, Alfred 17, 19–20
Huger, Anna Isabella (aunt) 47
Huger, Benjamin (father) 7–8, 10, 12, 14, 16, 23, 27, 38, 40–42, 123, 153, 180–83, 193; biography 149–63; children 152; court of enquiry 181–82; description 130; duties 114–116, 119, 121, 124; Harpers Ferry, command 173–75; meets Czar 151, 193; opinions 119, 122, 124; ordnance 152, 165–72; siblings 149; spurs 32, 145; testimony before Congress 176–80; Trans-Mississippi 53, 59, 64, 84, 114, 154–56
Huger, Celestine Pinckney (sister) 8, 16, 60–61; *see also* Preston, Celestine P. (née Huger)
Huger, Cleland (uncle) 101, 106, 151
Huger, Daniel 21
Huger, Daniel (great-great-grandfather) 7
Huger, Daniel (great-great-great-grandfather) 7
Huger, Elizabeth (aunt) 47
Huger, Elizabeth Celestine (née Pinckney) (mother) 8, 52, 80, 112, 114, 161–62
Huger, Eustis (brother) 8, 16, 76, 83–84, 112, 114–17, 119, 120–23, 183
Huger, five brothers 7, 149
Huger, Francis Kinloch (cousin) 101, 133
Huger, Francis Kinloch (Frank) 7–8, 11–12, **28**, 36–37, **50**, 63, 70, **85**, 97, 110; advice to father 55–56; artillery battery 34, 44, 49–50, 58, 69–70, 95–97; battalion 66, 82–94; capture 137–43; civilian career 127, 132–33; family 147; field pieces 44; foreign parts 62, 65; Gettysburg 62–67, 128, 135, 147; lack of food 72–73, 112; literary interests 71, 73, 112; optimism 110–11; ordered to protect guns 102; ordnance 56–57, 79; prices, inflation 77, 87, 118; promotions 32–33, 35, 52, 81, 83, 153; slaves 45–46, 48, 72, 85, 91, 101, 108; spurs 32, 77, 145; wants battle flag 75; wedding cake 61; West Point 22, 25–33; young women 35, 53, 61, 73, 75, 83, 85–87, 100, 107–8, 111
Huger, Francis Kinloch (grandfather) 8, 149
Huger, Francis Motte (cousin) 101
Huger, Frank K. 101
Huger, Harriot Horry (aunt) 47
Huger, Harriott Lucas (née Pinckney) (grandmother) 149
Huger, Isabella Johannes (Middleton) 7
Huger, Joseph Alston 47
Huger, Mariamne (née Meade) 18–19, 99
Huger, Mary (Dunkin) *see* Mary Dunkin
Huger, Mary Ester (aunt) 47
Huger, Meta 19
Huger, Thomas Bee 18–19
Huger, Thomas Pinckney (brother) 8, 16, 51, 71–72, 86
Huger, Thomas Pinckney (uncle) 112–13, 151
Humphreys, Andrew A. 88
Hunt, Henry J. 54
Hunter, David 92
Hunton, Eppa 137–38, 141

ice machine 128
Imboden, John D. 92

Ingraham, Alfred 99
Ingraham, Mrs. Alfred 99
Iroquois 18
Izard, Ralph 9, 49

Jackson, Ms. 59
Jackson, Thomas J. "Stonewall" 44, 51, 58–59, 70–71
Jenkins, Micah 89
Jessie 57, 65, 96–97, 100, 141
Johnson, Bradley T. 99
Johnson, Bushrod 99
Johnson, Edward 92, 95
Johnson, J.P. 154–56, 158
Johnston, Albert Sidney 68, 72
Johnston, Joseph E. 38, 46, 54, 56, 59, 61, 66, 82, 100, 181
Joint Committee on the Conduct of the War 105
Jones, Frank Freeman 49, 55
Jones, John M. 89
Jones, William G. 69
Jordan, Tyler C. 44, 109, 111, 140

Kautz, August 93, 97
Keifer, J. Warren 138
Kendall, Amos 17
Kerr, Fannie 52, 118
Kerr, John B. 81
Kershaw, Joseph B. 78, 92, 95, 138
Knoxville & Ohio Railroad 133
Knoxville, Tenn. 67, 74, 76, 78–79, 82
Krick, Robert K. 33, 71, 81, 121

Lafayette, Marquis de 8, 149
Lane, James H. 54
Leadbetter, Danville 78
Lee, Fitzhugh 93, 97, 134
Lee, George Washington Custis 138
Lee, Robert E. 12, 24, 41–43, 57, 82, 88, 140; Gettysburg 60, 67, 106, 135–36; Petersburg 98, 139
Lee, Stephen D. 51, 65, 71
Legs *see* Smith, Alfred T.
Letcher, John 33, 92
Limerick plantation 7
Lincoln, Abraham 112–13, 119
Long, Armistead L. 90
Longfellow, Henry Wadsworth 13
Longstreet, James 38, 46, 48, 53, 56, 67, 69, 81, 85, 88, 131; criticism 133–34; Gettysburg 135–36; Knoxville 74, 76, 80, 82; Seven Pines 153; wounding 89, 95
Longwood plantation 17
Lookout Mountain, Tenn. 74, 78–79
Louisa Court House, Va. 53

Mackay, Aeneas 9
Macomb, Mrs. Alexander 10
Macon (Georgia) Arsenal 154
Magruder, John B. 92, 160
Mahone, William 93, 97, 105, 128–29, 132, 140–41
Mallet, John W. 154
Malvern Hill, Va. 42, 60, 64, 96
Manning, John L. 153
Marshall, Tex. 156–58
Martin, William 52
Martinsburg, Va. (now West Virginia) 45
Martinsburg Pike 44
Maryland 46
Maryland Guards 162
Mason, John 27
Maynadier, William 175
McClellan, George B. 47, 106
McCrea, Tully 24–25, 30–31
McCreery, J. Van 146, 148
McCreery, William J. 146
McCreery, William W., Jr. 54, 63
McDowell, Lillie 85
McEvoy attachment 78–79
McLaws, Lafayette 63, 67–68, 81, 136
McRae 18
Meade, George G. 18–19, 62, 68, 88–89, 99, 103–4, 143–44
Meade, Richard Kidder, Jr. 99
Mexico City 152, 162
Middleton, Oliver H., Jr. 123
Middleton, Oliver H., Sr. 123
Minié, captain 166–67
Minié principle 166–67
Molino del Rey 152
Moody, George V. 142
Moody, Thomas 150
Moore, Joseph D. 49, 52
Moore, Samuel Preston, Dr. 45
Mordecai, Alfred 10, 150, 161, 174, 193; letter from 173
Moseley, Edgar F. 38

Nag's Head, N.C. 40
National Compensation Emancipation Society 24
national foundry 192
New York Times 7, 22
New York Tribune 117
Nitre Mining Bureau 116, 155
Norfolk, Va. 8, 46, 77, 181
Norfolk & Western Railroad 132
Norfolk battery 52–53
North Anna River 91

Old Point, Va. 10
Olmütz, Austria 8

Index

Orange Court House, Va. 43, 68
Ord, Edward O.C. 138
Ordnance 150; Confederate 56, 69, 78, 98, 119, 122, 151
Ordnance Board 11, 152
Ordnance Corps 185
Ordnance Department 152, 165, 193

Page, Richard C.M. 90
Paixhans, Henri Joseph 8
Panic of 1857 23–24
Paris, Va. 43
Parker, William Watts 55, 63, 71, 142, 147
Parkers Store 94
Parrott guns 56, 79, 98
Paul, D'Arcy W. 99
Paul, Samuel B. 99
Paul, Sophronia W. 99
peace commissioners 112–13
Pemberton, John C. 73, 117
Perry, Edward A. 141
Petersburg, Va. 98, 102–4, 106, 110–11
Pettigrew, James J. 54, 66
Pickett, George E. 63, 137, 139–42
Pierce (colonel) 10
Pikesville Arsenal (Md.) 22, 153, 162, 166
Pillow, Gideon 81
Pinckney, Rosetta Ella (aunt) 49
Pinckney, Thomas 149
Pleasants, Henry 102–4
Pocahontas coal mine 132
Poinsett, Joel R. 8, 10, 21, 24, 149–50, 161, 192
Poitiaux, B.E. 148
Polk, James K. 15
Polk, Leonidas 81, 125
Porter, David D. 18
Porter, Horace 137–38
Potomac River 56
Potter, Robert 103
Preston, Celestine P. (née Huger) *see* Huger, Celestine Pinckney
Preston, John Smith, Jr. 45, 51, 62, 65, 71, 75
Preston, John Smith, Sr. 106
Preston, Mary Cantey 109, 111
Preston, Sally Buchanan 52, 73, 75, 86; *see also* Buck
Preston, Susan Frances Hampton (Trudy) 81
Preston, Uncle John 94
Preston, William (nephew) 109, 112–13
Preston, William (Willie) 21, 64, 100
Preston, William Campbell 72
Price, Sterling 117

railroads 67
Rains, George W. 123

Raleigh, N.C. 47–48
Ramsay, George D. 174
Ramseur, Stephen D. 23, **28**, 58–61, 63, 74–75, 90, 96
Randolph, George W. 181
Ransom, Robert, Jr. 78
Ravenel, Alfred Ford 47
Read, Isaac 155–56
Reagan, John H. 120
Red River Campaign 125
Rees, Henry 104
refugees 116
Reno, Marcus A. 26, 29
Reynolds, John F. 31
Reynolds, Thomas C. 121
Rhett, Andrew B. 63
Rhett, Robert Barnwell 21
Rhett, Thomas G. 59, 114–16, 122, 154–56
Richardson, John H. 181
Richmond, Va. 45–47, 59, 70–71, 75, 82, 90, 95, 108
Richmond Armory 49
Richmond *Dispatch* 69
Richmond *Enquirer* 69
Richmond *Examiner* 69
Ripley, James W. 175; implied 185
Rodes, Robert E. 59
Rosecrans, William S. 67, 69, 71
Ruther Glen, Va. 49–51, 55

Sailor's Creek 137–41, 144–46
Salem Church 49
San Antonio Arsenal 84, 115–17; *see also* Texas Arsenal
Santa Anna, Antonio Lopez 32
Saunders, John S. 84, 117
Schaff, Morris 30–31
Scott, Winfield 11, 32, 152, 161–62
Sedgewick, John 58
Seminole War, Second 9
Seven Pines 38, 44, 54, 56, 59, 91, 130–31, 134, 136, 153; report 181
Seward, William H. 112
Sharpsburg *see* Antietam
Shenandoah Valley Railroad 132
Sheridan, Philip H. 97, 138
Sherman, William T. 19, 83–84, 112–13
Shreveport, La. 157
Sigel, Franz 92
Silliman, Benjamin 24
Sinclair, Arthur 118
Sloan, Benjamin F., Jr. 45
small arms 165, 178–79; numbers made 179
Smith, Mrs. E. Kirby 114–15
Smith, Edmund Kirby 15, 112–13, 121–22, 154, 155, 159–60; surrender 183
Smith, Gerrit 24

Smith, Gustavus W. 54, 134, 136, 153
Sorrel, G. Moxley 102
Spottsylvania Court House 95
Springfield Armory 175–76, 179, 185–86
Stafford, Leroy A. 89
Steele, Frederick 117
Stephens, Alexander H. 112
Steuart, George H. 92
Stockton, P. 155
Stragglers 43
Stringfellow, Franklin 94
Stringfellow, Thornton 94, 100, 123
Stuart, James E.B. 93
Stubbs, James N. 92
Suffolk, Va. 53
Sumner, Charles 13, 23
Swinton, William 131
Sykes, George 92
Symington, John 168, 176

Talcott, George 15, 192–94
Talcott, Thomas M.R. 135
Taylor, Bayard 117
Taylor, Charles F. 117
Taylor, John S. 44, 66
Taylor, Osmond B. 141, 146
Taylor, Walter H. 45, 49, 59, 134–35
Temple, R.H. 156
Texas Arsenal 155, 157; *see also* San Antonio Arsenal
Thomas, George 69
Tige principle 166–67
Tilghman, (Lee?) 38, 43, 57, 70, 85, 110
Tilghman, Tench 38, 110
Trans-Mississippi 15, 49, 74, 107, 112, 153; description 116, 159–60
troops 48
Turnbull, William 12
Tyler, Tex. 153, 156, 158

U.S. Bank 11
U.S. census, 1850 16
U.S. Ford 58
U.S. House of Representatives 175

U.S. Military Academy 25, 26, 180; cadet routine 25; conditions 24; new buildings 24; *see also* West Point

Venable, Charles Scott 135
Vera Cruz, Mexico 152, 162
Vicksburg, Ms. 60–61, 65, 112
CSS *Virginia* 153
Virginia Military Institute 92

Wade, Benjamin F. 105
Wade, William 10, 150, 193
Waggaman, Eugene 42
Walker, James A. 90
Walker, L. Pope 13, 153
Walker, Lindsay 140
Waltham Abbey 150
Warren, Gouverneur K. 92, 95
Warrenton, Va. 43
Washington Artillery 55, 147
weather: cold, rainy 48–50, 79, 82, 95, 110; dry, hot 9, 61, 106; good 9, 53; rain 9, 64–66, 70, 72
Weir, Robert W. 26
West Point 22–37; *see also* U.S. Military Academy
West Point Foundry 9
Whistler, James McNeill 26–27
White Oak Swamp 59
Whittier, John Greenleaf 13
Whitworth, Joseph 54
Whitworth gun, artillery 54
Wigfall, Louis T. 114, 121
Wilcox, Cadmus M. 45
Wilderness, battle of 87–88, 90, 94–95
Wilkinson, James 149
Winchester, Va. 45, 61, 65
Winthrop, Stephen 76
Wise, Henry A. 40–41, 99, 181
Wise, Mrs. Tully 19
Wool, John 153
Woolfolk, Pichegru 148
Wright, Horatio G. 138
Wright, Moses H. 69, 79

www.ingramcontent.com/pod-product-compliance
Ingram Content Group UK Ltd.
Pitfield, Milton Keynes, MK11 3LW, UK
UKHW042002140426
5217IPUK00015B/933